Fighting for Democracy

Fighting for Democracy

BLACK VETERANS AND THE STRUGGLE AGAINST WHITE SUPREMACY IN THE POSTWAR SOUTH

Christopher S. Parker

PRINCETON UNIVERSITY PRESS

PRINCETON AND OXFORD

Published by Princeton University Press, 41 William Street, Princeton, New Jersey 08540
In the United Kingdom: Princeton University Press, 6 Oxford Street,
Woodstock, Oxfordshire OX20 1TW

LIBRARY OF CONGRESS CATALOGING-IN-PUBLICATION DATA

Parker, Christopher S., 1963–
   Fighting for democracy : Black veterans and the struggle against white supremacy in the
postwar South / Christopher S. Parker.
      p. cm. — (Princeton studies in American politics : historical, international, and
comparative perspectives)
   Includes bibliographical references and index.
   ISBN 978-0-691-14003-2 (hardcover : alk. paper) — ISBN 978-0-691-14004-9 (pbk. :
alk. paper)   1. Civil rights movements—Southern States—History—20th century.
2. African Americans—Civil rights—Southern States—History—20th century.
3. African American veterans—Political activity—Southern States —History—20th
century.   4. Southern States—Race relations—History—20th century.   I. Title.
   E185.61.P25 2009
   323.1196073—dc22   2009002597

British Library Cataloging-in-Publication Data is available

This book has been composed in Sabon

Printed on acid-free paper. ∞

press.princeton.edu

Printed in the United States of America

10 9 8 7 6 5 4 3 2 1

FOR CARMEN

Contents

List of Illustrations

Preface and Acknowledgments

I happened upon the idea for this book many years ago, somewhere in the vastness of the Pacific Ocean, aboard a U.S. Navy ship on which I served. As a twenty-one-year-old supervisor of the Combat Information Center—the central nervous system of a U.S. warship—I was senior in rank, if not age, to almost all of my charges, all of whom were white. This was a far cry from my grandfather's experience a half century earlier during the Second World War. Similar to many other black men who served in the navy at the time, as a steward he was forced to act as a valet to white officers. During a particularly boring seven-hour watch, as I considered the differences between my circumstances and his, I wondered what motivated blacks—especially those like him, a black Southerner—to serve the country and join a Jim Crow military. Ultimately, some felt duty-bound; others sought to escape crushing poverty; still others felt like they had no other choice—that is, comply or go to jail. Regardless of the circumstances under which these men had come to be in the military, it was a transformational experience. In fact, it was so transformative that it ultimately helped democratize the South.

Fighting for Democracy illustrates how black veterans contributed to the process. For generations, structural impediments underwritten by social, political, and economic domination all but guaranteed a lifetime of subordination for black Southerners. However, as I will argue in this book, war stimulated what ultimately proved an insatiable appetite for equality—especially among black Southerners. To fight Nazism in one war, and communism in the next, American elites drew heavily upon the American creed to mobilize the masses for combat. By juxtaposing the American creed with rival ideologies, these American elites hoped to rally the nation. The strategy worked on both occasions. But the emphasis on the egalitarian norms of America accomplished nothing if not to stir the black militancy that had been simmering ever since the end of World War I, when much in the way of racial progress failed to materialize.

While the desire for equal treatment in postwar America was widespread, black veterans, I argue, were especially motivated to seek change. After all, they were the ones who bore the burden of service, enduring an avalanche of taunts from whites in the ranks as well as mistreatment from the white officers charged with leading and training them. Most important, they were the ones who fought, sweat, bled, and died in the name of democracy overseas but were prevented from enjoying its fruits upon their return from military service. Even so, their collective blood and sacrifice irrevocably vested them in America.

Fighting for Democracy reveals how and why black servicemen from my grandfather's generation both fought on behalf of democracy and fought to achieve it for themselves and the black community upon their return from military service. If, as some claim, the postwar South was a collection of authoritarian enclaves, and the success of the civil rights movement signaled the arrival of democracy, we can say that black veterans were successful in their fight to achieve democracy. In the end, this book shows how and why they were successful. Through interviews, black veterans who served during either the Second World War or the Korean War (sometimes both) convey both their frustration with the conditions in the South to which they returned, and their resolve to correct them, findings certified with survey data. By virtue of their sacrifice, black veterans believed themselves—and the black community—to be entitled to first-class citizenship. Since this wasn't forthcoming, military experience gave them the confidence to take it. Compared to what they were forced to endure in the military—that is, fighting the enemy in addition to racism in the ranks—black veterans were eager to fight Jim Crow upon their return, something at which it's clear many of them excelled.

. . .

This book began as a doctoral thesis at the University of Chicago, where I was introduced to boot camp for the second time. Believe me, Uncle Sam's boot camp's got nothing on the one in Hyde Park. At the University of Chicago I benefited from the guidance of the Department of Political Science's exceptional faculty, and especially that of my doctoral committee. Mark Hansen and John Brehm, the latter of whom joined the committee relatively late, were exceptionally generous with their time and advice. For this I remain in their debt. Michael Dawson, my principal advisor and now friend, pushed me from the very beginning to pursue a question that was of intrinsic importance to me instead of one of the fads that tends to capture the attention of the discipline from time to time. Since then, he has challenged me to raise the theoretical stakes of this book. Because he's always right, I did it. Thanks to him, this book, and my work overall, is much better.

Faculty isn't the only source of knowledge in graduate school. Fellow students can also make or break the experience. I had the privilege of keeping company with extraordinarily talented scholars who are also cool people. Sarita Gregory, Zoli Hajnal, Rob James, Taeku Lee, Hyacinth Miller, Mark Sawyer, and Nick Young all made Chicago a demanding yet fun place to be in graduate school. Mark and Taeku, especially, helped to shape the direction of this book in its latter stages. Kathy Anderson was more than support staff; she really helped me better understand the dynamics of the department. Rob Brown, Darren Davis, and Vince Hutchings have all served as friends and mentors to me during graduate school at time when, like many others, I had doubts about whether or not this business was for me. These guys always had the right answer when I asked them the (in)famous "Why am I doing this?" question, encouraging me to continue grinding it out. Thanks.

I finished the book at the University of Washington, where I've profited from the collegiality and support from my new colleagues. Bethany Albertson, Matt Barreto, Lance Bennett, Luis Fraga, Brian Jones, Margaret Levi, George Lovell, Steve Majeski, Mike McCann, Mark Smith, and Chip Turner have all made me feel welcomed from the start. Though he's since departed for Stanford University, Gary Segura provided outstanding leadership for the Washington Institute for the Study of Ethnicity, Race, and Sexuality. Earlier drafts of the book were completed at the University of California–Santa Barbara, where generous grant support funded time off and provided the resources for me to travel to the South and conduct the interviews so crucial to this project. Erstwhile colleagues Aaron Belkin, Kent Jennings, Rose McDermott, Lorraine McDonnell, Cedric Robinson, Eric Smith, Steve Weatherford, and John Woolley always gave freely of their time, offering sage advice. I made fast friends with Bruce Bimber and Garrett Glasgow upon arriving on campus. These friendships have endured even since my departure to Washington. Fernando Lopez-Alves, Earl Stewart, and Howard Winant were quick to offer wisdom and quicker to laugh. Melvin Oliver, the dean, always supported whatever I did.

Through the years, many friends and colleagues took the time to read and comment on all or part of the manuscript. For this, I thank Bruce Bimber, Tony Chen, Mike Creswell, Darren Davis, Peter Digeser, Garrett Glasgow, Bob Gooding-Williams, Vince Hutchings, Kent Jennings, Taeku Lee, George Lovell, Suzanne Mettler, Rob Mickey, Naomi Murakawa, Dan O'Neill, Mark Sawyer, Derek Stafford, Chip Turner, Steve Weatherford, and Nick Young. I had the good fortune of presenting parts of the book at various talks at UC–Berkeley, UC–Irvine, UCLA, and the University of Iowa. From these talks I received great advice from Joel Aberbach, Jack Citrin, Bernie Grofman, Laura Stoker, and Katherine Tate. Thanks also go to Ruth Homrighaus, who read and edited an early version of the manuscript.

Along with many others, I am also indebted to the Robert Wood Johnson Foundation for the time and space provided that allowed me to expand and polish the book. The Berkeley site of the Robert Wood Johnson

Health Scholars Program, led by John Ellwood, was an ideal place to learn health policy, and to begin work on a health-related project that remains dear to me, that of veterans and combat-related post-traumatic stress disorder. Bob Anderson, Jonah Levy, and Neil Smelser did an excellent job of opening my eyes to the ways in which social science informs health policy. Joan Bloom and Jack Citrin kept me focused on my project, and were kind enough to introduce me to Cal basketball. For two years at Berkeley, I shared space and had more fun than the academy should allow, with a group of young scholars that will surely help shape economics, political science, and sociology for years to come. For permitting me to bask in their brilliance I thank Karen Albright, Michael Anderson, Tony Chen, Seema Jayachandran, Sandra Kalev, Jordan Matsudaira, Rob Mickey, Naomi Murakawa, Aaron Panofky, Michael Schwartz, and Rob Van Houweling. I'd like to single out Tony and Rob, from whom I learned a lot, and with whom I laughed even more. Props to Seana Kelly and Claudia Martinez, on the administrative side, for making life easier for all of us.

This book would not have been possible without the cooperation of the many veterans I interviewed. I thank all of you for your participation. I owe special thanks to my liaisons in Houston and New Orleans, Ernest Shaw and George Jones, respectively. Without these guys' assistance, the interviews wouldn't have happened. The following students provided superb research assistance over the years: Heather Arnold, Jackie Bona, Kuang-hui Chen, and Derek Stafford. I'd like to thank Chuck Myers, my editor at Princeton University Press, whose patience and generosity are very much appreciated. Chuck's confidence in me isn't something I'll soon forget. Thanks also go to Ruth Homrighaus, who copyedited an early version of the manuscript.

Friends and family kept me sane as I wrote this book. Butch, Keith, Reggie, Rommel, and Stephanie Agee all kept me grounded, never allowing me to forget from whence I came. Long conversations with Willie Agee, who served during the Korean War, helped to inspire this book. Shawnye Anderson and Shannon Jackson are like sisters to me. Harold Bettis Jr. has inspired me from the start. Harriette Bettis and Ava Mitchell, Southern belles, keep me connected to my roots. I've known Eric Atno, John Lee, Nayan Patel, and Ed Trahan for many years; they've always had my back, and I theirs. To Arthur and Maxine Mayo, my father- and mother-in-law, thanks, first, for Carmen (I'll get to that in a minute). Beyond that, you've treated me like a son, and for that I remain grateful; I always look forward to the time we spend together. I hope there are many more such occasions. To my brother, Chauncey, another veteran I admire; we've been through a lot together. I hope you like this book. To my daughters, Britanni and Bryanna, I appreciate your patience with me; it's taken a while, I know, but Daddy's finally done with this book. I look forward to spending more time with you. My mother, Helen Agee, and her mother and father, Mollie and James Agee, made me who I am. Though you're now departed, there's not a day that passes that I don't think of you.

Ultimately, this book is dedicated to my darling wife, Carmen. What can I say? If for no other reason than the fact that this book has been with us for the duration of our relationship, you've been the most patient and understanding of all. The years that we've been together have been the best of my life; I look forward to many, many more. Although I'm the professor in this relationship, there's no doubt that I've learned much more from you than you from me. Since I know that words will fail to do justice to how I feel about you, I won't go any further. Just know that having you in my life, on my side, puts me way ahead of the game. I can only hope that my presence in yours brings similar meaning.

Seattle, Washington
September 2008

A version of chapter 6 was published as "When Politics Becomes Protest: Black Veterans and Political Activism in the Postwar South" in the *Journal of Politics* (vol. 71, no. 1, January 2009).

Fighting for Democracy

This is the country to which we soldiers of Democracy return. . . . But by the God of Heaven, we are cowards and
jackasses if now that the war is over, we do not marshal every
ounce of our brain and brawn to fight a sterner, longer, more
unbending battle against the forces of hell in our own land.
We return.
We return from fighting.
We return fighting.
—W.E.B. DuBois, "Returning Soldiers"

I have always had a feeling that I was just as much entitled to
register to vote as anybody. This thinking seemed to take on
momentum after getting out of the service, knowing the price I
paid . . . my life had been at stake . . . why shouldn't I have the
rights and privileges of any citizen? . . . If I could go over there
and make a sacrifice with my life, I was willing to do it here,
[even] if it meant death.
—William Bailey, World War II veteran,
quoted in Adam Fairclough, *Race and Democracy:
The Civil Rights Struggle in Louisiana, 1915–1972*

Beginning in the late 1940s, black Southerners grew increasing force-
ful in their rejection of white supremacy. Consider 1946, a year in
which black Mississippians publicly challenged white dominance on at
least two occasions. First, they contested the legitimacy of one of Mississippi's most popular politicians, U.S. senator Theodore Bilbo. Bilbo,
who was seeking a third term in the Senate, was accused of scaring
black Mississippians from the polls during the 1946 campaign. Upon
lodging a complaint, the local chapter of the NAACP, along with other
black organizations, looked forward to ousting from the Senate a man
who had opined on the campaign trail that "the best way to keep the
nigger from voting [was] to do it the night before the election," hinting
that, " 'Red blooded men know what I mean' " (quoted in Dittmer 1994,
2). Faced with a courthouse packed with whites who shared Bilbo's
sentiment, two hundred black Southerners from throughout the state
testified, at great personal risk, to the obstacles they had encountered
while trying to vote. Bilbo agreed not to take his seat in the upper

chamber until the matter was resolved. Ironically, he died of cancer of the mouth before the Senate came to a decision. This was a symbolic victory for the black Mississippians who denied one of the more racist politicians in the South the right to (mis)represent them for a third term.

That same year black Mississippians again sought to challenge white authority. This time, however, they did so with weapons. On the morning of July 2, 1946, twenty-one-year-old Medgar Evers gathered a group of young black men and headed for the courthouse in Decatur, Mississippi, intent on voting in the Democratic Party primary. Twenty armed white men blocked the group, warning them to end their quest. Feeling humiliated, the black men went home, retrieved small arms of their own, and returned (Dittmer 1994). Outnumbered, Evers and his contingent declined to continue, but their defiance sent a powerful message. Their actions suggested that they were prepared to take by force, if necessary, their right as American-born citizens to have a say in how the country was run.

While Evers and his group ultimately decided to avoid using weapons to contest white supremacy, other black Southerners relied on armed resistance as a tactical response to its violent strains. Elsewhere in the South, a year later, in 1947, black Southerners defied the Ku Klux Klan. In Monroe, North Carolina, Klan members planned to mutilate the body of Benny Montgomery, a World War II veteran who had killed his white boss after the man attacked him. Following Montgomery's conviction and execution, the Klan sought to express its disrespect for the man, and the black community of Monroe, by stripping the flag from Montgomery's coffin and dragging the veteran's body through the streets. A man named Robert F. Williams, along with other black men who lived in Monroe, refused to let this happen. When Klan members approached the funeral home to seize the body, they found the gun sights of more than three dozen rifle-wielding black men trained on them, at which point the Klan declined to engage. Another encounter between Williams and the Klan occurred ten years later. Williams, along with some of the members of the Monroe chapter of the NAACP, of which he was the leader, repelled an attack by the Klan on the home of one of the chapter's officers. The men defended the home behind fortified positions and coordinated rifle fire. As a result, city officials convened an emergency meeting during which they agreed to ban the Klan from assembling in public (Tyson 1999, chap. 3).

There were others who believed in the necessity of armed resistance. In response to threats from the Klan and local authorities, Earnest "Chilly Willy" Thomas founded the Deacons for Defense and Justice in 1964 to protect the black citizens of Jonesboro, Louisiana.[1] Consider one example of how the Deacons serviced the black community: On a cool morning in March 1965, black high school students in Jonesboro prepared to assemble their daily picket line. The police, already on site, called the fire department to help disrupt the demonstration by dousing the students with water from high-pressure hoses. As the firemen retrieved their hoses from the truck and returned, a car full of the Deacons arrived. The men exited the vehicle and loaded their rifles with buckshot in full view of the police. As the firemen prepared to spray the students, one of the Deacons instructed the other three: " 'Here he comes. Okay. Get ready. . . . When you see the first water, we gonna open up on them. We gonna open up on all of them.' " Turning to the police, he warned, " 'If you turn that water hose on those kids, there's gonna be some blood out here today' " (quoted in Hill 2004, 69). The police officers and firemen retreated before a shot was fired. Without the Deacons to protect them, moreover, the Congress of Racial Equality's (CORE's) efforts to register voters and desegregate public facilities in Louisiana would have been jeopardized (Fairclough 1995; Hill 2004).

• • •

What motivated these individuals and others like them to risk their lives by challenging white authority? Why were they willing to chance the violent reprisals to which black Southerners were often subjected when they tried to vote, much less openly testify against one of the most powerful politicians of the time? More important, why did they run the risk of death or economic ruin to which wielding weapons against whites exposed them? One answer is that black civic institutions—churches and secular civic organizations—provided those black Southerners who did resist with the social and psychological armor they needed to withstand threats. This explanation fits the first intervention, suggesting why

---

[1] Chartered in 1965, Deacons for Defense and Justice were an armed self-defense group. According to their charter, they proposed to " 'instruct, train, teach, and educate Citizens of the United States and especially minority groups in the fundamental principles of the republican form of government and our democratic way of life' " (quoted in Hill 2004). According to Hill (2004), the defense motive was buried deep in the text of the charter: " 'This corporation has for its further purpose, and is dedicated to, the defense of civil rights, property rights and personal rights of said people and will defend said rights by any and all honorable and legal means to the end that justice may be obtained' " (quoted in Hill 2004, 60–61). Originally formed to protect CORE workers and civil rights activists from Klan terror, the group's mission expanded to protecting from the Klan or the police anyone who required its help.

black Mississippians stood fast to challenge Bilbo. But churches and other black civic organizations typically shied away from armed resistance.[2]

How, then, do we explain why some black Southerners chose this mode of resistance? If we pay close attention, these vignettes suggest another source of strength on which some black Southerners drew: military experience. The protagonists of each of the incidents of violent resistance described above had either fought in or served during the Second World War or the Korean War. Medgar Evers, for instance, served as part of the famed Red Ball Express, the famous post–D-Day logistical operation that allowed the Allied forces to roll across Europe during the Second World War. His brother Charles and the other men who accompanied him that day in Decatur, Mississippi, had also served during World War II. Moreover, the majority of those who testified against Bilbo were also veterans of the Second World War (Dittmer 1994). Robert F. Williams served first in the army, during the Second World War, and later in the marines. Indeed, most of the men who had assisted him in fending off the Klan, on both occasions, were also veterans of World War I, World War II, or the Korean War. He recruited veterans to his chapter of the NAACP because, in his opinion, veterans "don't scare easy" (Williams 1998, 14). And Earnest "Chilly Willy" Thomas, along with many of those who took up arms to defend the students in Jonesboro that day and on later occasions, was also a veteran: he served in the Korean War while other Deacons had served in World War II, as well as in Korea.

This book explores why these and many other black "soldiers of democracy" followed the exhortation of W.E.B. DuBois, issued at the close of the First World War and reproduced in the first epigraph of this introduction, to fight for equality. My central argument is that black veterans' willingness to challenge white supremacy and resist Jim Crow rested to a significant extent upon their military experiences. They drew, first, on their perception that their service in the military made them full members of the political community; it merited full citizenship. Second, they drew on their military experiences, which exposed them to opportunities that bolstered their sense of agency and opened their eyes to the possibility of black-white relations in which they were considered equals. Finally, the

---

[2] This is not to say that some citizens, who were involved in local movement activities, also renounced armed resistance. The reluctance to employ armed resistance is a philosophy with which national civil rights organizations generally agreed, though CORE and the Student Nonviolent Coordinating Committee (SNCC) eventually reconsidered this position (Hill 2004; McAdam 1988).

confidence they gained from serving during wars in which they were forced to fight against the enemy in the field at the same time that they battled racism in the ranks sustained their commitment to fight white supremacy as well as their confidence to do so.

MILITARY SERVICE AND INSURGENCY

If we adopt the conventional views of military service and insurgency, and the conduct typically attributed to each, it is difficult to believe that military training could have resulted in challenges to authority. Scholars have identified several traits inculcated by the military that would seem to be anathema to protest. The military profession is typically associated with order, for instance, while insurgency and protest are associated with *relative* chaos. Scholars also argue that the military places a premium upon obedience, resulting in a preference for social order among soldiers that endures long after their separation from active duty (Janowitz 1960; Schreiber 1979). Insurgents use protest as a means to challenge authority, but challenging authority is forbidden in military circles. Finally, scholarly convention holds that a stint in the military breeds conservatism and reverence for tradition, neither of which is conducive to change (Abrahamsson 1970; Huntington 1957; Janowitz 1960; McClosky 1958; Segal et al. 2001), whereas insurgents by definition seek to change the status quo.

Military service is also believed to promote several normative values, among them national loyalty and fraternity (Janowitz 1983; Snyder 1999). In the early days of the American republic, patriotism and a preoccupation with national defense temporarily suspended class cleavages, sowing the cohesion necessary to defeat the British in the Revolutionary War (Chambers 1987; Cohen 1984, chap. 5). On the eve of the First World War, ex-president Theodore Roosevelt and his confederates insisted that military service would cure what they perceived to be flagging national cohesion and a lack of discipline among American youth, while it would also "Americanize" millions of immigrants (Chambers 1987, chap. 3; Gerstle 2001). Some thirty years later, as the Second World War drew to a close, universal military training as a means of creating a more homogenous and virtuous citizenry emerged once again as a subject of public discussion. In the 1940s and '50s, proponents of this idea argued that the ability of military training to promote democratic ideals, encourage a sense of fraternity and national unity through fulfillment of a common obligation to the country, and develop character merited its institutionalization. In consequence, Congress seriously considered passing the

Universal Military Training Act in the late 1940s and '50s, which would have mandated military service for all adult males.[3]

How, if at all, can the values and attitudes imparted by the military be harmonized with protest and, in some cases, civil disobedience? If the military promotes a preference for the status quo, social order, and for national unity and fraternity, how can we explain some black veterans' resistance to Jim Crow? In the context of the South, was not resistance inconsistent with the status quo and social order? Moreover, how is it that the military, an institution not known for its democratic practices, helped overthrow what some (e.g., Mickey, forthcoming) call authoritarian rule in the South? In this book, I make sense of the relationship between military service and resistance by considering how the civic education soldiers receive in the military affects their postservice attitudes. Indeed, through socialization and education, it is believed that soldiers are instilled with strong feelings of fraternity, a belief in the importance of national unity, and reverence for the democratic values for which they are prepared to die (Burk 2002; Cohen 1984, chap. 5; Janowitz 1983).[4] If black veterans bought into the republican version of citizenship, in which citizenship is earned through civic and martial practices (Snyder 1999), their views may have changed on a range of issues. Such veterans would have returned to the South feeling entitled to the equality for which they had fought.

The performance of military duty, furthermore, would have brought them to identify more strongly with the nation and its values. In other words, fighting *on behalf of* democracy ultimately resulted in black veterans fighting *for* democracy. Fighting for the preservation of freedom and equality elsewhere heightened their consciousness of racial differences when they returned to a South that failed to acknowledge, much less appreciate, their sacrifices. From this perspective, then, insurgency flowed from veterans' race consciousness, their sense of entitlement, and the shift in their political identity, according to which a perception of

---

[3] Several investigations have sought to assess the effect of military socialization on postservice attitudes and behavior (Bachman and Jennings 1975; Campbell and McCormick 1957; Christie 1952; Dorman 1976; Ernest and French 1955; Jennings and Markus 1976, 1977; Lippert, Schneider, and Zoll 1978; Roghmann and Soduer 1972; Segal and Segal 1976). Notwithstanding the inconsistent findings—that is, that some of these works identify service-induced differences while others fail to do so—none of these studies is sensitive to the issue of race. Of the studies that are sensitive to racial considerations, the evidence was collected well after the civil rights movement (Ellison 1992). See also Leal (1999), which assesses the effect of military service on Latino political activism.

[4] Janowitz (1978) has argued that after World War I the connection between military service and citizenship weakened. Nuclear weapons, Janowitz believes, made it difficult for the individual to imagine his importance to the pursuit of war.

their improved standing in the political community amplified their determination to achieve the equality they believed they had earned. Thus, some argue, veterans' activism ultimately rested on their perceived relationship to the national community: As full members, they insisted upon fighting for the rights they had earned (Brooks 2004; O'Brien 1999; Tyson 1999).

Political scientist Ronald Krebs's (2004, 2006) interrogation of this line of argument—indeed, of the very proposition that military socialization can produce veteran activism—is perhaps the most thoroughgoing to date. Krebs questions the ability of the military establishment to induce, via socialization, a shift in the identification of veterans of the sort required for political activism. Military service, he argues, is incapable of producing the sort of social transformation that people like Theodore Roosevelt have attributed to it. Unlike Janowitz (1983), who argues that the military is a principal source of civic education, Krebs argues that the military is not a "school for the nation." In his book *Fighting for Rights* (2006), in which he ultimately gauges the relative ability of blacks in America, and the Druze in Israel, to leverage military service as a means of achieving first-class citizenship, Krebs argues that military experience lacks the capacity to launch veterans toward meaningful interrogation of the status quo. Beyond the usefulness to minority groups of referring to wartime contributions as a rhetorical device with which to secure postwar benefits, he believes that military service, through the direct intervention of veterans, is incapable of reshaping the nation. If military socialization is to galvanize disparate groups of men into a cohesive whole, Krebs contends, it must persuade them to reconsider who they are, and how they define their political community. In the American case Krebs suggests, however, that a lasting commitment to a new, more American, identity is difficult to forge through military service for at least two reasons. First, veterans return to and rejoin social networks in which the regimentation associated with the military is not appreciated. Once they return, moreover, pressure is placed upon them to conform to civil societal norms and leave their military experiences in the past. Second, the endurance of identity shifts brought about by military socialization is limited by the fact that veterans typically leave the military prior to the age at which their political attitudes settle, foreclosing the ability of military service to have a lasting effect on the individual. In short, Krebs suggests that the radicalization of black veterans would have to rest on their having formed new and lasting identity commitments (i.e. identification with the nation) while serving in the armed forces. He maintains that such commitments are not formed; it follows that black activism is unlikely to have been prompted by the radicalization of black veterans while in the military.

Both of the approaches to the activism of black veterans just described have merit, yet each is limited by the fact that the extent of veterans' overall participation in the civil rights movement remains unclear. Consider the approach in which military service is believed to stimulate activism. A few narratives in which veterans' military service appears to have promoted their participation in the movement offer valuable insight into veterans' motives for challenging white supremacy, but they are limited to specific cases, such as, say, those of Tennessee or Georgia (Brooks 2004; O'Brien 1999). Furthermore, the scope of these inquiries is often limited to veterans of the Second World War. Thus, we cannot make any general claims regarding black veterans' activism based on these accounts, because we have no way of knowing the extent of their activism throughout the South, beyond the small cadre who were typically among the leadership of black civic organizations.[5] Nor do we know definitively if black veterans' civil rights activism was largely confined to those who served in the Second World War or if veterans of the Korean War also challenged white supremacy. Finally, before we can trumpet the relationship between military service and militancy, we must account for alternative explanations of resistance, such as those that attribute it to education, income, membership in black civic organizations, and racial solidarity (Marx 1967; Rochon 1998). Without accounting for these alternatives, it is difficult to gauge the extent to which military service affected the activism of black Southerners.

Krebs marshals an impressive array of social scientific evidence to interrogate the means by which many believe veterans become radicalized through their military experience. Yet none of it offers a *direct*, systematic test of his claim that military service fails to promote activism, particularly among black veterans. To be fair, the main thrust of Krebs's work centers upon the indirect effect of military service on social progress. He does a fine job of illustrating how and why the Druze were able to take advantage of the cultural capital associated with military service, and why blacks failed to do likewise.[6] Nonetheless, to arrive at this conclusion, Krebs must first demonstrate the impotence of the *direct* effect of military service in which veterans' military experience propelled them toward insurgent behavior, a claim that rests on suggestive, though far

[5] See also Dittmer (1994), Edgerton (2002), and Lawson (1976), all of whom suggest that black veterans were committed to activism across the South—after the Second World War. See also Payne (1995) for veterans' activity in Mississippi, Tyson (1999) for North Carolina, and Fairclough (1995) and Hill (2004) for Louisiana. Again, however, this issue is whether or not veterans were active beyond notables like Robert Williams, Medgar Evers, and Hosea Williams.

[6] See Krebs (2006) for reasons why military service failed as a rhetorical tool for African Americans.

from conclusive, evidence. In the absence of more compelling evidence, can we say for sure that veterans failed to contribute to insurgency in the South? What is needed is an approach conducive to an examination in which a range of factors may be considered.

This book takes such an approach. It does so by showing that, regardless of locale, many black veterans challenged white supremacy in the period following the Second World War and the Korean War. Equally important—as I will detail below—the book accomplishes this task by bringing to bear more systematic evidence on the question of whether or not military service, particularly one's military experience, produced activism among black veterans, independent of more well-known sources of insurgency. In the end, this book theorizes and tests a mechanism through which military service sparked insurgent attitudes and behavior—an approach that thus far remains absent from the literature.[7] It shows how the meaning and experiences associated with military service combined to produce citizens willing to fight for their fair share of the democracy for which they had sacrificed so much.[8]

Recasting Military Service and Resistance

I take the position that military service and insurgency are indeed compatible. To do so, however, I must shift the explanation of the relationship between military service and resistance away from military socialization to one that pivots instead upon the *meaning* associated with military service. This is necessary because it is a common belief that military

[7] Mettler's (2005a, 2005b) work also examines the politicization of black veterans. Her work interrogates the ways in which the GI Bill affected the political activism of black veterans. While she shows that the policy feedback effects of the GI Bill boosted the political engagement of veterans, her investigation concentrates on veterans, since they were the only group eligible for benefits. In short, Mettler seeks to discriminate between veterans on the basis of GI Bill usage. My project seeks to discriminate between veterans and nonveterans, the latter of which functions as a control group of sorts.

[8] While military experience contributed to insurgency in this way, the social history of the civil rights movement reveals that one need not have been a veteran to resist Jim Crow segregation. Indeed, from Martin Luther King Jr. and Stokely Carmichael to Ella Baker and Fannie Lou Hammer, we are more familiar with the deeds of activists who were without military experience. Of course, Dr. King led the Southern Christian Leadership Conference (SCLC) while Carmichael served as the voice for the more militant SNCC. Baker and Hammer, it seems, were versatile in their respective abilities to be counted among the leadership of several organizations during their respective lives. Baker was involved with the NAACP and the SCLC, and was key to the foundation of the SNCC (Ransby 2003). Hammer, a native of Mississippi, was also involved with the SNCC and was a founding member of the Mississippi Freedom Democratic Party.

socialization, with its putative ability to produce good citizens, eventually gives way to political socialization, which, with its emphasis on "learning . . . those values, attitudes, and modes of behavior that help people 'fit in' to their political systems" (Conover 1991, 131), in turn, is more in tune with maintaining the status quo, something the veterans in the vignettes presented earlier clearly sought to upset. Instead of political socialization, these black veterans seemed to be driven by something else. That "something," I believe, was political learning. Political learning, a process best described as one by which individuals come to apprehend knowledge of the political sort, departs from political socialization in at least two ways: the lessons learned need not support the existing political order, as is required for political socialization; nor is there a requirement that the lessons learned be of the deliberate kind, the product of pedagogy. Put differently, political learning "refers to the learning of any politically relevant material regardless of whether or not this learning promotes support for the existing political regime . . . [and] regardless of whether or not the learning is deliberate" (Conover 1991, 131).[9]

The meaning attached to military service, for African Americans, is one way to explain the source of black veterans' political learning. Historically, African Americans have used military service as a strategy for achieving equality, so much so that the utility of military service to achieve equal rights had "become an article of faith" among African Americans by the mid-twentieth century (Nalty 1986, 10). This is why, as Stouffer and colleagues (1949, chap. 10) discovered during the Second World War, black soldiers in that conflict believed their service would be rewarded with more equal treatment in postwar America. Indeed, as we shall see in chapter 1, black Americans' military service has contributed to racial advancement in the past.

But to fully understand the dynamic through which African Americans' military service has positively influenced the struggle for civil rights, we must also consider how the experience of military service itself transformed veterans. Fighting for democracy (or, for those who never had the opportunity to fight, simply serving), I contend, symbolized the equality to which African Americans aspired. Bearing arms to preserve America's democratic ideals, in the eyes of black (and white) Americans, had come to be associated with first-class citizenship; this meant full membership in the political community, which included the enjoyment of civil as well as political equality (Conover, Searing, and Crewe 2004). Wearing their nation's uniform likewise represented veterans' attachment to the nation and reflected

---

[9] Theoretically, political socialization is subordinate to political learning to the extent that the latter is the broader, more capacious concept. For more on political learning see Jennings and Niemi (1974, 1981) and Siegel (1989).

their improved social standing. Consequently, many black veterans believed that they deserved treatment commensurate with this standing.

The symbolic effect of military service provides the normative rationale for black veterans' resistance, but it fails to explain the conduct of the veterans in the vignettes given at the opening of this chapter, because it fails to identify the positive impetus for their actions. Why, in other words, did veterans decide to act on their beliefs? Surely other black Southerners felt moral outrage, but many were not in the practice of confronting domination with weapons. Military experiences, I argue, are what separated black veterans from nonveterans and, for many veterans, furnished this impetus. For black Southerners, service in the military exposed them to people, places, and circumstances that perpetual civilians never encounter. As we shall see, these experiences also provided black servicemen with a fresh perspective on their station in American society. While serving overseas, many black veterans were often treated by the dominant racial group with a measure of respect to which they were unaccustomed. Of course, segregation and discrimination within the military created hardships and resentment among black soldiers, the effects of which cannot and should not be minimized. Nevertheless, black soldiers—especially those hailing from the South— were often assigned responsibilities that required them to think and perform in new and different ways. Accomplishing challenging and novel tasks in the context of defending liberty, I argue, gave black soldiers an enhanced sense of agency. Moreover, many of them looked on their years in the service as an achievement that gave them confidence and the strength to resist white supremacy on their return to the South.

In sum, I argue that for black veterans, military service instilled a set of normative beliefs and experiences that motivated them to act to secure their rights as citizens. Normatively, fighting, or the willingness to do so, conveyed to black servicemen a sense of equality; the performance of citizenship, in other words, transformed black veterans into citizens of the first rank (Snyder 1999). Their service-linked belief in their entitlement to all of the benefits of American democracy created, as I will show, a moral warrant to pursue change. On the positive side, their military experiences fueled these veterans' sense of agency and introduced them to the possibility of change. The confidence they gained from bearing arms and resisting subordination in the military spilled over into their postservice lives. Witnessing new patterns of race relations overseas likewise alerted them to the possibility of change. These experiences encouraged many black veterans to participate in local struggles in which "ordinary people" challenged white supremacy (Brooks 2004; Dittmer 1994; Fairclough 1995; O'Brien 1999; Payne 1995; Tuck 2001; Tyson 1999).

Theory and Method

My argument about the political effects of military service is based on a theoretical approach that resembles the one adopted by Lieberman (2005) in his comparative analysis of government policy. Drawing on his synthetic approach, *Fighting for Democracy* combines ideational and institutional approaches to explain the political attitudes and behavior of black veterans. In the context under consideration here, military service—and its association with democratic citizenship (Burk 1995; Janowitz 1976; Krebs 2006; Salyer 2004; Snyder 1999)—served as a cultural resource on which black veterans drew for the purpose of advancing claims on America for the redress of grievances.[10] When Southern civil society, as well as state and local authorities, failed to recognize these service-based claims, however, this failure motivated veterans to act. Thus, the meaning of military service represents the ideational component of my approach.

But military service entailed more than just ideational consequences, furnishing black veterans with the motivation to act; it *enabled* them to act. Institutions, as taken-for-granted scripts and standard operating procedures, among other things, shape individuals' preferences (Meyer and Rowan 1991). More important, however, institutions are capable of empowering individuals (Smith 1992), creating the conditions for agency through symbolic action (DiMaggio and Powell 1991). Black veterans' experiences within the military, I submit, ought to be considered as interactions with an institution that empowered them to participate in and even help lead the postwar civil rights struggle. After all, courage, discipline, and leadership, all of which are institutionalized in the military, were drawn upon by black veterans who either led or founded key civil rights organizations (Brooks 2004; Carson 1981; Forman 1972; Hill 2004; see also appendix D for examples). Enduring institutionalized discrimination and segregation while in the military also prepared black veterans for insurgency upon returning to civil society. Many of them, as we shall see, became accustomed to challenging white supremacy while still in uniform. Thus, the military as an institution was a source of agency for black veterans.

If the theoretical approach of *Fighting for Democracy* is synthetic in nature, so is its methodological approach, which applies qualitative and quantitative methods to the analysis of new and existing sources of evi-

---

[10] For more on the ways in which culture promotes agency, see Archer (1988); Laitin (1988); Sewell (1992); Swidler (1986); and Wedeen (2002).

dence on the political attitudes and behavior of black veterans.[11] The most original source of evidence is a series of semistructured interviews I conducted with twenty-five veterans, all of whom served during the Second World War, the Korean War, or both. The interviews serve two purposes: first, they permit me to examine how, if at all, military service is reconciled with postservice militancy; second, my analysis of the interviews generates hypotheses that are subsequently tested using quantitative data in the latter chapters of the book. To test these hypotheses, I draw on the superb, if underemployed, data collected by Donald Matthews and James Prothro in the South during the early 1960s for the Negro Political Participation Study. This appears to have been the most complete survey instrument administered in the South during the civil rights movement; it contains attitudinal and behavioral items that measure everything from Southern traditionalism to political participation. Using data contemporaneous with the movement provides a basis for perhaps the most systematic investigation to date of the ways in which military service influenced political attitudes and behavior in the South during the movement. Moreover, this data also permits me to explore the external validity of the interview findings, as well as grapple with competing explanations for militancy among black veterans.

BROADER CONTRIBUTIONS

Exploring the political attitudes and behavior of black veterans during the latter stage of the civil rights movement in the South contributes to at least three streams of research. First, it advances our understanding of the relationship between war and racial progress by adding a much-needed individual-level explanation to existing work. In some accounts, war helped shape racial policy in America, forcing political elites to respond to world opinion in the context of the Cold War by addressing, if not correcting, racial injustice in the South (Borstelmann 2001; Dudziak 2000; Kryder 2000, Skrentny 2002). Others have demonstrated that the ideological reasons for war mobilization, the scope of the mobilization, and the consequences of each have also fueled racial progress (Klinkner and Smith 1999; Kryder 2000). Doug McAdam's work (1999) likewise cites factors beyond the individual level, arguing that, among other things, the economic push and pull of war and the concomitant interregional and

[11] A mixed-method approach is becoming increasingly popular in political science (Cohen 1999; Harris 1999; Harris-Lacewell 2004; Hochschild 1995; Lee 2002; Mettler 2005b; Sawyer 2006).

intraregional migration from rural areas to Southern metropolises sparked postwar change.[12] This book, by contrast, highlights the ways in which military service transformed *individuals* first into soldiers and then into activists who fought for more equitable treatment. It shows how mobilization for war may also lead to postwar micromobilization for change.

Another research agenda to which this book contributes is one in which war affects the development and vibrancy of American civil society. Some scholarship demonstrates the ways in which patriotism underwrote the growth of civil society. For instance, Robert Putnam's (2000) observations on the effect of World War II and Theda Skocpol and colleagues' (2002) findings pertaining to the Civil War and World War I both document the growth of civic associations in America. From a different perspective, Suzanne Mettler (2005b) shows the same thing. More to the point, her work highlights the ways in which military service, through the GI Bill, strengthened democratic civil society through the political activism of veterans who served during the Second World War. These veterans, buoyed by their appreciation for the opportunities bestowed upon them by the state, decided to continue their service to America by vigorously discharging their obligations as citizens. This book adds to this burgeoning literature by showing a means through which war helped to develop and expand black civil society. Although some black veterans chafed at the relatively conservative, buttoned-down culture of the NAACP (Forman 1972; Henry 2000; Hill 2004; Tyson 1999; Williams 1998), many others helped expand its membership in the Deep South in the postwar years (Payne 1995). Black veterans also helped found and lead other, more grassroots civil rights organizations that were important to the success of the movement, including the Deacons for Defense and the Mississippi Freedom Democratic Party (Brooks 2004; Carson 1981; Henry 2000; Hill 2004; see also appendix D). This book outlines a mechanism, one that differed from patriotism or policy-feedback effects, that contributed to the development and expansion of democratic civil society.

Fighting for Democracy also connects with the literature on the civil rights movement by demonstrating that black civic institutions were not the only sources of insurgent attitudes and behavior among black Southerners. It remains undeniable that black churches, civil rights organizations, and fraternal groups were the principal institutional sites through which black Southerners contested white supremacy in the South (Harris 1999; McAdam 1999; Morris 1984; Skocpol, Liazos, and Ganz 2006). Nonetheless, the comment of William Bailey in the second epigraph for

---

[12] See Sawyer (2006) for an excellent comparative perspective in which he combines macro and micro approaches to explain racial dynamics in Cuba.

this introduction, indicates why military service furnished black veterans with additional motivation to challenge the status quo. Bailey suggests that as an American, he had always felt entitled to participate in the political process, yet military service and the sacrifice it entailed had a transformative effect on his attitudes toward citizenship. In light of his sacrifice, exercising his civic rights assumed a sense of urgency he had not felt before serving. He was willing to die for that to which he felt himself entitled.

This conviction, I contend, is what separated Southern veterans from nonveterans, giving the latter additional motivation to resist white supremacy. While it was not a contemporaneous source of agency, as were churches and black civic organizations, the military nonetheless ought to be viewed as an "agency-laden institution" of the kind referred to by Aldon Morris. Such institutions, Morris explains, "generate cultural materials [that] . . . produce and solidify trust, contacts, solidarity, rituals, [and] meaning systems . . . of members embedded in their social network" (2000, 447). Military service, for African Americans, produced similar outcomes. Indeed, *Fighting for Democracy* suggests that military service was an important source of agency for black veterans.

PLAN OF THE BOOK

The exploration that follows begins with the historical and theoretical foundation upon which the balance of the book rests. Chapter 1 introduces the historical context of African American military service, tracing the relationships among race, war, and citizenship since the American Revolution and demonstrating why, in the mid-twentieth century, African Americans tended to view military service as a means of advancement for the race and the individual as well as a way to earn the respect of whites. The chapter reveals a republican narrative in that African Americans benefited from military service only when their efforts during wartime were at least appreciated, if not necessarily celebrated, by the nation. When, on other occasions, they were either denied the opportunity to serve or their service was maligned, African Americans' social progress tended to stall or even regress. More important, the chapter shows that black veterans' insurgent attitudes and behavior predated the Second World War, highlighting a pattern by which black servicemen and veterans grew increasingly intolerant of the domination to which they were subjected.

Chapter 2 elaborates my theoretical argument, building a framework through which we may apprehend black veterans' resistance and activism. If the first chapter is about revealing the consistency of black veterans' resistance, chapter 2 ventures to explain why these veterans continued to challenge white supremacy. As I have already suggested, this book draws on a combination of cultural claims and institutionalism to support its theoretical argument. I argue that the normative meaning of military service, in concert with the institutional experience associated with the military, was conducive to the development of a worldview among black veterans consistent with what I term "black republicanism," which, as I conceive it, describes a set of beliefs and values that drew on republican principles—adapted to fit blacks' experience in America—as a means of guiding black veterans' attitudes and behavior on their return to Southern society.

Chapters 3 and 4 lay the empirical foundation for the balance of the book. The third chapter examines the symbolic meaning of military service by considering the experiences and views of seventeen of the black veterans with whom I conducted in-depth interviews over a two-year period. This chapter gives life to their experiences within the military as an institution. The veterans discuss their struggles serving in a Jim Crow military and the mistreatment to which they were subjected. But they also go into some detail about how they fought back—sometimes quite literally. The chapter also reveals how military experience gave veterans a fresh perspective on the world and a sense of self-confidence. In chapter 4, I probe the contours of black republicanism in light of these interviews. In doing so, the chapter highlights the normative dimension of military service. While many of the veterans I spoke to identify with the country and its values, they rarely hesitated to criticize America. In most cases, they used republican rhetoric to frame their respective criticisms of the country. Many argued that the sacrifices that they made for themselves—and on behalf of the black community—should have cleared the way for more equal citizenship for African Americans. In several instances, as we shall see, this instigated the activism that I associate with black republicanism.

In the next two chapters, I explore the attitudinal and behavioral implications of military experience for black veterans of the Second World War and the Korean War living in the South. These chapters generalize the findings from the interviews to black veterans in the mass public. Relying on the Negro Political Participation Study, an exceptional, if underappreciated source of data, chapter 5 examines the insurgent attitudes of veterans and compares them to the attitudes of nonveterans, who serve as a baseline group. Ultimately this chapter illustrates that black veterans' military experience inoculated them against a preference for the Southern status quo—against the reluctant acceptance of white supremacy as a fact of life. These findings confirm, on a larger scale, what many of the interviews suggest: black veterans were committed to change.

In chapter 6, I turn to the examination of insurgent behavior. It is one thing to harbor democratic *attitudes* in the midst of a society committed to white supremacy. It is quite another thing, however, to act on these beliefs, especially when doing so often risks jeopardizing one's livelihood, even one's life. For the purposes of this study I argue that political mobilization in the context of white domination is a good proxy for insurgent behavior. Indeed, to the extent that mainstream political mobilization prior to the ratification of the Voting Rights Act in 1965 challenged white authority, it should be considered a form of insurgent behavior. This chapter shows that the activism described by my interviewees was not confined to a handful of veterans. Veterans' active challenge of white supremacy, we shall see, carried over to at least two modes of conventional political participation: voting and political activism. Regardless of the perceived danger associated with the mode of participation, black veterans as a group insisted on using the mainstream political process to challenge white supremacy. These results lend support to the activist claims I make concerning black republicanism.

In the book's conclusion, I revisit issues raised in this introduction and summarize the main findings. Substantively, I find that taking seriously the effects of black veterans' military experience adds to our stock of knowledge about the civil rights movement. The book shows that black veterans' military experience furnished another source of resistance, one that until now has largely remained confined to the many local struggles in which black veterans helped provide leadership. However, this book also suggests that black veterans did more than provide leadership during key campaigns, as historians have clearly shown to be the case. *Fighting for Democracy* also indicates that veterans were a significant segment of the struggle's rank and file. I then proceed to consider the broader implications of the book and directions for future research. For instance, the book highlights the use of republican rhetoric as a means of guiding the pursuit of reform. In this way I also show that military service, true to its republican roots, was conducive to democratizing the South. Black Southerners, however, used it as a means to wrest freedom and equality from enemies within, instead of protecting them from threats originating elsewhere.

CHAPTER 1

War, Military Service, and the Prospect for Change

A GLANCE AT HISTORY

> *The Crisis* says, *first* your country, *then* your rights! . . . Certain
> honest thinkers among us hesitate at that last sentence. They
> say it is all well to be idealistic, but is it not true that while we
> have fought our country's battles for one hundred fifty years,
> we have *not* gained our rights? No, we have gained them
> rapidly and effectively by our loyalty in time of trial.
> —W.E.B. DuBois, "The Reward"

> Shall we be citizens in war, and aliens in peace? Would that be
> just?
> —Frederick Douglass, "What the Black Man Wants"

From Crispus Attucks to Colin Powell, African Americans have always answered the call to the colors and have fashioned a long, exceptional history of military service. Examples of African American wartime heroes are legion and include the Massachusetts Fifty-Fourth Regiment during the Civil War; the Buffalo Soldiers during the Spanish-American War, who saved the hides of Theodore Roosevelt and his Rough Riders; the Tuskegee Airmen, who never lost a bomber over Italy during the Second World War; and the 761st Tank Battalion under General George Patton. Given the historic oppression of African Americans, why have they always answered the call?

One standard explanation for why citizens serve in the military rests upon the rights-obligations trade-off that is part of the American conception of citizenship (Janowitz 1980; Kerber 1997). According to this model, citizens who enjoy the benefits of democracy during peacetime are obligated to defend it during times of national crisis. Another explanation, offered by Margaret Levi (1997), suggests that if the state has demonstrated that citizens' contribution will not be wasted and if current policy and its implementation are deemed fair, individual citizens will be likely to answer the call as long as other citizens are doing so. Both theories are helpful in understanding why white males serve. For blacks, however, we need an alternative explanation.

We cannot explain black Americans' willingness to serve in terms of their desire to fulfill an obligation of citizenship for periods in which black Americans did not have the rights of citizens.[1] In the absence of equal citizenship—first at the federal level, and more recently at the state level—black Southerners remained excluded from the highest rank of membership in the political community (Karst 1989; Shklar 1991; Smith 1997). With this in mind, until relatively recently, blacks had no real moral obligation to serve in the military. Political alienation is sufficient reason to relieve individuals of the obligation of military service to a nation in which they are not part of the decision to make war (Walzer 1970, chap. 3). In Levi's view, compliance with conscription is based at least in part upon the perceived fairness of the government, including its past practices. History, however, taught African Americans to trust the federal government only as a last resort, and thus they had little reason to serve on the basis of trust.

Why, then, did blacks desire to fight for a country in which they remained second-class citizens? The principal explanation lies in the perceived benefits of military service, many of which lay squarely within the republican tradition. As this chapter's epigraphs suggest, black leaders from Frederick Douglass to W.E.B. DuBois were aware of the relationship between citizenship and military service.[2] They subscribed to the belief that blacks' willingness to share the burdens of war would be rewarded in postwar America. In some cases, as DuBois indicates, the strategy worked. As we shall see, changes in the legal status of blacks following the War of Independence and the Civil War were tied directly to African American participation in these conflicts. By this, I mean that social

---

[1] Make no mistake; I am not claiming that black veterans were exceptional in their willingness to serve. Blacks have not been exempt from the draft during most American conflicts, and those who have chosen not to serve have been subject to the same punishments as whites. African Americans have also been attracted to service in the military by material incentives, among them the opportunity to escape suffocating poverty, to travel, to make use of the GI Bill, and to learn valuable vocational skills (Katznelson 2005, chap. 4; Modell, Goulden, and Magnussen 1989; Mettler 2005a). Nevertheless, given their historically subordinate position in American society, black Americans' willingness to fight is laudable. Indeed, from the American Revolution through the Korean War, many—though certainly not all—black servicemen were adamant about fighting, not merely serving (Barbeau and Henri 1974; Bogart 1969; Cornish 1987; Fletcher 1974; Nalty 1986; Stouffer et al. 1949; Wynn 1993).

[2] DuBois's words are attributed to an editorial, penned in the *Crisis*, titled "The Reward." (1918). Douglass's observation is attributed to a speech titled, "What the Black Man Wants" (1865).

change was guided by the federal government (Marwick 1974), which rewarded African Americans for their service. In other cases, however, the strategy failed. After the War of 1812, the Spanish-American War, and World War I, the social position of blacks deteriorated (Klinkner and Smith 1999, chap. 1).

In this chapter I will trace the relationships among race, military service, and citizenship. My purpose is not so much to lay out a theory of these relationships; there is sufficient scholarship that does this well (Klinkner and Smith 1999; Nalty 1986; Wynn 1993). More to the point, existing work establishes a pattern by which military service, among other factors, often contributes to racial progress (Klinkner and Smith 1999). Rather, my purpose here is to examine whether or not the observed resistance of black veterans in the 1940s, '50s, and '60s was particular to their service during the Second World War and the Korean War. After all, the Second World War is often cited as the point at which the freedom struggle took a militant turn (Dalfiume 1969; Klinkner and Smith 1999; Sitkoff 1971a; Wynn 1993).[3] Moreover, it remains possible that black servicemen's willingness to challenge Jim Crow treatment during the Second World War was driven by the general mood of the black public (Thomas 1993). An alternative explanation holds that resistance on the part of black servicemen and veterans was part of a more general pattern, one that predated the Second World War and the rise of black militancy. In short, black veterans' militancy had less to do with *when* they served and more to do with the fact that they had served at all. As it turns out, black servicemen and veterans began to resist white supremacy long before the mid-twentieth century and the rise of mass African American militancy.

The Promise of Military Service in the Early American Republic

From 1619 through 1789, the political and legal status of African Americans remained fluid. Even prior to the institutionalization of slavery beginning around 1705 with Virginia's slave codes, Virginia law recognized differences between whites and Africans, with tangible consequences.[4] A 1669 statute, for instance, allowed slave masters to kill unrepentant

---

[3] For an alternative perspective, see Finkle (1973) and Sitkoff (1997).

[4] The Virginia slave codes spanned the years 1705–92, and covered every domain of slave life. They governed everything from who slaves were allowed to marry, the religions they followed, and which clothes they wore to what they were allowed to eat (Higginbotham 1996).

slaves because the latter were considered the property of the former (Higginbotham 1996). Since slaves were considered property, "common sense," according to Virginia code, suggested that one would not purposely destroy part of one's estate. Therefore, the death of a slave was treated as an accident with no legal consequences.[5] Despite this bleak official picture, however, scores of African Americans managed to transform their legal status prior to the Revolutionary War by winning manumission through service in colonial militias, aiding whites in their frequent skirmishes with Native Americans. Slaves were first called for service in the militia of South Carolina, for example, in 1703. By 1715, they were awarded with freedom upon presenting proof of having killed Native Americans. Slaves continued to serve in the South Carolina militia until 1750, when concerns about arming enslaved blacks began to outweigh fear of Native Americans (Berry 1977, chap. 2).[6]

A few decades later, the Revolutionary War presented an opportunity for the advancement of African American interests. Beyond the limited number of African Americans who were already serving in 1776 as members of militias, however, their efforts to enlist were not welcomed. American "patriots," it seems, did not wish to fight alongside "undesirables"—African Americans among them—whom they believed did not have a stake in the outcome of the war (Berry 1977, chap. 2). Out of fear and a perception of superiority, whites refused to even consider the prospect of arming slaves (Quarles 1961). Following the Lexington and Concord campaigns of 1775, during which they performed well, blacks were excluded from serving in the Continental Army.

The British decided to tap into this pool of manpower that the Continental Army seemed intent on wasting. In response to Lord Dunmore's promise to free any slaves willing to fight on the Crown's behalf, approximately 100,000 blacks aligned themselves with the loyalist cause. The soldiers of the Ethiopian Regiment, as they had come to be known, wore a sash on their British uniforms on which "Liberty for Slaves" was written. In response to the pressure Dunmore's offer created, General George Washington eased restrictions on African American enlistments in 1775, and by 1777 blacks—both slaves and freedmen—were permitted to serve on the side of the colonies without restriction, and often without the impediment of segregation (Berry 1977; Quarles 1961).

In what would become a pattern, the wartime service of these African Americans resulted in postwar progress. By the end of the war, over five

---

[5] The Virginia legislature added the "accident" clause in its 1705 draft.
[6] White officials also contracted Native Americans to hunt fugitive slaves (Berry 1977).

thousand African Americans had served in the Continental Army and Navy, earning their freedom in the process. In some quarters, slave masters attempted to return these veterans to servitude. In the eyes of many white elites, however—including the governor of Virginia—the military service and sacrifice of the men in question overrode the self-interest of white Southerners, revealing that republicanism transcended a form of government. Republicanism also represented a suite of values, Sara Purcell (2002) argues, on which American national identity would come to rest: self-sacrifice, military heroism, love of liberty, and benevolence. Perhaps this is what drove Virginia's chief executive to honor the service of Virginia's slaves. Governor Benjamin Harrison promised to " '[l]ay the matter before the [state] assembly, not doubting that they [would] pass an act giving to those unhappy creatures that liberty which they [had] been in some measure instrumental in securing to us' " (quoted in Quarles 1961, 183). The Virginia state legislature promptly passed a measure emancipating all slaves who had served.[7]

Aided at least in part by the performance of blacks in the Continental Army and Navy, the spirit of the Revolution (liberty for all) caused many—though certainly not all—whites to interrogate the institution of slavery in the North (Quarles 1961, 183–200), stimulating the emergence of several abolitionist societies. By 1804, every state north of the Potomac River had abolished slavery. Between 1776 and 1790, moreover, several Northern states also changed their laws to allow free blacks to vote.[8] Revolutionary ideology failed to penetrate south of the Mason-Dixon Line, however, where the North had to capitulate to Southern demands and allow slavery to remain intact if the new law of the land was to take root. In this regard, progress wasn't universal; it was limited in the main to blacks residing outside of the South, a minority of the black population in America.

War and the Declining Status of African Americans in the Antebellum Period

Between 1790 and 1860, the limited gains achieved by African Americans in the aftermath of the American Revolution started to erode, and

---

[7] In a twist of irony, there were actually more slaves who were liberated from slavery by supporting the British than those who supported the cause of the patriots. British ships spirited away as many as 20,000 slaves (Schama 2006). Some, however, were simply resold into bondage by loyalists or British officers upon arriving in the West Indies. Others managed to escape to Canada.

[8] New Jersey was the first, in 1776, allowing free blacks to vote as long as they met property requirements. Vermont and New York followed suit; in 1790, Pennsylvania became the last state in the North to ease voting restrictions on free blacks.

the civic and legal status of blacks began a steady regression to the status of nonpersonhood. The process began with the ratification of the Militia Act in 1792. It called for the participation of all white males of ages eighteen to forty-five in the state militias. Blacks were excluded from service in the state militias by this act, for at least three reasons. First, the militia served as the first line of defense for the nation, and blacks were deemed unfit to serve in this capacity. Second, state militias were to be employed as the principal safeguard against slave insurrection. Indeed, with the Haitian Revolution underway, it's quite possible that arming slaves was something planters wished to avoid (Foner 1974, chap. 2). Finally, according to the republican ideology under which the new nation operated (Bailyn 1967; Wood 1969), service in the state militia was reserved for those who were part of the political community, a status not enjoyed by the vast majority of blacks.

If there was any doubt at this point about whether blacks were to be understood as members of this community, it was removed the following year. The legal sanction of slavery embedded in the Fugitive Slave Act (1793), which bolstered the three-fifths clause already written into the nation's Constitution, indicated that blacks were not to be considered part of the political community. To be sure, African Americans were allowed to serve in the ranks of the regular armed forces; but such service earned little respect, as the regular army was perceived to be a place for undesirables (Berry 1977, chap. 3). Free blacks, many of whom had been freed during the Revolution, suffered additional setbacks in the years that followed the war. Beginning in 1802, for instance, the state legislatures of Connecticut, New Jersey, New York, and Ohio rescinded African Americans' voting rights.

The War of 1812 initially promised to at least forestall the racial retrenchment taking place in postrevolutionary America. By serving in the military, blacks hoped to regain the ground they had recently lost. But the government insisted upon enforcing the Militia Act, barring blacks from participating as part of the first line of defense.[9] Only Louisiana was exempt from complying with this legislation: the Treaty of Purchase for the Louisiana Territory (1803) allowed Louisiana to continue its tradition of arming small numbers of free blacks. Thus, in 1814, when General Andrew Jackson, commander of the U.S. Forces for the Gulf Coast region, faced a shortage of manpower, he enlisted the assistance of 350 free black men in the Battle of New Orleans. After the battle, the

[9] Once again, the British recognized the value of black troops, training two hundred former slaves as Royal Marines for eventual assaults upon Maryland and Virginia. They performed so well that they were soon absorbed into the regular British army (Edgerton 2002, chap. 1).

future president praised the service of these men: "'The two corps of colored volunteers,'" he said, "'have not disappointed the hopes that were formed of the courage and perseverance of their duty'" (quoted in Nalty 1986, 25). Ultimately, however, the black soldiers failed to receive the federal pensions and land that white veterans of the war received. They were also barred from marching in parades commemorating the Battle of New Orleans after they refused to perform what they perceived a demeaning chore: building levees, not a month after helping Jackson to secure victory.

Shortly after the war ended, African Americans suffered two further setbacks from which they would not recover until the Civil War. First, a War Department memorandum declared blacks unfit to serve with the "American soldier," officially segregating the U.S. military. And in 1820, secretary of war and white supremacist John Calhoun of South Carolina excluded African Americans from the regular army. African Americans were now barred from military service altogether: they were not allowed to serve in the militia, the U.S. Volunteers, or the regular army. Subsequently, they lost the right to vote in five additional states between 1821 and 1838. And as the middle of the nineteenth century approached, black Americans were branded *persona non grata* in the Midwest. In Illinois, Iowa, and Kansas, fully 80 percent of white residents voted for laws excluding blacks from entering their states (Klinkner and Smith 1999, chap. 1).

The political tensions of the 1850s produced a rash of additional restrictions on African American citizenship that it would take a civil war to remove. First, Congress passed a new Fugitive Slave Law in 1850 that allowed slaveowners to enlist the services of the U.S. Marshals in pursuing runaways—free of charge. The act also removed the statute of limitations on the pursuit of runaway slaves: as long as slavery received legal sanction, runaways could lose their liberty even decades after they had escaped the South.

But it was the *Dred Scott v. Sandford* case that dealt the most serious blow to African American citizenship. The *Dred Scott* decision (1857) institutionalized the exclusion of African Americans—both freedmen and slaves—from the national community. In stinging prose, Chief Justice Roger B. Taney argued in the Supreme Court's majority opinion that blacks, free or otherwise, could never be citizens because they were "[an] inferior and subordinate class of beings" with "no rights that whites are bound to respect" (*Scott v. Sandford*, 407). This claim was partially tied to military service: Scott's petition for citizenship was denied in part because he had never performed even a day of military service. Speaking for the Court, Taney referred to the Naturalization Act (1790) and the

Militia Act (1792) as proof of black Americans' lack of fitness for citizenship. Worth quoting at length is his interpretation of the Militia Act, which reads, "The language of this [law] is . . . plain and significant. . . . It directs that every 'free able-bodied white male citizen' shall be enrolled in the militia. The word 'white' is evidently used to exclude the African race, and the word 'citizen' to exclude unnaturalized foreigners; the latter forming no part of the sovereignty, owing it no allegiance, and therefore no obligation to defend it. The African race, however, born in the country, did owe allegiance to the Government, whether they were slave or free; but it [the African race] is repudiated, and rejected from the duties and obligations of citizenship in marked language." (*Scott v. Sandford*, 421) The Militia Act was indicative of the United States' move to a more bounded citizenry as the republic entered the nineteenth century. As part of a broader pattern, blacks were excluded from participation in one of the foundational obligations of American citizenship—service in the militia. And since blacks were excluded from the state militias, they were also fair game to be excluded from the wider political community.

Union Blue over Confederate Gray

As North and South faced off, Frederick Douglass insisted upon African Americans having a hand in the liberation of the race. Given the rationale for the decision in *Dred Scott*, Douglass knew that black participation in the war was the best way for African Americans to achieve equality. But there were other reasons why he urged blacks to serve, including appeals to manhood and citizen duty: if they were men they must make a stand. Moreover, if they were citizens, or hoped to be one someday, black men must observe the duties associated with citizenship. Douglass also believed that serving would help black men recover a sense of self-respect, and allow them to demonstrate courage to whites who remained skeptical of their worthiness as potential citizens. In short, military service during the Civil War was an opportunity for black men to prove something to themselves as well as whites (Quarles 1948, chap. 12).

The quickening pace of the war eventually provided black men the opportunity to see if Douglass was right. Upon realizing that successfully prosecuting a civil war would require the use of all able-bodied males, Congress passed a new Militia Act (1862) permitting President Abraham Lincoln to enlist free and enslaved blacks on a limited basis. However, the legislation failed to address the issue of equal pay between black and white soldiers, something that would eventually become an issue. The following year, the Emancipation Proclamation (1863) opened the door to the North's unencumbered accession of black soldiers. For both administrative and social purposes, the United States Colored Troops (USCT) were established in May 1863; approximately 75 percent of the soldiers were drawn from the slave population (Costa and Kahn 2005).

During the war, the USCT were partitioned into approximately 140 regiments. Not all of these units saw combat. In some cases, prejudice prevented black units from engaging the enemy; other times, there was simply a paucity of action. Black troops did, however, engage the enemy 449 times, and 39 of these engagements were major battles (Cornish 1987). By the end of the war, over 178,000 black soldiers and sailors had donned the Union blue, 144,000 of them from slave states. All told, black troops accounted for 10 to 12 percent of Union manpower. More than one-third (70,000) of the black troop members who served during the war were either killed in action or died from subsequent wounds or disease (Cornish 1987).

As it turned out, Douglass was correct in his assessment of how black participation in the war would be received—at least in the North. Benjamin Franklin Butler, a Union general who commanded black troops, cited the battlefield deeds of blacks to justify the extension of civil rights to them. In congressional testimony in 1874, the general recounted the scene that crystallized his support for equality:

> There, in a space not wider than the clerk's desk and three hundred yards long, lay the dead bodies of 543 of my colored comrades, slain in the defense of their country, who had laid down their lives to uphold its flag and its honor, as a willing sacrifice. . . . [A]nd as I looked at their bronzed faces upturned in the shining sun, as if in mute appeal against the wrongs of the country for which they had given their lives, and whose flag had been to them a flag of stripes, in which no star of glory had ever shone for them—feeling I had wronged them in the past and believing what was the future duty of my country to them—I swore to myself a solemn oath: "May my right hand forget its cunning, and my tongue cleave to the roof of my mouth, if ever I fail to defend the rights of the men who have given their blood for me and my country this day and for their race forever." And, God helping me, I will keep that oath. (Quoted in Edgerton 2002, 37)

African American participation did more than earn the gratitude of the general: it was a decisive factor in the outcome of the war (Berry 1977; Cornish 1987; DuBois 1935, chap. 5; Foner 1988, chap. 1). In return, African Americans received freedom from slavery and formal recognition as full citizens following the war. Many believed that the Civil Rights Acts of 1866, 1870, and 1875, along with the Thirteenth, Fourteenth,

and Fifteenth Amendments to the Constitution, would at least dampen—
if not extinguish—the effects of the black codes and white supremacy.[10]
The Civil Rights Act of 1866 and the Fourteenth Amendment invalidated
the black codes within a year of being ratified by state legislatures across
the South. The legal status of African Americans, it seemed, had changed
once and for all.[11]

While it was true that reform had taken place, it had failed to take root
in the South. Most white Southerners remained stubbornly attached to
the Southern way of life. Though the black codes devised by recalcitrant
white Southerners that sought to regulate freedmen were rendered in-
valid, most white Southern attitudes about the rightful place of blacks
failed to change (DuBois 1935; Foner 1988; Franklin 1961; Litwack
1979, chap. 1). With the exception of Tennessee, the former Confederate
states at first refused to recognize the Fourteenth Amendment. The South's
intransigence resulted in its occupation by Union forces, complete with
detachments of black soldiers, many of whom were former slaves who
were eager to "repay" selected planters and their minions for their brutality during slavery (Litwack 1979). With black troop strength either rival-
ing or outstripping the presence of white troops (Valelly 2004), Southern
white society felt itself unnecessarily insulted by the North with the presence of black troops. Certainly, the confidence, pride, and fearlessness
with which former slaves carried themselves threatened Southern sensibilities (DuBois 1935; Fletcher 1968; Foner 1988; Franklin 1961; Litwack
1979). But white Southerners feared and resented black soldiers for at
least four additional reasons: (1) whites feared that black former slaves
might wish to seek revenge; (2) as noted above, whites feared the insubordinate behavior of black soldiers; (3) armed blacks undermined the notion of black inferiority on which the "legitimacy" of white supremacy
rested; and (4) black troops inspired hope among black civilians (Fletcher
1968; Foner 1988).[12]

---

[10] Of course, black participation in the war wasn't the sole reason for the burst of reform.
Both political and humanitarian motives animated radical Republicans' desire for pushing
reform, ramming it through congress over President Andrew Johnson's objections (Franklin
1961).

[11] It should also be noted that the Freedman's Bureau was established in 1865. Among
other things, it was charged with easing the transition of former slaves from a state of dependence to one of self-sufficiency (DuBois 1935). Ultimately, the bureau established or
provided funding for schools at all levels. It also established forty hospitals for the care of
African Americans (Franklin 1961). Because the bureau was not granted permanent status
by President Johnson and was reviled by the South, however, it was dissolved in 1872.

[12] Military rule also facilitated the growth of political power among black Southerners. Loyalty oaths and loyalty challenges managed to mobilize blacks while demobilizing

In January 1866, there were approximately sixty thousand black soldiers spread throughout the South. By June of the same year, however, drastic troop reductions cut black troop strength by three-quarters, leaving approximately fifteen thousand soldiers of the USCT to help police the South (Fletcher 1968). Often, local police and militia members resented the presence of armed black troops in the South and sought to mistreat these soldiers whenever possible. Perhaps the most significant instance in which black troops resisted such mistreatment occurred in Memphis, Tennessee, around 1866. When the Memphis police attempted to arrest a black soldier for disorderly conduct, fifty black soldiers witnessed the event. Tired of police harassment, these soldiers followed the police as they escorted the prisoner to jail, wresting him from police custody. When police tried to arrest two black veterans later that same day, shooting broke out as the veterans chased the policemen down a boulevard. When the officers returned with reinforcements, they were met by over 150 veterans, who eventually returned to their post. The next day, whites took out their frustration on black civilians, killing forty-six unarmed black civilians and burning ninety-one homes, four churches, and twelve schools (Ryan 1977).

. . .

Taking the first century or so of U.S. history as a whole, the connection between military service and racial progress is evident. In general, when African Americans were permitted to serve, positive change in their citizenship status ensued; when they were prevented from serving, such change was not forthcoming. As the Memphis riot suggests, however, the changes that resulted from military service were not limited to improvements in legal status, and they were not all granted to blacks by whites. Almost all of the black soldiers who served during the Civil War were former slaves who had always depended upon whites for sustenance. Serving alongside free blacks exposed them to a different mind-set—one that pushed them to think beyond the narrow confines of the South and to absorb the identity of freedmen with whom they served (Costa and Kahn 2005). These veterans, who were prominent in the subsequent occupation of the South, were no longer content with the limits that had been imposed upon them. Like the Northern freedmen with whom they had come to identify, they took pride in their service. The sight of armed black troops, furthermore, was a source of pride for local blacks throughout the South (Foner 1988).

---

enough whites during military reconstruction to gave blacks a majority in the South (Valelly 2004).

Colonel Thomas Moore, regimental commander of the Fourteenth USCT, appreciated what military service achieved for blacks. The performance of his troops during the Battle of Nashville moved the commander to report, " 'A new chapter in the history of liberty had been written. It had been shown that marching under the flag of freedom, animated by a love of liberty, *even the slave becomes a man and a hero*' " (quoted in Cornish 1987, 289; emphasis added). Black soldiers were well aware of their role in the victory (Foner 1988); it should come as no surprise, then, that their contributions to this victory seem to have affected how many black veterans felt about their capabilities. Indeed, the educational and leadership opportunities provided by their military service, prepared many black veterans of the Civil War with postwar positions of some significance, some of which included elected office in state legislatures (Cornish 1987; Holt 1977, chap. 4).

DIMINISHING RETURNS AND INCREASING MILITANCY, 1876–1918

During the roughly forty-year period from 1876 through 1918, the struggle for equality shifted from a national-level battle to one with a regional focus, in which the state governments of the former confederacy undermined reform initiated by the national government. During this period, the social, political, and legal status of black Southerners resembled that of the slavery years. The withdrawal of federal troops from the South as part of the Hayes-Tilden Compromise, as well as narrow legal interpretations of Civil War legislation in the civil rights cases of 1883, stripped black Southerners of the physical and legal protection they had enjoyed during Reconstruction. With black troops present, whites were reluctant to harass or abuse black civilians (Fletcher 1968), but once those troops were removed, the abuse of Southern blacks resumed and grew worse (Litwack 1979, chap. 2).

In the civil rights cases of 1883, the Supreme Court successfully retarded the recognition of African Americans as citizens, diluting the impact of the Civil War amendments and the Civil Rights Acts of 1866 and 1875. The Civil Rights Act of 1866 had been designed as a corrective to the more general Thirteenth Amendment, in which neither equal rights nor the prospect of black citizenship were specified. The Fourteenth Amendment (1868), Fifteenth Amendment (1870), and the Civil Rights Act of 1875 were intended to serve as bulwarks against subsequent encroachment upon African American rights. The 1883 civil rights cases were a direct challenge to the constitutionality of the 1875 act, which outlawed discrimination on account of race within inns, public conveyances, and theaters. In essence, the Court ruled in 1883 that as long as the federal government was not complicit in discriminatory action, it was permissible for private concerns to discriminate. The Court reasoned that the right not to be discriminated against is a "social right" that does not affect its victims' more fundamental rights that constitute the core of citizenship and the ability to enjoy it (Higginbotham 1996).

In the Court's judgment, congressional enforcement of the Thirteenth Amendment was limited to incidents in which involuntary servitude could be proven. In the absence of such enforcement, however, the continuing stigma of slavery, which the Thirteenth Amendment was intended to proscribe, remained for black Southerners. Questions concerning due process and equal protection also triggered an interrogation of the Fourteenth Amendment. In this case, the Court limited congressional enforcement of the amendment's guarantee of equal protection to the prevention of state-based encroachment upon the enjoyment of public conveyances and inns, omitting the enforcement of the right of individuals to equal protection in all areas of life.

But it was the decision in *Plessy v. Ferguson* (1896) that gave the constitutional cover to segregation that completed the installation of white supremacy—especially in the South. Taking their collective cue from the Supreme Court, state governments of the former Confederate South added legal, economic, and political exclusion to the roster of inegalitarian practices imposed upon black Southerners. A combination of the white primary, poll taxes, literacy tests, residency requirements, and the grandfather clause systematically stripped black Southerners of the ability to vote, extinguishing their political power.

The Cuban Campaign

The Spanish-American War (1898) furnished African Americans with an opportunity to recover from the social setbacks inflicted on them by the *Plessy* decision and win relief from mob violence—lynching had roughly doubled in frequency since Reconstruction (Tolnay and Beck 1995). African American editor E. E. Cooper believed that black Americans' service in the Spanish-American War would ultimately redound to the benefit of the race. In his estimation, black participation would usher in "an era of good feeling the country over and cement the races into a more compact brotherhood through perfect unity of purpose and patriotic affinity [where whites would] unloose themselves from the bondage of racial prejudice" (quoted in Nalty 1986, 64). Other black leaders disagreed. Henry M. Turner, senior bishop of the African Methodist Episcopal Church, believed that in the context of war, patriotism presumed that one had a home to protect. In his view, however, blacks "'had no home [in America] and never [would] have one.' " Turner advised against " 'rushing into a death struggle for a country that cares nothing for [black men's] rights and manhood,' " concluding that " 'Negroes who are not disloyal to the United States deserve to be lynched' " (quoted in Nalty 1986, 64). Moreover, black leaders who were sympathetic to Turner's view also rejected the Cuban and Philippine campaigns on ideological grounds: they represented imperialism, pure and simple. More to the point, they knew what the Cubans and Filipinos were in for, and were against the idea of spreading white supremacy beyond America's borders (Brown 1997; Gatewood 1987b).

If the response to President William McKinley's call for volunteers is any indication, however, most of black America agreed with Cooper. Black volunteers from several states rushed to demonstrate their patriotism. Since black troops were thought to be especially well-suited to deal with the tropical diseases American forces were expected to encounter in Cuba, five "immune" regiments of black volunteers were organized. The regular army's Ninth and Tenth Cavalry regiments, along with the Twenty-Fourth and Twenty-Fifth Infantry regiments—all four of which had been designated as standing "colored units" by an act of Congress after the Civil War—fought bravely on the southwestern frontier.[13] On one occasion in particular, black cavalry rescued Theodore Roosevelt's Rough Riders from certain doom. Speaking of their gallantry upon his return to America, the president-to-be recalled, " 'The Spaniards called them 'Smoked Yankees' but we found them to be an excellent breed of Yankees. I am sure that I speak the sentiments of officers and men in the assemblage when I say that between you and the other cavalry regiments there exists a tie which we trust will never be broken' " (quoted in Gerstle 2001, 35). Roosevelt's political ambition and social beliefs required that he deny the contribution of black soldiers in Cuba, however, going so far as to suggest that black soldiers were cowards.[14] Nevertheless, black soldiers earned five medals of honor and more than twenty certificates of merit for their bravery in Cuba. Moreover, their accomplishments in Cuba—particularly, saving the future president's skin—were an important source of pride and sustenance for black Southerners (Fletcher 1974).

[13] The Army Reorganization Act (1866) ensured a continued African American presence in the Army by calling for the maintenance of these four permanently segregated regiments.

[14] According to Gerstle (2001), Roosevelt's vision for the American nation galvanized by war had no room for the heroic deeds of black soldiers. Since Roosevelt believed in the citizen-soldier ideal, he placed a premium upon battlefield heroism, which signaled bravery and the makings of a citizen of the first rank. His vision of an American nation at the turn of the century excluded all but those with ancestral ties to Europe.

Despite black soldiers' service in the Spanish-American War, however, black Southerners were scarcely better off as the nineteenth century concluded than they had been when the century began. True, many were no longer enslaved, but the rise of Jim Crow dashed any hopes of fair and equal treatment. Lynching, a means of social control (Tolnay and Beck 1995), increased in frequency to approximately one hundred per annum in the aftermath of the Spanish-American War. Suffrage restrictions imposed in the post-Reconstruction South were zealously enforced in the eleven former Confederate states (Key 1949; Kousser 1974; Woodward 1955).

The war, nonetheless, created a segment of the black population that was capable of fighting back. Prior to shipping out to Cuba, black troops encountered Jim Crow customs in the Southern towns in which they were encamped. But much like the previous generation of black soldiers who had occupied the South after the Civil War, the all-black units were intolerant of white supremacy. For instance, when soldiers from the four black regiments were ordered to Florida from their posts in more tolerant regions for staging prior to their deployment to Cuba, some of the black soldiers discovered that drunken white soldiers from an Ohio unit had used a two-year-old black child for target practice. In retaliation for this atrocity, the black soldiers destroyed all of the segregated businesses in town and beat every white soldier with whom they came into contact.

Another incident that suggests black soldiers' unwillingness to accept white domination occurred after the war. In 1906, soldiers of the Twenty-Fifth Infantry Regiment were encamped at Brownsville, Texas, where black soldiers were warned not to lounge in parks or patronize businesses. They were routinely assaulted by the police for the smallest infractions. After one such episode, some of the soldiers fought back: 150 shots were fired, one white man was killed, and two more were wounded. Although there was not enough evidence to warrant the trial of the African American soldiers who had participated in the incident, President Theodore Roosevelt took matters into his own hands, dishonorably discharging all 167 of the black soldiers who allegedly participated in the incident; fourteen were eventually reinstated.

The Great War

On the eve of the America's participation in the First World War, white supremacy was ascendant in the South. Jim Crow statutes and customs deprived black Southerners of the ability to vote, live, learn, and earn a reasonable living as full citizens of the United States (McMillen 1989; Ransom and Sutch 2001). White-on-black violence was rampant: from

1916 to 1917 sixty-five lynchings took place in the South (Tolnay and Beck 1995). Furthermore, the bravery of black soldiers in the Spanish-American War had been downplayed, and the practice of segregation in the federal governmental departments drew support from the newly elected Woodrow Wilson in 1913 (King 1995). But when the United States entered the Great War, the country once again needed to tap the black community for its support.

Black leadership was divided on the issue of whether to encourage black men to enlist. W.E.B. DuBois urged African Americans to "close ranks" with whites. He believed that black participation in the war effort would result in postwar gains:

> This is the crisis of the world. For all the long years to come men will point to the year 1918 as the great day of Decision, the day when the world decided whether it would submit to military despotism and endless armed peace—if peace it could be called—or whether they would put down the menace of German militarism and inaugurate the United States of the World. We of the colored race have no ordinary interest in the outcome. That which the German power represents today spells death to the aspirations of Negroes and all darker races for equality, freedom and democracy. Let us not hesitate. Let us, while this war lasts, forget our special grievances and close our ranks shoulder to shoulder with our own white fellow citizens and the allied nations that are fighting for democracy. We make no ordinary sacrifice, but we make it gladly and willingly with our eyes lifted up to the hills.

DuBois implored black Americans to fight, arguing, "Our country is at war . . . if this is OUR country, then this is OUR war." From black soldiers' collective sacrifice, he asserted, "the right to vote and the right to work and the right to live without insult" would emerge (DuBois 1918, 111).

DuBois's stance on the war was controversial and came as a surprise to many blacks who had come to identify him as a staunch militant, a leader who typically condemned accommodation (Ellis 1992). William Monroe Trotter, publisher of the *Boston Guardian* and one-time Harvard University classmate of DuBois's, was one public figure who disagreed with his contemporary's position on the war.[15] Trotter argued that the United States should concentrate upon " 'making the South safe for Negroes [instead of making the] small nations of Europe' " safe

---

[15] Some questioned DuBois's motive for urging African American cooperation with the war effort after it was discovered that he was offered an army commission in exchange for his work (Ellis 1992; Lewis 1993).

for democracy (quoted in Jordan 1995, 1574).[16] A. Philip Randolph, who would later become the president of the most powerful black labor union, the Brotherhood of Sleeping Car Porters, also spoke out against black participation in the impending war. Randolph believed that the black elite should concern themselves with local issues. He suggested the black leaders who supported black participation in the war should " 'volunteer to go to France if they [were] so eager to make the world safe for democracy.' " For his part, he " 'would rather fight to make Georgia safe for the Negro' " (quoted in Barbeau and Henri 1974, 12), a sentiment with which Marcus Garvey, a DuBois rival, agreed (Grant 2008, chap. 5).

Most of black America sided with DuBois and complied with the draft: over 370,000 African Americans served in the First World War. African Americans constituted 13 percent of all draftees and 9 percent of the total American troop strength (Barbeau and Henri 1974; Chambers 1987). The military rewarded black soldiers for their willingness to serve by attempting to downplay the contributions of African Americans to the war effort, something that happened during the Spanish-American War. Black troops suffered many indignities during World War I. The most experienced units—the regulars of the Ninth and Tenth Cavalry and the Twenty-Fourth and Twenty-Fifth Infantry—were ordered to remain in the Philippines, Hawaii, and the American Southwest, robbing them of the opportunity to prove their mettle in Europe. Moreover, only 20 percent of the 200,000 black troop members who were deployed to France were allowed to participate in combat operations (Nalty 1986, 112), and many of these men were not allowed to fight alongside whites. In France, moreover, four regiments of the all-black Ninety-Third Division were "lent" to the French by General "Black Jack" Pershing, who, ironically, had earned his moniker commanding—and praising—the black troops of the Tenth Cavalry regiment during the Spanish-American War.

In France, black soldiers were frequently undermined by American commanders alarmed by the relative ease with which black troops mixed with the less race-conscious French, who afforded them a measure of dignity and respect. Fearing the future effects of such egalitarian treatment, American commanders devised a plan to ensure postwar racial harmony in the United States. The army distributed a document titled "Secret Information Concerning Black American Troops" to French officers and civilians who were likely to come into contact with black soldiers. It "advised" the French that the races must be kept apart so as to not encourage liaisons between black soldiers and white women. According to the document, race-mixing constituted an affront to American national

---

[16] Ellis (1992, 1995) and Jordan (1995) engage in a lively debate concerning DuBois's motivation(s) for encouraging black support for the war.

values, and tolerant treatment of blacks would furnish them with " 'intolerable pretensions to equality' " (quoted in Barbeau and Henri 1974, 115). It was necessary, the document argued, to keep blacks in the place to which they were accustomed in order to avoid "spoiling the Negroes."[17]

Black conscripts were not the only recipients of poor treatment. As a symbolic gesture intended to secure African American support for the war (Barbeau and Henri 1974, chap. 4), the army agreed to train black officers as long as black and white troops were trained at separate facilities. Even with the separate training arrangements, the move was welcomed by many in the black community, including DuBois. Trotter and most of the black press, however, decried the segregated camp (Jordan 1995). To them it was another slap in the face. Nevertheless, one commentator called the Officer Training School in Iowa "the one constructive movement for the Negro since the Fifteenth Amendment" (Quoted in Barbeau and Henri 1974, 57–58). Yet black officers never received a fair opportunity to lead. Few of the army's senior commanders perceived blacks as leadership material; others feared the social implications of black officers' commanding white troops. Still others believed that black enlisted soldiers would not listen to black officers because the enlisted yearned for white leadership. Official and unofficial barriers were erected to ensure the failure of black officers. On the official side, black officers only constituted 0.7 percent of officer strength, even though 13 percent of all conscripts were black. Unofficially, discrimination played a major role. Many of them eventually faced charges of incompetence, so as to rid the army as much of that 0.7 percent as possible. And those black officers who remained were denied promotion beyond the rank of captain (Barbeau and Henri 1974, 58).

When black officers were promoted, the military took steps to prevent the customs of segregation from being violated. The only black field-grade officer, West Point graduate Colonel Charles Young, was selected for promotion to brigadier general, but he was medically retired a day before he was to receive this promotion, apparently because his rank would have placed him in a high-level divisional command post in which he would have commanded at least two dozen white officers. In other cases when a black officer approached a promotion that would make him senior to white officers in his unit, his white commanding

---

[17] As Colonel J. A. Linard, one of Pershing's staff officers, stated in a document to the French commands, " 'White Americans consider blacks to be lacking in intelligence, judgment, and civic and professional morals. . . . It is necessary to avoid any intimacy, beyond civil politeness, between French officers and black officers; the French should not eat with them nor shake hands with them, nor visit or converse except as required by military matters' " (quoted in Barbeau and Henri 1974, 114–15).

officer would simply have the black officer transferred, replacing him with a white officer of the rank to which the black officer would have been promoted. Finally, when black officers were made senior to white officers, they were often instructed not to require their white subordinates to salute them.

Discrimination of this type was also practiced overseas. During classroom instruction in France, black officers were ordered to allow their white classmates to be seated before they were permitted to sit. Black officers were not allowed to eat in the officers' mess with white officers, and they were required to use segregated latrines and showers. These experiences left indelible scars on the men who endured them, some of whom went on to wage war against Jim Crow upon returning home. Charles Hamilton Houston, a Harvard-trained attorney and later the architect of the NAACP's legal assault upon segregation, was among them. Due to the discrimination to which he and other black soldiers were exposed in the Jim Crow army, Houston vowed to fight white supremacy. In April 1919, he left the army, declaring, " 'My battleground is in America, not France' " (quoted in Linder 2000, 2).[18]

Stateside, black troops were less tolerant of the attempts made by whites to impose Jim Crow, as a July 1917 incident in Houston, Texas, demonstrated. The pursuit of Pancho Villa required a substantial southwestern military presence; the Third Battalion of the Twenty-Fourth Infantry Regiment drew the assignment.[19] While in Texas, the black soldiers of the Twenty-Fourth refused to observe Jim Crow, ignoring the attendant customs. Houston police responded by beating and generally harassing black soldiers whenever they saw fit. Soon, however, the soldiers became the aggressors. The conflict began when a black soldier happened upon two police officers beating a black woman. Upon protesting, the soldier was assaulted by the officers and arrested. After a second soldier was also beaten and arrested, word reached Camp Logan, where the soldiers were encamped. Over 100 soldiers armed themselves and marched into town looking for justice. During the conflict that ensued, 15 whites and 1 Latino were killed; among the deceased were 4 police officers. At the ensuing courts-martial, 156 black soldiers were tried and 13 subsequently hanged.

[18] For more on how Houston's experience during the First World War shaped his desire for equality, see McNeil (1983).

[19] Pancho Villa, the rebel Mexican general, attacked a detachment of the U.S. Calvary in Columbus, New Mexico. Villa led a raiding force of fifteen hundred that seized over one hundred horses and mules, burned the town of Columbus, and killed seventeen townspeople. Under the command of "Black Jack" Pershing, President Wilson dispatched twelve thousand troop members to hunt for Villa. After months of searching, American forces never found him.

Despite all of the obstacles encountered by black troops who served during the First World War, they managed to make their mark on the battlefield. The "Men of Bronze," as the 369th Infantry Regiment were called by the French, never yielded an inch of ground for over six months and never had a soldier taken prisoner. All told, 750 of the regiment's black soldiers lost their lives and over 5,000 were wounded. But it was the Ninety-Third Division, the one under French command, that suffered the bulk of the casualties. Of the approximately 10,000 soldiers in the division, about one-third were either killed or wounded in action (Barbeau and Henri 1974). In the end, three of the four regiments of the Ninety-Third Division that fought under the French flag were awarded the Croix de Guerre, an honor bestowed for bravery.

The long-term implications of black Americans' serving in World War I for the service-progress nexus were grave. The results remind us of the Spanish-American War after which efforts were made to undermine the contributions of blacks to the war effort. The principal reason for all but denying the contributions of black soldiers and sailors during the Spanish-American War ultimately rested on Roosevelt's justification of waging war in the first place: as a means of galvanizing the nation's whites, whom he believed to be the superior racial stock in America (Gerstle 2001, chap. 1). But he couldn't do this if he'd acknowledged the contribution of black troops during the war. Thus, the outcome for blacks after World War I was no less racial, though the motivation was somewhat different. This time the impulse to reduce blacks' contribution to the war effort drew on a desire to diminish their postwar claims on citizenship by virtue of their service. Only 11 percent of the black troops who went to war were allowed to fight, and many of these did so under French command, making it more likely that their achievements would be ignored by the mainstream American press. At the same time, less well-trained elements of the all-black Ninety-Second Division, which fought under American command, were blamed for a setback they experienced during the Argonne offensive when some of its units retreated under fire. The army and the mainstream press seized upon the misfortune and, according to some, overemphasized the failure because the unit was black (Barbeau and Henri 1974; Foner 1974; Nalty 1986). Indeed, elements of the all-white Thirty-Fifth Division also retreated. Even so, the incident seemed to confirm stereotypes that blacks were ill-suited for combat, their abilities more equal to tasks that didn't require much in the way of courage or ingenuity.

The most experienced of the black fighting forces, moreover—the regular regiments of the infantry and cavalry—were ordered to remain in the Pacific and the Southwest during the war, robbing all-black units of the chance to maximize their combat effectiveness. Most of the Ninety-Second and much of the Ninety-Third Divisions were manned by inexperienced conscripts, but the Ninety-Third enjoyed the relative benefit of fighting under the more tolerant French, who did not make a point of questioning the competence of black officers or troops. The Ninety-Second, on the other hand, was commanded by white American officers, many of whom were born and bred in the South. General Robert Lee Bullard, the commanding general of the Second Army, under which the Ninety-Second Division was organized, believed blacks were inferior and unfit for combat (Barbeau and Henri 1974; Nalty 1986). Naturally, his sentiments trickled down the chain of command, resonating most strongly with the general's Southern brethren. Perhaps this explains why the Ninety-Third performed better than the Ninety-Second, whose black soldiers were often berated by white Southern officers. Finally, black officers in the Ninety-Second Division were not given a chance to prove their worth as leaders. At every turn, they were reduced to near-irrelevance.

With the service of African Americans so thoroughly undermined, it is no surprise that black Americans failed to benefit from such service in the postwar period. In fact, conditions grew progressively worse. In the South, white repression increased in the aftermath of the war. If Senator James K. Vardaman's (D-Mississippi) sentiments are any indication, white Southerners were concerned about the return of black troops. Vardaman feared that black veterans would be spoiled, terming them "'French women-ruined . . . uppity niggers'" (quoted in Barbeau and Henri 1974, 175). He encouraged white Mississippians to form vigilante groups to prevent the "rape" of Southern white women. Instead of embracing the efforts of black soldiers who had endured many indignities while fighting for their country, many whites chose to focus instead upon the "new Negro" they feared would emerge from the war. Black veterans were routinely assaulted, shot, and in some cases lynched upon their return.

More generally, the need to restore the racial status quo in the South and economic competition elsewhere set the stage for the "Red Summer" of 1919. In 1918 and 1919, race riots exploded across America, affecting Chicago and New York in the North and Longview, Texas; Knoxville, Tennessee; and Elaine, Arkansas, in the South (Edgerton 2002). In the mayhem, over 135 African Americans were killed by white mobs, including 10 veterans who were lynched in *uniform*. Ultimately, though, the training they received in the military as well as the confidence gained from surviving the bloodshed in France, encouraged many veterans to lead protective and retaliatory efforts against whites who thought it okay to attack blacks, particularly in Chicago (Lentz-Smith 2005; Williams 2007).

Indeed, African Americans at home welcomed the demobilization and return of black soldiers. Since the soldiers had been armed, trained in the ways of war, and hardened by combat, it was presumed by at least some black Southerners that these "men [were] not afraid to die" and were accustomed to "killing white men." These men would lead the fight against white supremacy (Reich 1996, 1479). This optimism wasn't unfounded. Cadres of black soldiers who fought in the Great War would, two years later, stand to defend a black community in the midst of perhaps the most violent race riot—to that time—in American history. These veterans had come to believe the rhetoric promoted by President Woodrow Wilson: they had participated in the war to save democracy. As such, these veterans believed themselves entitled to a piece of democracy on their return to Tulsa, Oklahoma (Brophy 2002, chap. 1).

The Tulsa Race Riot, as it has come to be known, was precipitated by a misstep taken in an elevator by nineteen-year-old Dick Rowland. As the black teenager entered the elevator, he apparently stumbled into the young woman who was its operator. She screamed, claiming Rowland had assaulted her, and he fled. Rowland was later arrested. While he awaited trial, as many as two thousand of the town's whites assembled outside of the jail in which he was held, intent on lynching the young man (Halliburton 1972). As word spread to Greenwood, the black community in Tulsa, black men—many of them veterans of the First World War—donned their uniforms, armed themselves, and mustered at the jail. Other black veterans remained behind to defend Greenwood against any ensuing reprisals against the black community. During the conflict, the veterans displayed skills learned in the military, including digging trenches from which to fight, organizing fire teams, and posting snipers (Brophy 2002; Halliburton 1972). In the end, at least twenty-six blacks and ten whites were killed in the riot. The loss of property in the black community was enormous. Better than one thousand homes in Greenwood were destroyed by fire, and as many as forty city blocks were burned.

• • •

In the context of the rise of racism in the 1890s, when segregation was institutionalized and American imperial ambition drove the country to subjugate "racially inferior" people in the Philippines and Guam, the contributions of black soldiers to the Spanish-American War and the First World War failed to improve the condition of African Americans (Fletcher 1974). The country's need for manpower during the Spanish-American War and World War I was simply too great to deny blacks the ability to serve, but African Americans' contributions to both wars were undercut. Only small numbers of black troops were allowed to participate in combat roles, their competence was often called into question, and their valor was frequently downplayed or simply dismissed. These events robbed African Americans of the ability to claim equal rights on the basis of their military service. Consequently, state-sponsored change failed to emerge.

At both the national and state levels of government, black Southerners, who constituted the vast majority of the African American population (Gregory 2004), were betrayed. At the national level they were done in by the judiciary. With unfavorable decisions in the civil rights cases and *Plessy v. Ferguson*, black Southerners were stripped of first-class citizenship. At the state-level, the removal of federal troops allowed state representatives to rewrite their respective constitutions, devising legal and extra-legal means of removing franchise from black Southerners. In sum, black Southerners, once again, became objects of domination.

Donning the uniform seems to have changed at least some of the black servicemen who hailed from the South, however, making them less willing to tolerate white supremacy. The event that took place in Tennessee in the aftermath of the Civil War foreshadowed how black servicemen and veterans would react to the indignities associated with second-class treatment. As the events in Houston, Brownsville, and Tulsa suggest, black veterans were sometimes willing to put their military training to use, dying if they had to, to exact the justice, respect, and freedom to which they felt their military service entitled them. Moreover, we cannot overestimate the extent to which military service reinforced their sense of manhood and, therefore, confidence. The experience of bearing arms, and receiving more equal treatment from many of the French, including the women, made them feel like men, something they wouldn't soon forget (Lentz-Smith 2005).

Fighting on Two Fronts Twice: World War II and the Korean War

The social, political, and economic status of African Americans failed to change much in the two decades following the Great War. During the Depression, African Americans, like everyone else, sought relief from poverty and the prospect of starvation. President Franklin Delano Roosevelt's answer was the New Deal, but it was a raw deal for black Americans; discrimination initially affected the administration of relief and eligibility for social security (Katznelson 2005; Lieberman 1998; Sitkoff 1978). Later, Harold Ickes and Harry Hopkins intervened to ensure a more equitable distribution of benefits and access to programs (Sitkoff

1978, chap. 3), but this intervention alone failed to create economic equality. In 1939, 93 percent of African American families lived below the poverty line, as compared to 65 percent of white families, and in the South, black men earned only 44 percent as much as white men did. Educational disparities ensured the persistence of these gaps. In the South, individual states spent, on average, three times more to educate white children than black children (Jaynes and Williams 1989, 59). Since 75 percent of all black Americans lived in the South in 1940 (U.S. Bureau of the Census 1943), three in four African Americans remained disenfranchised and segregated from whites in all facets of life, including hospitals and cemeteries. White-on-black violence also continued to plague Southern African Americans. From 1930 through 1940, at least 142 blacks were victims of race-related homicides committed by whites.[20] While Roosevelt condemned lynching, calling it murder, his legislative priorities were elsewhere (Weiss 1983). As a consequence, antilynching legislation remained unfinished business on the eve of World War II.

The Second World War is often cited as an occasion on which Americans were forced to examine their values and beliefs (Higham 1997; Klinkner and Smith 1999; Myrdal 1944). The American creed was employed, at least in part, as a means to rally support for the war effort and the mobilization of the American military machine. It was difficult to reconcile democratic ideology with the plight of Southern African Americans, however. The ideological underpinnings of the war and the need for national unity signaled a desire for diversity and increased tolerance. The confluence of these factors, Philip Gleason (1980) suggests, crystallized—for the first time—a distinctive American national ideology. Gunnar Myrdal predicted in 1944 that a critical examination of American social practices in light of World War II sloganeering, in which the national ideology was emphasized, would force whites to bring social practice into alignment with cultural beliefs. Indeed, blacks were quite optimistic about their prospects in postwar America. For change to occur as it had in the aftermath of the Civil War, however, blacks believed they must have an active role in the war effort; they had to be allowed to fight.

Black elites sought to capitalize on the ubiquity of the American creed in the prewar discourse by fighting for the right to fight. They reasoned that tangible social progress was more likely to follow the war if black troops were allowed to participate fully in combat than if they were stuck in noncombat assignments—that is, if they were allowed to serve at all. As it became increasingly likely that America would join the fight in

---

[20] Data compiled by the author from the Espy File, a National Archive of Criminal Justice Data, deposited with the Inter-university Consortium for Political and Social Research.

Europe, therefore, the black elite made military service a central goal in the pursuit of civil rights (Dalfiume 1969; Nalty 1986; Wynn 1993). Whereas black Americans had been urged to offer unconditional support for the First World War, deferring resolution of their complaints until after its conclusion, support for World War II would be contingent upon black soldiers' full participation in the war effort. Instead of closing ranks with whites, many in the black elite adopted a new strategy prior to the Second World War: the Double V campaign. The two victories to which the campaign's name referred were victory abroad for the nation (over fascism) and victory at home in the struggle for civil rights (over racism).

The campaign began in 1938 with black opinion-makers calling for increased African American participation in the armed forces. To work toward the goal of "a more dignified place in our armed forces during the next war," the Committee for Participation of Negroes in the National Defense Program was formed in 1938 (quoted in Dalfiume 1969, 26). A joint venture between the influential *Pittsburgh Courier* and black officers from World War I, the committee sought to avoid the disappointments of the First World War and the immediate postwar period by ensuring African Americans' access to full, unencumbered military participation. Roy Wilkins, editor of the *Crisis*, sought to make clear to the secretary of war that there was " 'no other single issue—except possibly lynching—upon which there is a unanimity of opinion among all classes [of blacks] in all sections of the country' " (quoted in Dalfiume 1969, 27). If the president cleared the decks for the full participation of blacks in the military, Wilkins promised, the administration stood to reap electoral benefits in the fast-approaching 1940 presidential campaign.

Beyond the moral justification for rejecting the separation of races in wartime—that segregation and the doctrine of racial inferiority on which it rested were wrong—were more pragmatic justifications. Segregation denied black soldiers full participation in the war effort, resulting in poor morale and possibly impeding combat effectiveness. It was expensive and inefficient in that it required the construction and maintenance of separate (if not necessarily equal) facilities. Finally, segregation wasted manpower. While all-black units tended to be overstaffed, white units were more likely to become depleted. With segregation of the military in place, however, black troops could not be used to fill out white units (Dalfiume 1969; Lee 1966). Black leaders sought full and equal participation for blacks in the armed forces, including integration (Lee 1966).

The administration's response to the demands of the committee was mixed. Pressed by Republican candidate Wendell L. Wilkie, who pledged an assault on racism, President Roosevelt saw his relative popularity among the black electorate threatened. Consequently, he pledged to allow blacks to serve on an equal basis. As part of this concession, Roosevelt signed off on an antidiscrimination clause in the pending Selective Service Bill, agreeing to allow blacks to serve in the military in direct proportion to their representation in American society. He also agreed to permit all officers, black and white, to train together, and he promised to establish aviation training for black officers. In addition, Roosevelt agreed to permit black officers to command black troops—at the junior officer level. In comparison to African Americans' service in World War I, this was progress, but it was tempered by the administration's insistence on continued segregation of the military. Moreover, blacks would only be inducted if they were deemed mentally and physically fit for service and if separate facilities were available for them. Over the protests of black leaders, these conditions were codified in the Selective Service Act of 1940.

On the positive side, the president promoted Benjamin O. Davis to brigadier general, making him the first black general in the history of the American armed forces. Judge William Hastie, a Harvard-trained attorney and the first African American appointed to the federal bench, became assistant secretary of war, though the ongoing segregation of aviation officer training eventually triggered Hastie's resignation in 1943. Hastie believed integration of the armed forces to be of paramount importance to the national mission. As the judge reasoned, " 'Until the men of our Army . . . believe in and work for democracy with similar fervor and determination, we will not be an effective nation in the face of a foreign foe' " (quoted in Lee 1966, 140). Army leaders argued in response to such criticism that the pattern of established relationships between blacks and whites had to be retained in the army. To do otherwise was to risk " 'alienat[ing] the people from the army and lower[ing] their morale' " when both were " 'vital' " to " 'national needs' " (quoted in Lee 1966, 140–41).

Black leaders had other goals, one of which was to secure jobs in the booming defense industry for those who did not serve in the military. The international implications of American participation as a belligerent in the war presented African American insurgents with an opportunity to leverage American postwar international ambition into domestic social reform. Asa Phillip Randolph, the prominent labor leader, transformed the black public's residual anger about their treatment in the wake of World War I into a grassroots movement that threatened to undermine the facade of American unity on the eve of America becoming involved in the Second World War. He capitalized upon the ideological rhetoric of President Roosevelt by threatening a march on Washington in June 1941 if nothing were done to increase the numbers of African Americans in the defense industry. The president capitulated to Randolph's demands, avoiding what would have been an embarrassing protest on the eve of

American entry into the war. The result was the issuance Executive Order 8802 (Kryder 2000), outlawing discrimination in the war industry and establishing the Fair Employment Practices Committee (FEPC) to monitor compliance with the order.

The reasons surrounding Hastie's resignation notwithstanding, blacks were making progress. After winning what they perceived at the time were two major concessions from the administration in the form of the antidiscrimination clause as part of the Selective Service Act and Executive Order 8802, and Davis's promotion, blacks had reason for optimism. Moreover, black servicemen and women incidentally benefited from the Soldiers Vote Act (1942). There were some in Congress who thought it unpatriotic that people serving in the military were prevented from casting a ballot in the state in which they were registered. Most in Congress were fine with allowing service members to cast absentee ballots. What managed to raise the hackles of many members of Congress, though, was an amendment that proposed to temporarily suspend the poll tax for service members with Southern roots. With the exception one or two Southerners, Southern Democrats were outraged at the prospect of approximately 400,000 black service members having unfettered access to the ballot. However, with the nation at war, and anticipating a bitter, protracted fight over the permanent abolition of poll taxes in the general public, the Southern Democrats conceded the Soldiers Vote legislation in the hopes of holding the line on the general poll tax bill to come (Lawson 1976, chap. 3; Sullivan 1996, chap. 4).[21]

The respite was short-lived. On the home front, race riots exploded across America in 1943 as blacks continued to grow weary of their subordinate position in American society, while whites continued to believe blacks were content with their lot (Stouffer et al. 1949). Blacks, moreover, thought the government should be doing more to help them; whites, for the most part, thought the government's efforts were sufficient (Klinkner and Smith 1999). With the ensuing riots, ignited by deplorable housing conditions in Detroit and police brutality in New York City's Harlem, the misunderstanding between the nation's black and white populations was on full display. However, owing to a mix of inter-racial cooperation following the Detroit riots of 1943 that resulted in a push for a more moderate approach to grievance redress, and the desire of black newspaper editors to preserve prospects for postwar equality by tempering their fight for social justice with support for the war, the heat

---

[21] Because ballot requirements varied across the forty-eight states, there were unanticipated administrative problems, resulting in only 28,000 ballots cast by deployed service members. When another bill was proposed to facilitate the voting of over eleven million service members for the 1944 campaigns, Southern democrats blocked it (Sullivan 1996).

of black militancy cooled toward the middle of the decade (Finkle 1975; Sitkoff 1971a, Sitkoff 1997).

Black servicemen, however, could not afford to relax. As America's involvement in the war deepened, black soldiers were scarcely welcome in the United States. Over half of the base commanders in the North and 70 percent of their counterparts in the South refused to host all-black units (Dalfiume 1969; Lee 1966; Nalty 1986).[22] As it had during the First World War, local hostility toward black soldiers bred mutual contempt between the locals and black GIs. Whites attempted to impose Jim Crow segregation upon black GIs who possessed the temerity to venture into town. As they had done during the Spanish-American War and the First World War, however, black soldiers balked at the imposition of Southern convention. The moral inconsistency of representing Uncle Sam while enduring Jim Crow created a combustible situation between the races, threatening to ignite racial powder kegs on and around Southern military installations.

Eventually, the repeated attempts of Southern whites to break the spirit of black GIs deteriorated into a series of racial confrontations, some of them violent. All told, over 209 racial incidents involving black GIs and authorities (civilian and military) occurred during the war, two-thirds of them at Southern bases (Kryder 2000). Judge William Hastie offered an eloquent, succinct account of the racial confrontations that plagued the military at this time: " 'It is impossible,' " Hastie said, " 'to create a dual personality which will be on the one hand a fighting man toward the enemy, and on the other, a craven who will accept treatment as less than a man at home' " (quoted in Klinkner and Smith 1999, 167). A more direct, if brusque, expression of this sentiment came from a black GI who reasoned, "If this is Uncle Sam's army, then treat us like soldiers and not animals or else Uncle Sam might find a new Axis to fight" (McGuire 1983, 11). Some of the returning black veterans followed through on this threat and catalyzed race riots in Alabama, Mississippi, and Tennessee (Robinson 1997).

At least a portion of their resentment, one could posit, resulted from blacks' frustration with their chronic under-representation in the armed forces. Until 1940, African Americans who wished to join the military were permitted to do so only by filling vacancies in one of the four all-black units. In 1940, there were approximately thirty-six hundred black soldiers and five black officers in the regular army, three of whom were

---

[22] Similar conditions obtained overseas, where many of the field commanders in North Africa and Europe refused to accept black units. Segregation did little for the morale of black troops and led to less-than-positive perceptions of black troops by white GIs (Stouffer et al. 1949).

chaplains (Nalty 1986). The two nonchaplains were the aforementioned General Davis and his son, Benjamin O. Davis Jr., a lieutenant colonel in the Army Air Corps and a West Point graduate. Upon America's entry into the war, approximately one hundred thousand black soldiers donned the uniform (Lee 1966). By the end of the war, approximately one million African Americans had ultimately served, either voluntarily or through conscription, two-thirds of them from the South, where most had been drafted (Stouffer et al. 1949).

Despite the impressive number of African Americans who served, black troop strength never reached the army's stated target level of 10.6 percent (Lee 1966), the proportion commensurate with the size of the country's black population. It averaged 8.6 percent during the war, 2 percent below the target. More disturbing, however, is the extent to which black troop members were relegated to auxiliary units and the manner in which their service was demeaned. Because many theater commanders retained the belief that black troops were inferior soldiers and superior laborers, a stereotype held over from the First World War, the army began to convert combat units into support units in 1943 (Lee 1966). As a result, black strength in combat units declined from a high of 38 percent in 1942 to 12 percent in 1945. Of course, this meant that black representation in support units increased from a low of 48 percent in 1942 to 75 percent in 1945 (Stouffer et al. 1949, 494).

As they had been in the First World War, black troops were also forced to deal with the charge of cowardice. The Ninety-Second Division again bore the brunt of the criticism, particularly because of its behavior during the Italian campaign. Led by white officers, almost all of them reared in the South, the division made repeated attacks against German forces that were dug in and had the advantage of high ground. The officers repeatedly ordered the black troops to execute frontal assaults that amounted to suicide runs instead of attempting to flank the position, a maneuver that would have significantly reduced casualties. Critics assert that black GIs disappeared during the fighting, but they only did so as they saw their white junior officers doing the same (Edgerton 2002). One platoon, however, stood and fought. Lieutenant Vernon Baker, one of the few black officers in the Ninety-Second Division, assumed command when his white captain deserted the platoon—in the heat of battle. The captain said he was going to get reinforcements, but the reinforcements never arrived, nor did he (the captain) bother to return. Lieutenant Baker was one of a total of six men from his company who ultimately survived the engagement.

When given a fair opportunity, black troops generally acquitted themselves well in combat. In the army, the 761st Tank Battalion, attached to General Patton's Third Army, was key to the Allied advance across

France and into Germany. On several occasions, the 761st was the lead element in Patton's assaults. All told, the men of the 761st earned eleven Silver Stars and sixty-nine Bronze Stars. In the Air Force, the 332nd Fighter Group—the renowned Tuskegee Airmen—never lost a bomber. Pilots of this group shot down 111 German aircraft and destroyed another 150 on the ground. For this, they earned over 1,000 medals, including 150 Distinguished Flying Crosses. In the process, seventy-six black pilots lost their lives in combat. During the Battle of the Bulge in 1944, a manpower shortage required the use of black soldiers in combat in tandem with whites. Over 4,500 troops from black units volunteered, but there was only room for 2,500. To avoid the spectacle of black noncommissioned officers giving orders to whites, black sergeants were required to relinquish their rank if they hoped to join the assault. Ultimately, 84 percent of the white officers and 81 percent of white noncommissioned officers with whom they served said that the black troops performed well (Stouffer et al. 1949), but when General Davis asked that these results receive publicity in order to strengthen the case for more permanent integration his request was denied (Dalfiume 1969).

In the aftermath of the war, some of the most important, if symbolic, legal changes that occurred to the status of African Americans were instigated by attacks by white Southerners on black veterans. In one incident, black veteran Roger Malcolm, his wife, her sister, and her sister's husband were murdered by the Ku Klux Klan after Malcolm was released from jail. It seems that he stabbed his white employer for making unwanted advances on his wife. To the Klan, Malcolm represented one of the " 'bad Negro' veterans who returned from war and were 'getting out of place' " (Lawson 2004, 8). In Louisiana, another black veteran, who was released from jail on a loitering charge, was burned to death with a blow-torch by whites—with the assistance of a sheriff's deputy.

One incident in particular shocked President Harry S. Truman, solidifying his resolve to combat racism and promote civil rights as a part of his political strategy for the campaign to come in 1948. In February 1946, Isaac Woodard, a recently discharged sergeant who had served in the Pacific theater, donned his uniform and boarded a bus from an army base in Georgia to head home to North Carolina. As the bus made its way through the South, the driver cursed the sergeant, accusing him of loitering for too long in the "colored" restroom at a stop in South Carolina. The veteran took exception to the harassment, sparking an argument between the two men. The driver alerted the local authorities, telling law enforcement that the sergeant was drunk, though in fact he was not a drinker. The officers who arrived at the next stop to arrest Woodard beat the sergeant with a blackjack, permanently blinding him when one of the officers jammed the end of a nightstick into his eyes (Nalty 1986, 204–5).

The NAACP saw to it that the incident received maximum publicity, and the attack on Woodard drew the ire of most of the nation, from both black and white people. The president resolved that he could not tolerate such treatment of veterans who had fought a war to preserve American values. This decision did not come easily to Truman; as a Missourian, his rearing did not predispose him to racial tolerance (Hamby 1995). But Truman's own military service in the First World War may have moderated his view of race insofar as he understood the sacrifice associated with defending the country. This much is evident in his declaration about the attack on Woodard: " 'When a mayor and a City Marshal can take a negro Sergeant off a bus in South Carolina, beat him up and put out one of his eyes, and nothing is done about it . . . something is radically wrong with the system. . . . I can't approve of such goings on and shall never approve of it. . . . I am going to try to remedy it' " (quoted in Klinkner and Smith 1999, 204).

Due in some part to the atrocities inflicted on black veterans in the aftermath of World War II, Truman appointed a commission on civil rights in December 1946 (Lawson 2004; Nalty 1986, chap. 15). Among the recommendations of the commission's report *To Secure These Rights*, which was issued in 1947, were the desegregation of the armed forces, the establishment of a permanent Fair Employment Practices Committee, antilynching legislation, and a bill banning poll taxes. Beyond claims about how he felt about black veterans coming under attack, however, the president had other reasons to press Congress to pass the reforms proposed by his civil rights commission. In both foreign and domestic spheres, he was pressured to do something about the condition of black Southerners. Cold War pressures, with the Soviets using every blunder committed by white supremacists as a means of interrogating America's fitness to lead the "free world," forced Truman to address the civil rights, if not the human rights, of African Americans (Anderson 2003; Borstelmann 2001; Dudziak 2000; Skrentny 2002). However, addressing civil rights pushed the Southern wing of his party to the brink of defecting from the national Democratic Party. Eventually, prudence and political survival dictated that the president court the black vote. Without it, he was advised, he'd be a one-term president (Dalfiume 1969; Lawson 2004; Nalty 1986). Faced with this possibility, he took the advice of his counsel and courted African Americans for their support, at the risk of losing the South (Sitkoff 1971b).

Dixiecrats, the disaffected Southern wing of the party—those who chose to defect from the Democratic Party instead of supporting a party platform in which the interest of blacks were represented (Frederickson

2001)—were not the only group dissatisfied with the president's position on civil rights. Several black leaders, DuBois among them, had grown tired of what they perceived as Truman's token attempts to address civil rights (Anderson 2003). Weary of the incessant foot-dragging on the part of the Truman administration to implement at least the reforms recommended by the President's Committee on Civil Rights, several black elites decided to pursue a different strategy. At the end of World War II, black leaders seized upon Roosevelt's initiative to institutionalize human rights by attempting to put an international bill of rights in the UN Charter. The bill aimed to highlight the discriminatory treatment suffered by people of color—worldwide.[23] The bill failed to pass, but it did manage to get human rights mentioned in the charter. In 1946, the National Negro Congress publicized the continuing oppression of African Americans by petitioning the UN Subcommittee on the Prevention of Discrimination and the Protection of Minorities. According to John David Skrentny (1998), the petition fell somewhat short substantively but focused the attention of the international community upon the continuing state of racial oppression in America. A year later, the NAACP employed a similar strategy, filing a document with the UN Commission on Human Rights titled "An Appeal to the World: A Statement on the Denial of Human Rights to Minorities in the Case of Citizens of Negro Descent in the United States of America and an Appeal to the United Nations for Redress." Though the appeal failed to prompt an institutional response from the UN, it drew widespread international attention—to the chagrin of the United States and the delight of the Soviet Union (Anderson 2003; Skrentny 2002).[24]

Exposing America—with its professed liberal ideals and grand aspirations of leading the free world—as a hypocrite, seemed a viable option at the time. Nothing else seemed to work—certainly not domestic political pressure because blacks continued to be murdered well after President Roosevelt declared freedom from fear as a right to which all people should be eligible. Drawing on human rights as a means of securing economic and social rights, goals that promised to correct the educational, occupational, and health disparities borne on the shoulders of blacks, in

[23] As several scholars illustrate, blacks also attempted to link African American oppression to a worldwide struggle against colonialism. For exceptional accounts of this strategy, see Plummer (1996); Singh (2005); and Von Eschen (1997).

[24] "An Appeal to the World" failed to register a larger splash due mainly to Eleanor Roosevelt's distaste for it. She claimed (probably correctly) that the Soviets would seize it as an opportunity to attack the United States. After she threatened to resign her seat on the NAACP's board of directors in protest, Walter White—much to the displeasure of DuBois—pulled his support from the document to placate Mrs. Roosevelt (Anderson 2003, chap. 3).

the context of the Cold War, did more harm than good. In the eyes of rabid anticommunists these goals were often intentionally conflated with communism, the ideology of the enemy. In this atmosphere, some civil rights organizations were forced to cut ties with allies on the left to avoid charges of treason and disloyalty. This forced the more radical faction of the movement to return to more traditional avenues of pursuing its goals of political and legal equality instead of human rights (C. Anderson 2003; Singh 2005; Von Eschen 1997). As a consequence, they were forced into taking the more conventional route, using pressure tactics to achieve their goals.

Certainly, one result is that blacks emerged from the war without much in the way of tangible gains. To be sure, on President Roosevelt's watch, the white primary was declared illegal, increasing black turnout at the polls in the South (Lawson 1976; Matthews and Prothro 1966). But Roosevelt's Executive Order 8802, outlawing employment discrimination in war industries and establishing the FEPC to ensure compliance with the order, was not sustained in the long run. After failing to secure enough congressional support as it ran afoul of a bipartisan coalition composed of Southern Democrats and conservative Republicans (Chen 2002; Katznelson et al. 1993), the FEPC was forced to fold in 1946.[25] With the exception of *Shelly v. Kraemer*, in which the Truman administration helped strike a blow for civil rights, filing a brief in support of outlawing racially restrictive housing covenants, many of Truman's proposed reforms failed to amount to anything concrete. For instance, the antilynching legislation submitted by Truman—as well as other recommendations of the president's commission—stalled, failing to receive enough support in Congress to become law, foiled once again by a bipartisan coalition of conservative Republicans and Southern Democrats (Katznelson, Geiger, and Kryder 1993).

This outcome understandably disappointed the black Americans whose participation in the war was key to its success—especially those who fought. Perhaps the greatest achievement of the Truman administration, and the high point for African Americans' aspirations for equality, was Executive Order 9981, which demanded the desegregation of the armed forces. Though at first the army balked at the presidential order, citing their belief that integration would harm military effectiveness, the president, through the Fahy Committee, a body charged with coordinating the desegregation of the armed forces, technically got what he wanted:

---

[25] Chen (2007) shows that although the FEPC was doomed at the federal level, it nonetheless galvanized a bloc of liberals who were eventually successful at pushing through fair employment practices legislation at the state level.

integration.[26] Still, the army refused to comply in a timely fashion as the president left it up to field commanders' discretion about when to desegregate their units. This resulted in three years of procrastination on the part of the army's senior commanders. It would take the exigencies created by another war, revealing the inefficiency of segregation, for real integration to occur (Dalfiume 1969; MacGregor 1981; Mershon and Schlossman 1998).

Even so, the war produced a group of black veterans who were reluctant to return to the status quo, and continued to fight for equality long after the decline of mass militancy in the mid-1940s. Perhaps this had to do with the rising educational levels of black servicemen as they entered the Second World War vis-à-vis their predecessors as they entered the First World War (Stouffer et al. 1949). It's also the case that black servicemen took advantage of the educational opportunities offered in the military. Several thousand draftees were given remedial academic training to make them better soldiers (MacGregor 1981). Moreover, the possibility also exists that the black press impressed upon black servicemen the importance of their sacrifice to the cause of civil rights (see appendix B for details).

Upon becoming reacquainted with Jim Crow, therefore, many turned toward activism, assuming leadership in some grassroots organizations and founding others that helped to sustain the civil rights movement. W. W. Law is one such veteran. Upon leaving the army after World War II, Law obtained his degree from Savannah State University and presided over the Savannah, Georgia, chapter of the NAACP from 1950 through 1976. During his tenure, he succeeded in his efforts to desegregate the public schools in Savannah and led boycotts, sit-ins, and wade-ins (the integration of Tybee Beach). World War II veteran Medgar Evers also fits this mold. Serving in France and England, Evers rose to the rank of sergeant while serving in Europe as part of the Red Ball Express, the post–D-Day

---

[26] The Fahy Committee wasn't the administration's only attempt at addressing the issue of military manpower after World War II. The Gillem Board, convened shortly after the Second World War, was charged with devising an efficient way of using African American manpower in the postwar army. The board recognized that blacks enjoyed the constitutional right to serve, and that the army needed to make efficient use of its manpower. But the board also deferred to the army's judgment on the capabilities of black soldiers. This allowed the army to maintain its system of quotas and segregation. The Chamberlain Board, convened in 1949, supported the conclusion of the Gillem Board (for details, see MacGregor 1981). It's worth noting that the black community, led by A. Philip Randolph, refused to accept this outcome. Along with several veterans from the Second World War, Randolph threatened to urge black and white youth to resist military service in the future if the army continued to refuse to desegregate.

logistical operation that helped the Allies win World War II; he went on to become indispensable to the NAACP in Mississippi. Before his assassination in 1963, he helped set up local chapters throughout the state and eventually rose to national prominence as the NAACP's first field secretary.

Hosea Williams, also a veteran of the Second World War, was part of an all-black unit attached to Patton's Third Army. After twice sustaining serious injuries, Williams returned to Georgia and completed high school (at age twenty-three); he then earned a bachelor's degree and a master's in chemistry from Atlanta University. In 1957, he joined with W. W. Law to integrate Savannah's Tybee Beach. Until 1962, Williams led the political arm of the NAACP, the Chatham County Crusade for Voters. After differences with the NAACP board of directors forced him to leave the organization, Dr. Martin Luther King tapped him to join the leadership of the Southern Christian Leadership Conference (SCLC). In 1965, the SCLC appointed Williams to lead the now-famous Selma-to-Montgomery march to protest voting inequality. The march culminated in what is referred to as Bloody Sunday. When the marchers crossed the Edmund Pettus Bridge in Montgomery, Alabama, state and local police beat and hospitalized dozens of them, including Williams and Student Nonviolent Coordinating Committee (SNCC) leader John Lewis. ABC News captured the spectacle, broadcasting it to a startled nation. The incident is credited with providing President Lyndon Johnson with the impetus to push the Voting Rights Act through Congress (Lawson 1976, chap. 11; Lee 2002, 4).

Amzie Moore, who served in the Pacific theater during the Second World War, represents a final example of black veterans' activism during the black freedom struggle. A Mississippi native, born in 1911, Moore helped SNCC's Bob Moses organize voter registration drives in the Magnolia State and supplied the original idea on which Freedom Summer was based. As president of the Cleveland, Mississippi chapter of the NAACP, he met Bob Moses, who would become one of SNCC's most creative field secretaries. Moore wished to enlist students for the purpose of registering black Mississippians to vote. Ultimately, he wanted to topple segregation through the ballot. Hence, it was Moore's idea on which Freedom Summer and voter registration were based (Carson 1981). Moore was also a founding member of the Regional Council of Negro Leadership (RCNL), an organization dedicated to promoting black self-help and entrepreneurship. Finally, his home served as a movement headquarters from which he helped coordinate, along with Moses, Freedom Summer and voter registration drives.

The Korean War

As the Cold War deepened, African Americans' struggle for reform grew increasingly difficult. Anyone who dared criticize America, as it remained locked in an ideological battle with the Soviet Union, risked being accused of harboring communist sympathies. Without the ability to bring more international pressure to bear on the Truman administration, segregation and discrimination continued to haunt African Americans (Anderson 2003). "Separate but equal" remained a guiding principle in the South. Moreover, on the eve of the Korean War, the army remained steadfast in its commitment to segregation—in principle if no longer policy.

As the Korean War got underway in June 1950, blacks constituted 25 percent of accessions to the army—more than twice the proportion that would have been admitted had the army been allowed to remain wed to its quota system. But because the military remained segregated, this shift in the racial makeup of the military created a problem: white units remained chronically undermanned, while all-black units were overmanned, in some cases by 62 percent (Dalfiume 1969). In the interest of efficiency, among other factors, white commanders in the field began to siphon excess manpower from black units, beginning the piecemeal integration of the army in Korea (Dalfiume 1969, 203–6). By all accounts, integration on a small scale worked well. Black and white soldiers fought well together, and there were few racial incidents (Nalty 1986). Still, General Mark Clark, the army chief of staff, resisted desegregation, as did General Douglas MacArthur, commander of forces in the Far East.

Two factors eventually coaxed the army into full compliance with Truman's order. First, General Matthew Ridgeway relieved MacArthur of command in the Far Eastern theater. For military and moral reasons, Ridgeway wished to desegregate the forces under his command. The second factor was a study commissioned by the army to assess the consequences of segregation and integration. Project Clear, conducted by social scientists with appointments at the Johns Hopkins University, commenced in the spring of 1951. It surveyed army commands in Korea, Japan, and the United States. Its findings cleared the way for Ridgeway to desegregate the forces under his command in the Far East. According to the report, over 75 percent of the army officers and enlisted men who had served in integrated units (in basic training and in Korea) praised the performance of black soldiers and officers. White officers and soldiers who had not served side-by-side with blacks were less open to the idea of integration (Bogart 1969). In other words, within units in which segregation had taken place, black servicemen were parts of a larger, more inclusive "us." In the stateside commands in which whites mainly served in segregated units, on the other hand, blacks continued to be perceived as "them," even though they wore the same uniforms.

Desegregation failed to guarantee that black soldiers would receive equal treatment and equal respect. They were subjected to manifold indignities while fighting on the Korean Peninsula. Operationally, black soldiers were routinely accused of displaying cowardice in the heat of battle. The all-black (until 1951) Twenty-Fourth Infantry Regiment absorbed the brunt of the criticism. Based in Japan prior to the escalation of hostilities in June 1950, the soldiers received better treatment from Japanese locals than they did from their white, mainly Southern-bred, commanders. When the unit was thrust to the front, the imperious, condescending attitudes of some of the white commanders needlessly imperiled their charges. George Lipsitz summarizes black soldiers' mistreatment at the hands of white officers during the Korean War:

> Black soldiers . . . talked about poor command decisions by white officers, inadequate equipment, insufficient rest periods, unfair and dishonest publicity and high casualty rates in battle. They pointed out that wounded white soldiers could expect evacuation by helicopters, but black GIs had to carry their wounded away from battle on stretchers. They noted that white units pulled back from battle enjoyed long rest periods, but that black outfits had to drill and stand inspection during their brief rest period before rushing back into combat. Many of the black soldiers . . . were convinced that white officers considered them expendable. (1988, 47)

On several occasions, black soldiers cited incidents in which white officers were so irresponsible as to all but walk them into friendly fire. On one such occasion, Lipsitz writes, "a white officer ordered his black soldiers to take a hill, then left them in combat while he reported back to company headquarters with a foot wound that his soldiers claimed was self-inflicted" (1988, 48).

Army discipline was also decidedly discriminatory. In the first months of the war, almost 25 percent of the front-line soldiers were black, but black GIs made up fully 90 percent of those charged with cowardice under fire—sixty black soldiers versus eight white soldiers accused between August and October of 1950 (Lipsitz 1988). Over 50 percent of the accused black soldiers were found guilty, and half of these men were either sentenced to death or to life in prison. Among whites, on the other hand, only two of the eight accused (25 percent) were found guilty, subsequently receiving light sentences of three and five years' imprisonment (Lipsitz 1988, 44–45). The sloppy application of military justice moved a young Thurgood Marshall, then the NAACP's chief counsel, to conduct an investigation in person. As Marshall later observed, " 'The life of a Negro meant nothing to those courts. Some soldiers who were charged were eventually convicted of misconduct under fire when they were not even near enemy lines' " (quoted in Lipsitz 1988, 45). Moreover, the black press corps reported the poor treatment of African American GIs to the black public stateside. (See appendix B for an analysis of how the *Chicago Defender* tied black soldiers' military service to its agitation for equal rights for black Americans.)

Black troops nevertheless distinguished themselves in combat. When the armistice was signed in 1953, over 600,000 black soldiers had served in the Korean War, constituting approximately 8 percent of the total strength of the armed forces. More than five thousand black soldiers died on the battlefield in Korea. Despite charges of cowardice that persisted throughout the war, black GIs were recognized for their bravery. Lieutenant Colonel Samuel Pierce Jr., for example, commanded what is regarded as the first successful American offensive in the war. In the same campaign, Captain Charles Bussey won a Silver Star for repelling an attempt by North Korean forces to flank the battalion. His platoon is credited with killing 250 of the opposing force. Of the twenty-five black aviators who served in the war, three earned the Distinguished Flying Cross. Among the recipients was Captain Daniel "Chappie" James, who went on to become the first African American to first wear three, and then four, stars. Two black soldiers were posthumously awarded the Medal of Honor: William Thompson and Cornelius H. Charlton, both of whom served in the maligned Twenty-Fourth Infantry regiment. In fact, Thompson was the first American of any color to earn it in Korea.

As the Korean War drew to a close, the black population of the United States was slightly better off than it had been prior to the war. The military was now truly desegregated in both word and deed. Race relations benefited from the integration of the forces, at least in the short term. Both black and white soldiers held higher opinions of the opposite group after serving together in Korea (Bogart 1969).[27] The Supreme Court would soon make its momentous decision in the *Brown v. Board of Education of Topeka* case. Despite these small steps forward, however, black Southerners continued to suffer under the lash of Jim Crow, and white Southerners went on terrorizing their black neighbors both physically and economically in response to the latter's attempt to enter political life and receive an equal education (Bartley 1969; Lawson 1976; Matthews and Prothro 1963; McMillen 1994; Salmon and Van Evera 1973).

---

[27] Unfortunately, this positive effect was confined to the Korean theater. Project Clear conducted a parallel study of attitudes in the military on American soil, where integration had not yet been implemented. In this part of the study, racial animosity and distrust remained (Bogart 1969).

Dwight D. Eisenhower replaced Truman in the White House and, in turn, passed the buck on civil rights, at least as it pertained to integration. The president, who failed to fully support the decision in *Brown* (Borstelmann 2001; Dudziak 2000), believed it wrong for the federal government to force integration on the South. In the long run, he thought it better if blacks achieved equality through the ballot, through political pressure. The franchise, after all, was guaranteed by the Constitution. For this reason, Eisenhower believed the franchise fair game for the use of state power to guarantee it (Lawson 1976). Though the former general dispatched troops to Little Rock, Arkansas, he did so under duress: it was a means of undermining Soviet criticism of American racial practices (Dudziak 2000).[28] Moreover, his support for civil rights bills in both 1957 and 1960 was also done in service to American foreign policy. As it had for Truman's administration, the Cold War forced Eisenhower's White House to give the appearance of bringing Jim Crow to heel lest America risk losing the global competition for allies to the Soviet Union (Borstelmann 2001; Dudziak 2000; Plummer 1996; Skrentny 2002).[29] Ultimately, both Civil Rights acts were flawed pieces of legislation; each lacked an enforcement mechanism capable of out-flanking Southern officials determined to retain political hegemony (Bartley 1969; Lawson 1976; Rosenberg 1991).

Nevertheless, the Korean War, like the war that preceded it, contributed its share of veterans to the fight against white supremacy. To give just two prominent examples, James Forman, a Korean War veteran, served as SNCC's executive secretary from 1964 to 1966. Without his unwavering leadership, and organizational skills, it's doubtful that SNCC would have achieved the success it did as the freedom struggle's "shock troops," mobilizing a new segment of activists (students) and serving as an inspiration to many black Southerners suffering under the weight of white supremacy (Carson 1981).

Earnest "Chilly Willy" Thomas was a founding member of Deacons for Defense and Justice in Jonesboro, Louisiana. As an airborne radio operator during the Korean War, exposure to a more egalitarian way of life beyond Louisiana steeled his resolve to realize such freedom at "home." Like Forman with SNCC, Thomas brought his military training to bear on the organization he led. His organizational and leadership skills steadied the

---

[28] Rogers M. Smith has also indicated to me that Eisenhower's reaction to the Little Rock crisis may have also been driven by the former general's desire to assert his authority as president over what he may have viewed as an insubordinate governor in Oval Faubus.

[29] Dudziak (2000) suggests that members of the Supreme Court appreciated the gravity of the Cold War, perhaps even taking international opinion into consideration as they decided the *Brown* case.

group for its clashes with the Klan. Through the use of force, and threats of it, the Deacons were, on more than one occasion, able to win important concessions from local, state, and federal political authorities (Hill 2004). With protection from the Deacons, moreover, the Congress of Racial Equality was able to proceed with voter registration drives and community organizing without much interference from the Klan (Fairclough 1995; Hill 2004).

From the beginning of the Second World War through 1960, real, tangible reform on civil rights remained elusive. Whether it was the Second World War, the Korean War, or the Cold War, American ideological consistency and national ambition demanded at least an attempt at racial progress, if not real racial reform. Postwar liberalism, with its emphasis on embracing blacks in the practice of the liberal creed, sought to eliminate antiblack racism and discrimination (Myrdal 1944). Applying the liberal creed to blacks would fulfill the promise of American democracy and rid the country of the hypocrisy with which it had lived for over three hundred years. This is one way to view Truman's reforms, as an attempt to institutionalize postwar liberal sentiments (Horton 2005). Indeed, if symbolism is commensurate with progress, progress indeed occurred on both Truman's and Roosevelt's watches. For Roosevelt, outlawing employment discrimination in the war industries, establishing the FEPC, and appointing some of the justices that declared the white primary elections illegal certainly counts for something. Similarly, Truman's move to desegregate the military and his willingness to run on a civil rights platform in 1948 was another sign of progress. Even Eisenhower can be credited with establishing the Civil Rights Division in the Department of Justice and pushing for the first civil rights legislation since Reconstruction. Rendering decisions that outlawed the white primaries, race-based housing covenants, and the notion of "separate but equal," the Supreme Court probably contributed most to progress.

War is related in some way to each of these executive orders, court decisions, and pieces of legislation, but it is not the only thing these attempts at state-led change have in common. Another trait shared by each of these remedies is that each was flawed in some way. Even the *Brown* decision, at least in the short term, failed to achieve tangible change (Bartley 1969; Orfield 2000; Rosenberg 1991; cf. Klarman 2006). Often, domestic political considerations limited the reach of racial reform as Southern Democrats and conservative Republicans, at the federal level, conspired to block legislation aimed to ease the suffering of blacks. Political expediency, personal ambition, and a steadfast belief in white superiority ensured that this arrangement received backing at both state and local levels of government (Bartley 1969; Mickey, forthcoming). Having said that, we should not underestimate the symbolic importance of the executive orders or the Court's decisions, for these small, largely symbolic victories signaled the presence of favorable political conditions that were conducive to the possibility of real change (McAdam 1999).

Even though change failed to materialize from above, it's worth noting that many black servicemen, like their predecessors, remained unbowed to white supremacy. From both the Second World War and the Korean War, black veterans emerged prepared to put their newfound skills to the test. As the brief biographies herein of black veterans who emerged from this period indicate, some of them played important parts in the rapidly unfolding black freedom struggle that would eventually lead to real reform in the South. However, they would help lead change from below, at the grassroots level.

. . .

This chapter has illustrated the connection—and sometimes the lack thereof—between military service and changes in the social status of African Americans. Black soldiers' service in the Revolutionary War and the Civil War had a direct, positive effect on the legal status of African Americans. In both conflicts, blacks served in relatively large numbers, and their service was a key factor in the victory achieved by the side on which they fought. Following the end of Reconstruction and the rise of militant white supremacy in the South, black GIs responded to the call during the Spanish-American War and World War I but were largely prevented from seeing combat. When they were sent to the front lines, they tended to be accused of cowardice, despite evidence to the contrary. On both occasions, blacks' claim to equal citizenship through service and sacrifice was either undermined by limitations placed on their participation or through questioning their mettle on the battlefield. Their service in these two conflicts resulted in no immediate effects for the cause of civil rights, but their resistance of white supremacy provided a glimpse of things to come. Veterans of the Second World War and the Korean War were given a greater chance to prove their mettle and were correspondingly much more successful in their efforts to overturn Jim Crow.

Another pattern emerges from this chapter's overview of black participation in American military conflicts. Though the evidence is suggestive rather than conclusive, it seems fairly clear that regardless of the presence or absence of state-sponsored change, black servicemen and veterans since the Civil War have tended to resist Jim Crow. In the post–World War II period throughout the South, veterans were among the chief agitators for change. Many were among the leadership in established civil rights organizations such as the NAACP (Dittmer 1994; Payne 1995;

Tyson 1999); others formed their own grassroots organizations (Brooks 2004; Hill 2004).

Several factors explain why the veterans of World War II and the Korean War were more successful in their challenges to white supremacy than their predecessors. First, they were far more educated than their predecessors (Stouffer et al. 1949). This likely led to more militant behavior, for they had a better appreciation for their participation in war and its significance in the wider context of the struggle for black freedom. Second, the rise of the Harlem Renaissance and Marcus Garvey's brief but influential Universal Negro Improvement Association movement furnished blacks with a sense of racial pride (Wynn 1993). Third, the veterans of these two wars had the experience of World War I on which to draw. Former officers of the First World War provided some of the leadership that resulted in Roosevelt's making key concessions on the eve of World War II. Each of these factors contributed to the recognition of political opportunity in the 1940s and '50s. Further, the international pressure created by the Cold War, electoral competition, and a divided government in the 1950s and early '60s forced a decline in repression and supplied hope to blacks seeking social change (Jenkins and Argonne 2003; McAdam 1999; Tilly 1978). Structural conditions, then, also made it easier for veterans of World War II and the Korean War to register their discontent than it had been for those who preceded them.

How did the military transform black Southerners, who as a matter of survival were raised to avoid directly challenging whites (Litwack 1998; McMillen 1989), into people who were no longer reluctant to publicly interrogate the status quo? Black veterans' tendency to refuse to abide racism stemmed, I believe, from their identification with the values for which they fought and the confidence they gained from military training and, in several cases, combat. The latter is one reason that Senator Vardaman protested the induction of black Southerners prior to the First World War. "'Universal military service means that millions of negroes . . . will be armed,'" Vardaman complained. "'I can think of no greater menace to the South than this'" (quoted in Barbeau and Henri 1974, 34–35). Though his implied vision of armed black men forcibly overthrowing white supremacy in the South was rather off the mark, Vardaman was right to fear that the experience of war would empower black GIs. In the next chapter, I propose a mechanism by which the military service of black veterans stimulated their postwar insurgency.

CHAPTER 2

Military Service and Resistance

Toward a Theory of Black Republicanism

> Just a few fools . . . of the race are taking the view . . . that the
> colored man has nothing to fight for in this country, where he is
> the subject to more humiliation, maltreatment [and] lynching
> than the treacherous, barbarous Spaniard, or the alien anar-
> chist, nihilist, or socialist. But now the country dearer to us
> than life is in peril, and everybody who thinks knows that
> Negroes have in every past crisis forgotten their little hardships,
> forgotten their chains even . . . and have unhesitatingly come to
> their country's call. They know that this is our country, that
> Negroes helped to make it what it is in war and in peace. . . .
> Negroes want to fight, are anxious to fight, but only on the
> same footing as the rest—they want an equal chance from start
> to finish to rise even to the highest possible place by merit. . . .
> The stars and stripes, the eternal emblem of Liberty, equality,
> fraternity, and justice to everybody must not, shall not touch
> the dust, if the black arms of ten million Negro Americans are
> given a full and fair chance to help hold it aloft. God save the
> nation, Washington, Attucks, Douglass, Lincoln, and McKinley
> by making it do right by all her children, black and white alike.
> —N. C. Bruce, Third North Carolina Volunteer Infantry
> (Negro), May 1898, quoted in Willard Gatewood,
> *"Smoked Yankees" and the Struggle for Empire:*
> *Letters from Negro Soldiers*

In chapter 1, I illustrated the manner in which military service affected
the social standing of African Americans. When blacks were allowed to
serve and their service contributed substantively to a war's positive outcome, they were rewarded with progress toward social justice. Conversely, on those occasions when they were not allowed to serve or their
combat-related contributions were minimized or flat-out denigrated,
their social status remained the same or even regressed. As I emphasized,
however, change was not limited to the top-down, government-sponsored
sort that occurred in the aftermath of the Revolutionary War and the

Civil War. As some of the actions of black servicemen mentioned in the previous chapter suggest, many of those who served had changed, even if society refused to do so, and these changes in turn helped to produce more widespread reform in the South.

To argue that black veterans returned home more willing to challenge white supremacy than they were when they left is not to say that nonveteran black Southerners failed to routinely contest their oppression. From everyday actions aimed at claiming dignity and self-respect to larger, more complex acts of resistance choreographed by movement organizations, black Southerners often demonstrated a willingness to resist white supremacy (Dittmer 1994; Kelley 1993, 1994; McAdam 1999; Morris 1984; Payne 1995; Tuck 2001). Nevertheless, I contend that the "radicalizing experience" of the military to which Eric Foner (1988) refers in his work on the Civil War supplemented black servicemen's and veterans' commitment to insurgency.

The epigraph to this chapter highlights the content of their radicalism. It expresses loyalty and commitment to American principles, as well as the demand that American society honor them. It is also worth noting that N. C. Bruce, a black soldier who served during the Spanish-American War, also mentions fraternity and justice, in addition to liberty and equality, as American principles that must be honored. His interpretation of the flag as a symbol of these principles, I argue, is a nod to blacks' desire to be part of the larger national political community in which they are viewed as equals. He also suggests that blacks were willing, even eager, to fight for their country. But the country had to allow them to do so under fair conditions. Black Americans, he argues, were willing to set aside their hurt and anger regarding the humiliation and brutality to which they were subjected in exchange for the opportunity to serve on an equal basis. Perhaps this sense of political agency, one that remained frustrated, explains the militancy of black veterans.

From the previous chapter we know how this particular story ends. Black units performed well in the Spanish-American War, even saving Theodore Roosevelt's Rough Riders from defeat. While their deeds did not become well known nationally, the soldiers who performed them remained proud of wearing the uniform, proud of their service to the nation (Fletcher 1974). They became increasingly militant as the pride and confidence associated with their military service continued to collide with the daily humiliations and subjugation of Jim Crow. Even as segregation hardened throughout the South around the turn of the century, some black soldiers and veterans challenged the prevailing racial norms to which pride and confidence did not permit them to submit. This resulted in violent clashes, often accompanied by gunplay (Christian 1995; Fletcher 1974).

In this chapter, I will elaborate a theoretical framework designed to explain the attitudes and behavior of such black veterans. I first examine the political and cultural underpinnings of the citizen-soldier ideal, which I argue is foundational to black veterans' claims to equality. I then take a two-pronged approach to explaining the effects of military service on veterans' political attitudes and behavior. I ground this approach in the symbolic meaning of black veterans' military experience. Normatively, black Southerners believed that wearing the uniform and serving the country made them the political equals of whites—full members of the political community. In this regard, military service had the symbolic effect of making black Southern veterans feel "more American." In this way, black veterans believed themselves entitled to the fruits of democracy for which they were prepared to die, including freedom and equality. They also drew symbolic meaning from their *experiences* in the military, which they associated with significant achievements and perseverance over the rigors associated with military life, as well as enduring discriminatory treatment even as they fought for democratic principles. Conquering both gave many of them an unshakeable sense of confidence. After examining the meaning of military service to veterans, I consider how their service shaped the belief system to which they subscribed, something I call *black republicanism*. I will then distinguish it from both mainstream republicanism and other competing black ideologies. As I argue below, black republicanism was a belief system that deployed the rhetoric of republicanism as a means of justifying claims to equality and the contestation of white supremacy.

THE CITIZEN-SOLDIER IDEAL

To fully appreciate why black elites like Fredrick Douglass and W.E.B. DuBois believed so strongly in the efficacy of military service in producing racial progress, we must first examine the place of military service in American political culture. Let us begin by considering the origins of the institution of the citizen-soldier, a cornerstone of republican citizenship.

The Citizen-Soldier Ideal: The Classical Model

Originating with Aristotle and later revised in the work of such thinkers as Cicero, Niccolò Machiavelli, Jean-Jacques Rousseau, and Baron Montesquieu, *republicanism* is a complex set of ideals and empirical assumptions about how citizens and institutions may secure the common good and protect political liberty. Among these ideals and assumptions is the notion that a virtuous citizenry is a necessary component of a free state. Unlike the liberty associated with liberalism, which aspires to freedom from interference and the unconstrained pursuit of self-perfection (Berlin 1969), republicans seek to free themselves from the arbitrary interference of others and to participate in their own political destiny (Pettit 1997; Skinner 1998). More concretely, liberals are concerned with preventing the imposition of limits on their freedom of choice. Republicans contend, on the other hand, that freedom as the absence of interference ultimately fails to square with real freedom. Indeed, Quentin Skinner, a leading republican theorist, maintains that "if basic rights and liberties may be taken away with impunity . . . they do not have the status of rights" (2002, 250). For one to remain an object of domination one does not need to actually have their freedom of choice curbed; the mere possibility that it *could be* curbed by another party is sufficient for domination to obtain. Theoretically, then, it is possible to enjoy freedom of choice and pursue self-perfection while remaining an object of domination. For republicans, thus, a free state is one in which the absence of domination is preferred to the absence of interference. The principal difference, therefore, is how one defines freedom: for liberals, it's the absence of constraint; for republicans, it's the absence of dependence or domination.

Domination may emanate from the outside or from within. Individuals may be subjected to internal domination by those within the state who arbitrarily curb their freedom, such as a corrupt government through its agents. War, on the other hand, presents an external threat to liberty, as it may result in a nation's occupation or its permanent loss of sovereignty. To avoid domination and the loss of their liberty, citizens are encouraged to put the needs of the republic before their private interests. Thus, the civic virtue of a republican citizenry is exhibited in its willingness to participate in politics, subsume self-interest to the common good, identify emerging threats to liberty—both internal and external—and come to the aid of the country, even if it requires the forfeiture of life. Republican liberty, in sum, is both realized and protected through participation in the public sphere, including military service (Snyder 1999).

If civic virtue is central to the realization and protection of political liberty, what can be done to engender a virtuous citizenry? Here, republicans have traditionally turned to a variety of institutional and social mechanisms (including mixed government, direct participation, education, civic religion, the avoidance of economic extremes, and the control of commercial interaction) in order to inculcate the proper virtues of citizenship. The military, which produces the citizen-soldier, is among these mechanisms. Indeed, many republicans have perceived the military to be the republic's primary school of virtue. Machiavelli, for example, believed that military service to the state has the capacity to transform people into better citizens because it ordinarily demands self-sacrifice and a concern for the greater good (Pocock 1975). Service members must be willing to exchange their safety for danger, comfort for physical hardship, and familial integrity for family separation. Enduring these hardships together with fellow citizens to protect the republic reinforces the importance of self-sacrifice for the good of the political community.

The idea that soldiers should be citizens, however, has been important to republican theorists for another reason: possession of a citizen militia allows the republic to avoid the corruption associated with a standing army. A professional army must justify its existence, possibly creating a conflict of interest, as it must press for an aggressive foreign policy, which in turn makes war more likely. With few exceptions, war threatens the political community and therefore the common good.[1] The militia not only makes a standing army unnecessary but inhibits the spread of corruption by preventing tyranny from above or unjustified revolt led by demagogues from below. Some theorists have considered an armed citizenry (a citizen militia) to be the only thing standing between a corrupt state and the interruption of republican liberty by the imposition of domination or servitude (Pettit 1997). Others see an armed citizenry as capable of denying factions led by demagogues the ability to undermine the pursuit of the common good. In a republic with widespread political participation, David Williams (1991) explains, the citizen militia was historically perceived to be utterly incapable of acting against the common good of the people, because "the virtue of the militia rested upon and reflected the virtue of the citizenry as a whole because they were one and the same" (579).

The Citizen-Soldier: In the American Context

The citizen-soldier was very much in evidence during the American Revolution. In fact, the early Americans favored a militia-based fighting force over a standing army because, like their European forebears, they believed the latter might just as soon promote corruption as stem it. Alexander Hamilton, in *Federalist Paper* 29, "Concerning the Militia," makes clear the republican concern for a standing army while arguing the merits of a federally regulated militia: "If standing armies are dangerous to liberty, an efficacious power over the militia . . . ought . . . to

---

[1] Machiavelli (1970), on the other hand, believed that an aggressive foreign policy and war were sometimes good for the republic because they can relieve internal unrest that was mitigated when plebes were sent off to fight.

take away the inducement and the pretext to such unfriendly institutions" (Hamilton 2005, 154). In the American colonies, moreover, republicanism was shaped by opposition to continuing British rule (Bailyn 1967; Wood 1969). In Gordon Wood's (1969) account, the American version of republicanism reflected the moral character of American society, in which civic virtue, equality of opportunity, and self-sacrifice anchored the pursuit of the public good. There is little doubt that these ideals motivated ragtag, poorly trained state militia units to take on the far superior British force. It's not a stretch to say that the militiamen drew upon the righteousness of their cause as means of enduring the financial and personal sacrifices entailed in repelling the redcoats (Chambers 1987).

That the colonists enjoyed their political liberty and were willing to die for the values underpinning it was revolutionary in its own right. There is, though, at least one additional reason why the American rebellion against the British should be considered a revolution: it remains the first modern attempt to create a broad-based republic in which ordinary people were given a voice in government in exchange for their service. The citizen-soldier tradition was a key part of this experiment. Prior to the war, the ability to vote was tethered to property ownership, excluding significant segments of the population. But it was exceedingly difficult for the colonial elite to reconcile the egalitarian spirit of the revolution with the contingent nature of the franchise (Keyssar 2000). The prevailing sentiment among men of all social ranks seems to have been that " 'every man in the country who manifests a disposition to venture all for the defense of its liberty, should have a voice in its council' " (Anon. [Thomas Young?], quoted in Keyssar 2000, 14). And so, as the eighteenth century drew to a close, military service was closely connected in the new American republic to the discourse of citizenship.

The service-citizenship nexus continued to be influential in the United States in the nineteenth and twentieth centuries. Suffrage expansion in the aftermath of the War of 1812 was attributed in part to military service. By agreeing to attach voting rights to military service—that is, to militia duty and army service—the social elite secured their interests while sidestepping the moral dilemma associated with the less fortunate shouldering the bulk of the burden of defense (Keyssar 2000, chap. 2). The Civil War, however, was a departure from the earlier conflicts. Unlike the War of Independence and the War of 1812, in which some men fought to gain franchise, refusing to serve during the Civil War, some believed, warranted a forfeiture of civil and political rights, including the right to vote. During the war, republicans argued that, when necessary, military service was an important obligation of citizenship (Chambers 1987). General William Sherman, a noted Civil War commander, went so far as to suggest that the American government should strip of all legal and political rights those who refused to answer the call to the colors. When New Yorkers resisted conscription, the state militia's adjutant remarked, "'Where the whole population participates in the rights, privileges, and immunities of a free people, they must share equally also in its burdens'" (quoted in Chambers 1987, 59). While draft dodgers were never actually stripped of civil or political rights, they were deprived of liberty: they were thrown in jail (Chambers 1987, 59).

The citizen-soldier enjoys a long, and some would say distinguished, history in American political development. Yet some scholars take issue with the status of the concept. Historian Richard Kohn, for example, maintains that the ideal American soldier is a myth, romanticized for the sake of inspiring patriotism. Kohn (1981) argues that only on rare occasion has the military truly been a reflection of American society. Sometimes, moreover, patriotism alone has failed to motivate sufficient numbers to join the fight. American history, Kohn reminds us, is also full of deserters, of soldiers who have fled from the fight or intentionally injured themselves to avoid combat. Even Peter Karsten's (1966) work on the citizen-soldier, which on balance is positive, reveals real deficiencies with the individuals who are charged with realizing the ideal of the citizen-soldier, some of whom were charged with collaborating with the enemy as prisoners of war.

These revelations should not be taken lightly. Every war has its share of people who, for various reasons, fail to join with their conationals, or are too weak to withstand interrogation. Nevertheless, the ideal of the citizen-soldier has been important in the development of American citizenship, regardless of the frequency with which some individuals deviated from it. Moreover, for symbolic and practical reasons, the citizen-soldier ideal retains currency in American citizenship discourse insofar as military service continues to be regarded as an obligation of citizenship (Conover, Crewe, and Searing 1991). Symbolically, it has represented membership in the political community, for service has secured right to vote for those who lacked it in most cases. In this regard, eligibility for military service—especially militia duty—has rivaled the vote as an indicator of social standing (Berry 1977; Shklar 1991). After all, it is irrational to risk one's life to defend a nation in which one has no say in the decision to go to war. To do so, contradicts republican logic in that those who defend the republic from external domination should not be refused the opportunity to participate in the institutions that promise to spare them from internal domination. Republican ideology demands that soldiers not be asked to fight for republican freedom abroad even as they are denied it at home.

THE SYMBOLISM OF MILITARY SERVICE

The citizen-soldier ideal suggests that military service represents political equality. It signals one's loyalty to the nation and its values, often resulting in the extension of the franchise to nonvoting groups that have used military sacrifice to prove their loyalty. For this reason, the citizen-soldier ideal was seized upon by black elites as a means of staking a claim to equal citizenship. Implicit in their championing of African Americans' military service was their assumption that the value of this service would be recognized and rewarded by the state. So popular in the black community was the notion that military service represented a path to equality for African Americans that it was taken for granted and eventually attained the status of folk wisdom among blacks (Burk 1995). Though scholars have often made this point, the symbolic meaning of military service for black soldiers has received less attention. To whites and blacks alike, military service signified loyalty; but to blacks it also represented their membership in the national political community, something that for much of American history has been contested (Smith 1997). Military service, especially for black Southerners, also represents the many experiences associated with serving Uncle Sam, including fighting and surviving two battles: one on the battlefield, the other on post.

Generally, symbols simplify and communicate often complex arrays of stimuli from which meaning is derived (Firth 1973). One source of stimuli to which symbolism may be applied is political culture. If culture is at least in part constituted by a system of symbols (Geertz 1973; Laitin 1988), we may think of political culture as a system of political symbols (Dittmer 1977). To the extent that political culture is in part about how one feels about politics (Almond and Verba 1963), it makes sense that symbols, as a means of indexing political culture, are laced with affect (Elder and Cobb 1983; Sears 1993). Indeed, symbols represent individuals' attachment to political culture insofar as they are at once part of political culture and tangible objects to which people within a given system attach meaning (Cobb and Elder 1972).[2]

Whether symbols are abstract or more concrete, they have at least one thing in common: they are subject to interpretation. More precisely, "the meaning of [a] symbol," as anthropologist Raymond Firth observes, is "a concrete indication of abstract values" (1973, 54). Among the ways in which symbols become tethered to values is through the production of meaning. Meaning, according to political scientist Lisa Wedeen (2002),

---

[2] For the pioneering work on the connection between politics and symbols, see Edelman (1985).

is the product of individuals' practices, symbols, and language. More to the point, she contends that "symbols are inscribed in practices that produce observable political effects." These political effects, in turn, confer meaning upon the symbol. Meaning can only be made, however, "as conventions become intelligible to participants through observable usages and effects" (Wedeen 2002, 722). Simply put, in the absence of a shared understanding of the relationship between symbols and practices, and the product of the two, meaning is difficult to achieve.

For my purposes, Wedeen's framework suggests that meaning is attributed to the observable political effects of military service as social practice. Historically, as I have shown in chapter 1, military service is often associated with improved social standing, especially if, as Judith Shklar (1991) has argued, standing is tied to the franchise. Service during the Revolutionary War supplied white men without property with the right to vote; the War of 1812 also extended the franchise to white males. For blacks, the American Revolution resulted in limited freedom for those who served, and the right to vote—albeit only temporarily—for free black Americans more generally. It almost goes without saying that the Civil War brought more widespread change for African Americans. Moreover, the periods surrounding the Revolution and the Civil War were times during which republican themes were very much a part of public discourse (Bailyn 1967; Chambers 1987; Smith 1997). We see, then, that military service, as a social practice embedded in the language of republicanism, produced tangible political effects, securing access to the ballot. Hence, we see a path by which military service has come to symbolize political equality.[3]

As tangible representations of political culture, symbols range from the abstract to the concrete. On the abstract end of the continuum are representations of the political community; the flag, the national anthem, and the Constitution are good examples (Baas 1979). Political authorities, such as a presidential administration, political actors, and particular policies, are more concrete, situational symbols (Elder and Cobb 1983). In this taxonomy of symbols, military service belongs with

[3] Political symbolism is more than a representation of political culture. Symbolic politics, as Sears (1993) calls it, also informs political attitudes and behavior. Sears argues that early childhood socialization creates affective attachments to objects that are essentially political symbols. Party identification, basic values such as equality and individualism, and racial prejudices are all symbols to which sentiments, positive and negative, are attached. These symbolic predispositions predict political attitudes and behavior when a symbol contained in the attitude object triggers the disposition with which it is associated. For example, for whites, busing, as an attitude object, triggers predispositions associated with race (Sears, Henslee, and Speer 1979).

the flag and the Constitution as a representation of the political community. Each is a commanding presence in American mythology and therefore within American political culture. With such cultural prominence comes enormous normative weight: the flag is associated with patriotism, the Constitution with the rule of law, and military service with first-class citizenship.

MILITARY SERVICE AS A SYMBOLIC EXPERIENCE

The symbolism associated with military service motivated black veterans by drawing upon the reproduction of American political culture, in which military service is equated with full membership in the political community. Emphasizing this normative component of military service, however, can only take us so far. The normative component helps to explain why veterans wanted change, but it fails to explain what ultimately moved them to act. If we wish to fully understand why black veterans acted on their beliefs we must examine their *experiences* in the military. This move does not require abandoning the symbolic political framework. Beyond mediating the relationship between individuals and their political culture, symbols are also capable of representing shared experiences and of summarizing and indexing knowledge (Dittmer 1977; Elder and Cobb 1983; Firth 1973). In what follows, I argue that the social practices and values that are part of the military's institutional culture, along with the confidence that comes with surviving service in a Jim Crow military, constituted the shared experience and stock of knowledge that spurred veterans to act on their frustration and sense of entitlement to equality.

Race-Neutral Military Experiences

No one can deny that military service, especially during war, is among the most challenging and enduring experiences life has to offer. After all, one is obliged to kill, and die if one must, for the nation (Walzer 1970). Since the military as an institution is charged with national defense, it must develop practices, procedures, and values commensurate with its mission. Like other institutions, the military operates according to well-defined scripts and rules (Meyer and Rowan 1991). Such scripts in the military include but are not limited to teamwork and self-reliance, both of which are key to achieving mission success (Gage 1964; Lovell and Stiehm 1989). It is also responsible for the inculcation of certain values conducive to the pursuit of war. Some studies indicate that discipline, duty, courage, and obedience, the suite of values on which military culture rests, are indispensable to the military's mission of national defense (Huntington 1957; Janowitz 1960). The military, as a total institution—especially during war—continues to reinforce these values for the balance of the service member's career.

To inculcate and reinforce these martial values and virtues, the military draws on constructions of masculinity. That military training draws on such constructions should shock no one; the West has almost always equated being a warrior with masculinity (Elshtain 1987). Some even suggest that martial virtue is a prerequisite of manliness (Mansfield 2006). While one need only consult the performance of American women in the current foreign entanglements in Iraq and Afghanistan to conclude that the marital virtue associated with military service isn't only reserved for men (Snyder 1999, 2003), masculinity remains purposefully linked to qualities believed to be coterminous with the successful pursuit of war (Goldstein 2001). According to this line of reasoning, an effective warrior is one who possesses courage, strength, skill, and honor, all of which map well onto traditional conceptions of masculine duty, part of which emphasizes the duty of men to defend women and children. Warriors must also learn to suppress emotion and the natural inclination to flee when attacked, which are solved through the application of discipline and courage, respectively. Soldiers are taught to aspire to possess all of these values lest national defense suffer.[4]

Military service also breeds confidence. As sites that present opportunities for self-realization, institutions serve as ideal locations for engaging in behavior that is likely to generate confidence and a sense of agency (Gecas 1982). The military should (and should continue to be) such a site for at least two reasons. First, it is often a challenging environment in which mastering difficult, complex tasks are essential. Successfully completing these tasks, studies show, increases one's sense of efficacy. Second, one's sense of efficacy is tied to how one's actions are appraised in the community (Bandura 1982). In other words, the subjective *meaning* of an act affects the extent to which one is able to gather confidence from it (Gecas and Schwalbe 1983). With the possible exception of Vietnam (Isaacs 1997), American veterans are typically celebrated by the Ameri-

---

[4] Military culture courts controversy, however, when masculinity is used as a means of motivating service members, especially trainees. The military has institutionalized manifold ways of training men to fight. However, successful performance of each aspect of this training, according to Hockey (2003), is identified with masculinity; failure is associated with femininity. As a result, weakness, fear, and a failure to focus—the opposite of discipline— are perceived as the antithesis of masculinity and are feminized. Recruits who do not measure up run the risk becoming feminized and thereby stigmatized in the eyes of their peers (Enloe 1993).

can public. It's no wonder, then, that veterans generally tend to emerge from the military with a keen sense of confidence (Elder and Clipp 1989; Mettler 2005a). Thus the practice of *practicing* for war—and in the case of battle, engaging in one—has at least one side benefit in that it boosts confidence.

Military Experience and Race

Discipline, courage, and confidence are important to military culture. Even masculinity has its place. All are important to the military's institutional identity. Each, however, is race-neutral in that these traits have come to be intrinsically associated with the military without regard to race. Once race is added to the mix, however, otherwise mundane military practices that would be of no consequence if the military were either all white or color-blind, become points of departure for action among black Southerners. Consider the acquisition of confidence. For whites, merely surviving combat was sufficient for boosting self-confidence (Elder and Clipp 1989). For blacks, an additional source of confidence, beyond the public's appreciation of military service, was attached to surviving Jim Crow policies in the military. During the Second World War, racism was institutionalized through policy; it remained so in practice during the Korean War. Hence, blacks were forced to endure antipathy from white soldiers, fight the institutionalized racism in the military, and confront the enemy on the battlefield. Logic dictates that, having bested " 'the man, the system, and the axis [powers],' " according to one anonymous veteran (quoted in Thomas 1993, 139), black veterans emerged from the military undeterred, and with abundant confidence.

We can look to masculinity for additional examples. Discipline and courage, both of which are constructed by the military as masculine traits, are indispensable for military service. But they were also important resources for black servicemen who sought to challenge the institutional racism to which they were subjected. In the absence of courage it's hard to imagine black soldiers challenging military authority during the Second World War.[5] Likewise, without discipline, one cannot conceive of the black veterans in the Tulsa Race Riots (see chapter 1) protecting their community by using fire teams and posting snipers.

The custom of overseas deployment, something that is a necessity even in peacetime, represents another source of insurgent attitudes. Travel—seeing

[5] The work of Katzenstein shows that women were also able to challenge military authority, mobilizing against sexism in the armed services. But the conditions under which they did so were quite different from when black veterans bucked authority. For more, see Katzenstein (1998).

new places and experiencing different cultures—often encourages one to think and go about business in new ways, especially if one has been raised in a traditional society (Grasmick 1973; Inkeles 1969). For white servicemen, travel overseas resulted in increased self-awareness (Elder, Gimble, and Ivie 1991). For black servicemen, especially from the South, experiencing life overseas went beyond self-awareness. Deployment during the Second World War and the Korean War exposed well over a million black Southerners—who were accustomed to discrimination and oppressive conditions (Litwack 1998; McMillen 1994; Woodward 1955)—to a model of race relations in which the indigenous, dominant group often treated them with a measure of respect. After witnessing more progressive cultures elsewhere, therefore, black servicemen had an additional reason (beyond the conviction that it was morally unjust) to question the legitimacy of white supremacy. As we shall see, exposure to more racially equitable societies made black veterans question the legitimacy of Jim Crow not only at home but also overseas. Black GIs were often forced to contend with the slanderous accusations of whites, even as they wore the uniform. Such experiences overseas and back home in the South, I contend, invited many of them to realize the stubbornness of white supremacy. If black veterans recognized the illegitimacy of Jim Crow prior to serving in the military, we can expect their perception of its illegitimacy to have intensified upon their return.

For African Americans, and especially for those from the South, military service during World War II and the Korean War also furnished an opportunity to escape crippling economic oppression. Prior to the elimination of segregation, the military represented one of few avenues of upward mobility for African Americans. To be sure, segregation was a formidable barrier to this mobility, and in some cases it devastated morale (Bogart 1969; Stouffer et al. 1949). Yet many black Southerners capitalized on the opportunities the military afforded them to rise out of poverty and relative illiteracy in spite of the demoralizing effects of institutional segregation. By learning new skills and becoming a part of a larger national organization, black servicemen were infused with a sense of self-confidence few had felt prior to their years of service (Katznelson 2005; Kohn 1981; Modell, Goulden, and Magnusson 1989; Moskos 1976; O'Brien 1999).

Many veterans, moreover, joined the military during a formative time in their lives, in their late teens and early twenties. Attitudes that are developed during these years tend to crystallize, remaining salient through middle adulthood (Jennings and Niemi 1981; Krosnick and Alwin 1989). Attitudes produced by momentous events also tend to remain with individuals for many years. If memories of the Second World War and participation in protests during the 1960s produced lasting effects (Jennings and Niemi 1981; Schuman and Scott 1989), so too should have military service.[6] And if attitudes developed under these circumstances are important—and they are—they should resist change, remain stable over time, affect cognition, and ultimately drive behavior (Krosnick and Petty 1995). We should expect the military experience, then, to have continued to structure the ways veterans thought, felt, and behaved for many years after their service.

To summarize, then, the military experiences of soldiers produce first a normative symbolic association; for African Americans, military service and fighting for democracy represented entrée to first-class citizenship. Second, they provided black Southerners with experiences, for which the military, as an institution, is responsible. Military service exposed African Americans to opportunities and situations that had the potential to result in enormous personal growth. Contending with and defeating institutionalized racism, both systemic and personal, should have only increased black veterans' confidence and assertiveness. Everyday exposure to military culture reinforced soldiers' confidence with discipline and a sense of courage generated by military training and its emphasis on the need for soldiers to demonstrate their masculinity. These experiences instilled many black veterans with a sense of achievement and of confidence, as well as an awareness that there were places in the world in which blacks and whites were more equal.

SKETCHING A BELIEF SYSTEM FOR BLACK VETERANS

The experience of military service made black veterans a relatively unique group in the Jim Crow South.[7] Certainly, like all black Southerners, veterans were socialized within black institutions that reinforced identification with the race. Their socialization experience nonetheless significantly departed from that of nonveterans. For starters, black veterans were exposed to and became accustomed to a measure of equality while in the service. This is not to say that segregation and discrimination within the military were not major problems; they were. But if the socialization experience of black Southerners who lacked military service

[6] It should be noted that upon comparing the residual effect of military service with protest participation during the 1960s, Jennings and Niemi (1981) found that the latter had a larger impact upon subsequent attitudes and behavior than the former. They also note, however, that the difference may be due to the populations from which each joined. Protestors were self-selected, while veterans were not.

[7] Group formation requires that members are cognizant of their membership in the group, aware that it is based upon commonly held values and experiences, and emotionally invested in it (Brewer 2001; Tajfel 1981, 1982).

is the baseline for assessment, black veterans were exposed to relatively egalitarian conditions that empowered them.

Like whites, blacks were allowed to bear arms in defense of the country, a signature right of republican citizenship (Kerber 1998; Williams 1991). The decision in *Dred Scott v. Sandford*, in which Scott's petition was denied at least in part because he was barred from the militia, reminds us of the importance of arms bearing—especially in defense of the political community—to citizenship.[8] Though with few exceptions blacks were not allowed to serve in the same units with whites prior to the Korean War, black and white soldiers sometimes fought side by side.[9] Even if we leave aside occasions on which they fought and died together, that they fought on the same battlefield was indicative of rough equality.

Many black servicemen, as we have seen, were not given the opportunity to fight. Yet even this did not prevent them from experiencing more equal conditions and treatment than was afforded to black Southerners with no military experience. Indeed, black soldiers often perceived themselves to be elevated to the level of their white compatriots simply by donning any garb bearing the initials "U.S." (Glatthaar 1990; Thomas 1993). White lynch mobs implicitly acknowledged this symbolic function of the uniform when they sought to lynch black GIs who possessed the temerity to wear it in the South. Perhaps the uniform represented a level of equality which with these white Southerners were uncomfortable.

Another cleavage in the experiences of black veterans and nonveterans resulted from the former having encountered the paradox of military service. By this I mean the experience of actively fighting for democracy while being denied its fruits, such as equal treatment. As I have indicated, fighting and wearing the uniform were rough indicators of equality, but they were also sources of pride and confidence. To be sure, black nonveterans were familiar with the constraints imposed by white domination, and many were proud of their race (Litwack 1998; Matthews and Prothro 1966; Rochon 1998). But it remains difficult to imagine a comparable experience among nonveterans in which such a sense of empowerment was juxtaposed with oppression.

The military experiences of black veterans supplied the raw material for the formation of a viable social group. To the degree that group formation and identification requires that members are cognizant that they

---

[8] I have gone into the *Dred Scott* decision in a bit more detail in chapter 1.

[9] The Battle of the Bulge, the German counteroffensive through the Ardennes in 1944, is an occasion in which black units, at the battalion level, were integrated with larger white units, at the regimental or divisional level (Lee 1966).

belong to the group, are aware that membership is based upon commonly held values, and are emotionally invested in the group and its values (Tajfel 1981), veterans constitute a social group. For a social group to remain viable, however, it needs a belief system to bind it together. Ideology serves this purpose. As a system of beliefs, values, and attitudes (Rokeach 1968), ideologies bind individuals to groups, which coalesce around common cognitive orientations (Converse 1964; Lane 1962; Harris-Lacewell 2004). They also perform an important cognitive function, informing perceptions of the social world and conditioning how one reacts to it (Dawson 2001). Ideologies, in short, provide a rationale for group interests (Lane 1962).

Ideological Contenders

Identifying the ideology of black veterans requires first turning to Michael Dawson's seminal work on black ideologies.[10] In *Black Visions* (2001), Dawson identifies six ideologies that have historically served as the basis of African American political thought: radical egalitarianism, disillusioned liberalism, black Marxism, black nationalism, black feminism, and black conservatism. I begin to assess the compatibility between black veterans and the ideologies identified by Dawson with nonliberal ideologies, ways of seeing the world that are at variance with the ways black veterans see it. For instance, it would be difficult to square the sensibilities associated with black feminism, a way of seeing the world in which correcting race- and gender-based oppression takes priority, with black veterans. It seems to me that black veterans would have no problem opposing the oppression of black women. Indeed, they sought to protect black women. And though they thought it their duty to protect black women, the desire to do so smacks of patriarchy, something rather inconsistent with feminism, much less black feminism. Beyond that, black veterans, like other African American men who sought to challenge the status quo, believed that women should assume a relatively subordinate role in the movement (Hill 2004; Ransby 2003; Tyson 1999). For black veterans, however, given the masculinity inculcated as part of their military training, and the affirmation of their manhood through arms bearing and more equal treatment overseas (Lentz-Smith 2005), it is likely the case that their patriarchal impulses were pushed beyond those that were associated with nonveterans.

---

[10] I draw on Dawson's historical exploration of black ideologies as a point of departure because it is the definitive work on black ideologies of the period of time covered in this book. Harris-Lacewell's (2004) work on black political ideologies is an exceptional piece of scholarship, but hers is a work centered upon contemporary ideologies.

Black Marxism, with its emphasis on class conflict and distrust of capitalism, has even less to offer black veterans. With few exceptions, and as long as their postwar status improved, blacks veterans, at least implicitly, sought to preserve capitalism as part of the American way of life. A related point, one that bears directly on class, is the advancement blacks sought through the use of the GI Bill (Mettler 2005a). It seems that a desire to move into the middle class—and higher, if possible—would prevent most black veterans from embracing black radicalism.[11]

The last of the nonliberal ideologies is not so easily dismissed. Black nationalism, especially the community variant, may appeal to black veterans in at least three ways. First, black nationalism prizes self-reliance, something with which black veterans are indeed comfortable (Moskos and Butler 1996). Like black nationalists, many black veterans also harbor a deep distrust of the state—at all levels of government. Third, black veterans, similar to all nationalists, also believe that men should lead the charge for reform, women assuming a subordinate role (Hill 2004; Tyson 1999). The attraction between African American military service and black nationalism, however, is not without limits. More militant versions of black nationalism, ones that insist upon land, or separation from American society, fail to appeal to black veterans (Parker 2001). Even community nationalism, a strain of black nationalism committed to the development of black autonomous institutions (Carmichael and Hamilton 1967; Dawson 2001, chap. 2), if not complete social separation from whites, isn't compatible with black veterans' military service. One reason for the incompatibility is that community nationalism fails to tolerate diversity: blacks should be for blacks and no one else. This contradicts findings that suggest military service in mixed units increased racial tolerance (Bogart 1969; Stouffer et al. 1949). Another point of departure between the tenets of community nationalism and the behavior of black veterans rests upon allegiance, and to whom it is owed. Black nationalists, including community nationalists, preach allegiance to the black community (Carmichael and Hamilton 1967). Yet this philosophy fails to square with the views of many black veterans in the postwar South who expressed allegiance to both the black community *and* the national political community (McMillen 1997; Parker 2001).[12]

---

[11] Two notable exceptions are Harry Haywood after World War I, and Robert F. Williams during the 1960s. After serving during the First World War, Haywood joined the African Blood Brotherhood, an organization that combined black nationalism with socialism (Dawson 2001). After falling out of favor with the NAACP over his preference for armed self-defense, he fled to China, and eventually settled in Cuba.

[12] For an examination of black nationalism from a normative perspective, see Shelby (2005). For other empirical explorations see Brown and Shaw (2002) as well as Davis and Brown (2002).

That leaves us with the black ideologies that Dawson associates with liberalism: radical egalitarianism, disillusioned liberalism, and black conservatism. Of these ideologies, black conservatism is easiest to dismiss. Because military service stimulates racial pride and self-confidence, black veterans may have supported the emphasis on self-reliance of black conservatives (Dawson 2001). But black conservatism in the context of Jim Crow also meant accepting white supremacy (Marx 1967). Black conservatives were, in the 1950s and '60s, satisfied with the speed of change, and they rejected civil rights activism. As other scholars have pointed out, however, many black veterans refused to observe tradition, challenging white supremacy on several occasions throughout the South (Brooks 2004; Hill 2004; Nalty 1986; O'Brien 1999; Tyson 1999). Black conservatism cannot account for this activism.

It may be that black veterans subscribed to the ideology Dawson calls "disillusioned liberalism." One can imagine that serving in a segregated military under the command of racist Southern white officers might have caused black servicemen to conclude that whites were fundamentally racist, one of the tenets of this ideology (Dawson 2001, chap. 6). As a tactical solution to the tenacity of racism, disillusioned liberals counseled separation from American society as well as the political and economic empowerment of the black community. Black veterans certainly supported the empowerment that disillusioned liberals called for. They believed, for instance, that blacks should be in charge of their own institutions, including businesses and schools (Parker 2001). But they could not abide entirely separating from American society, even as a tactical solution to American racism (Ellison 1992; Parker 2001). Indeed, many veterans remained committed to America even after suffering discrimination during their service (McMillen 1997; Moore 1996). For better or for worse, black veterans cast their lot with American society; many of them had served and risked death in order to gain entrée into this society (Stouffer et al. 1949, chap. 10).

We now arrive at radical egalitarianism, the ideology most consistently embraced by African Americans (Dawson 2001). What we know about black veterans suggests that radical egalitarianism adequately describes a number of important aspects of their attitudes and behavior. Radical egalitarianism combines "a severe critique of racism in American society [with] an impassioned appeal for America to live up to the best of its [liberal] values" (Dawson 2001, 16). Dawson notes radical egalitarians' insistence upon individual liberty and uplift as well as self-reliance. Moreover, radical egalitarians adhered to Douglass's famous admonition to would-be insurgents, "Without struggle, there is no progress." Emancipation, in other words, required activism at the polls and in the streets. Wartime, Dawson contends, offered an ideal opportunity to lobby for racial justice because "black actions during war constitute the repeated proof necessary to demonstrate black worthiness for full economic, social, and political equality and participation in American society" (2001, 260).

The experiences and aspirations of black veterans appear to have been relatively consonant with this description of radical egalitarianism. As chapter 1 suggested, veterans of all eras were critical of America's failure to realize its national ideals, a criticism that resulted in their activism. But there are a few tenets of radical egalitarianism with which black veterans seem to have disagreed. The first is the preference of radical egalitarians for a strong central state. It makes perfect sense for black Americans to prefer a strong state as a safeguard against the misdeeds of state and local governments. Given veterans' discriminatory treatment in the military, though, it is plausible to presume that they would not have trusted central state authority to the same degree as those without military experience. Because the central government was slow to respond to Southern terror, moreover, some veterans preferred to rely upon themselves to ensure their liberty (Hill 2004). Second, while it is true that black veterans were committed to activism, there was a line they refused to cross. Many veterans participated in protests, for instance, but if "taking it to the streets" entailed rioting, veterans were reluctant to do so (Parker 2001).

Another disconnect between black veterans' worldview and radical egalitarianism involves gender. It was not uncommon for black veterans to emphasize their masculine identity (Tyson 1999). Military service, after all, has historically served as a rite of passage through which young men prove their fitness for manhood (Gill 1997). Add to this the emasculated position of black men in the South and the centrality of masculinity to military socialization culture (Enloe 1993; Goldstein 2001; Hockey 2003), and it is no mystery why black men sought to certify their manliness by participating in combat (Stouffer et al. 1949). Yet the manliness associated with the military conflicts with radical egalitarianism's stance on equality insofar as women were largely excluded from the institution.[13] Due in part to their military training, black veterans were deter-

---

[13] Dawson doesn't make any direct claims that radical egalitarianism is gender neutral. However, on the grounds that one of the major tenets of radical egalitarianism is equality, it implies universalism, that equality is for everyone. Also, Ida B. Wells, one of the most prominent black activists of the early twentieth century, is among the most noteworthy practitioners of radical egalitarianism (Dawson 2001). In theory, therefore, radical egalitarianism's universalism should include women. But in practice, it is not at all clear that women were perceived as equal by some of the other twentieth-century radical egalitarians, chief among whom are W.E.B. DuBois and Martin Luther King Jr. (Dawson 2001). In DuBois's case there is evidence to support claims that he believed in gender equality in

mined to protect the women and children in the community as they challenged white supremacy. Their conceptions of gender roles shaped what they believed to be the appropriate forms of social action for men and for women (Brooks 2004; Hill 2004). At least some black veterans, then, might have taken issue with the gender neutrality suggested by radical egalitarianism.

The Case for an Ideological Alternative

None of the above-mentioned ideologies, it seems, is fully capable of accommodating the behavior of black veterans. Black veterans were critical of the American polity, yet they maintained a desire to be counted as part of it. They chose activism, but many preferred activism without civil disobedience. Veterans believed in the importance of the black community's economic autonomy, but they rejected the necessity of full-blown social and political autonomy. Many black veterans, indeed, were also relatively militant, but not alienated (Parker 2001). It appears that black veterans sampled the menu of black liberalism, taking bits and pieces from conservatism, disillusioned liberalism, and radical egalitarianism without committing to any one of them.

What on the surface appear to be attitudes and behaviors without much coherence, however, are actually quite intelligible when considered as part of an ideology not identified by Dawson. Three general themes emerge from an examination of black veterans' worldview. First, black veterans were often critical of America. Sometimes during wartime, but more often after it, veterans voiced their disappointment at the glacial pace of racial progress. Second, black veterans possessed the courage to act on their convictions. In the face of white domination and intimidation, they continued to press claims to equality. Finally, veterans were ultimately committed to America and American ideals, even after suffering discrimination in the military.

BLACK REPUBLICANISM DEFINED

The ideology of mainstream republicanism appears more than capable of encompassing these three themes associated with black veterans' attitudes and behavior. Republicanism, for instance, calls upon citizens to criticize the state lest corruption take root. Citizens of the republic are also required

---

principle and practice, as well as critics who believe otherwise (Carby 1998; Lewis 2000). King, according to Ransby (2003), believed that women were best suited for supporting roles in the movement.

to participate in public life to ensure the maintenance of the common good; political activism is the lifeblood of the republic. Finally, republican citizens are required to love the values and institutions on which the republic rests, as patriotism ensures the fidelity of citizens to the nation.

If, however, one takes seriously the purpose for which republican theory was developed—to describe a means of self-governance that can ensure citizens' freedom and equality—it is apparent that conventional definitions of the ideology cannot apply to black Southerners. It is only in the last forty years that African Americans have been able to participate in self-governance in the absence of domination. Ratification of the Civil Rights Act in 1964 and the Voting Rights Act a year later outlawed public segregation, brought Southern educational institutions into compliance with the *Brown v. Board of Education of Topeka* decision, eased political participation, and promoted the political representation of black Southerners (Alt 1994; Handley and Grofman 1994; Kousser 2000; Lawson 1976; Matthews and Prothro 1966; Orfield 2000). Thus, any conception of black citizens' republicanism must acknowledge the domination to which black Southerners reluctantly became accustomed.

It is helpful, therefore, to define black veterans' republicanism as a separate type, which I will call *black republicanism*, and to elucidate some of the contradictions and elisions that separate it from the more conventional version of republicanism. As the following chapters illustrate, some of these contradictions and elisions open the door to new and interesting ways of interpreting the attitudes and behavior of black veterans.

Distinguishing Black Republicanism from Conventional Republicanism

Black republicanism, as I conceive it, is a response to the domination that was imposed on black Southerners during the Jim Crow era (Morris 1984). By any standard, Jim Crow crippled black Southerners' ability to exercise freedom of choice, violating a chief tenet of liberalism: noninterference. Indeed, the government and its agents, at the state and local levels, actively interfered with black Southerners' ability to vote and to live where they wished, and hampered their access to equal education. But liberalism's principle of noninterference fails to fully capture the invidiousness of Jim Crow and white supremacy because, in the absence of active interference, according to liberalism, there can be no domination. This leaves us without the ability to account for the threats against black Southerners that are associated with white supremacy, something that can be accomplished without actual interference.

If liberalism cannot fully account for the totality of domination, republicanism can pick up the remaining slack. Unlike the former, the latter does not require *active* interference on the part of the state to affect one's freedom or even freedom of choice. What makes even the late Jim Crow period—the time immediately preceding the civil rights legislation of the mid-1960s—one of domination is the *possibility of interference from* white authorities. For republicans, according to Phillip Pettit, "the dominating party can interfere on an arbitrary basis with the choices of the dominated . . . in particular on the basis of an interest or opinion that need not be shared with the person affected. The dominated party can practice interference . . . at will and with impunity: they do not have to seek anyone's leave and they do not have to incur scrutiny or penalty" (1997, 22). Under these conditions, the possibility remains that the master will fail to interfere with the slave's choices. The slave may even have a "benevolent" master; but the fact that he *may* interfere is sufficient to make one susceptible to domination (Skinner 1998).[14] Thus, in the late 1950s and early '60s blacks, in some parts of the South, weren't deterred from voting through manifest acts of violence; they needn't bear witness to it. By the 1950s, after decades of violence visited upon members of the community who sought to vote, they were deterred by the mere *possibility* of violence (Matthews and Prothro 1963).[15]

Even as domination robbed black Southerners of freedom it promoted a sense of solidarity and attachment to the black community. Economic exploitation and discrimination in their various forms—the shared experience of tenant farming under Jim Crow rules, the institutional discrimination that followed black Southerners to the cities in the South and North—fused together the black community (Broman, Neighbors, and Jackson 1988; Demo and Hughes 1989). Physical domination and vulnerability to indiscriminant violence also bred a sense of solidarity (Demo and Hughes 1990; Litwack 1998). The development of black institutions within which black Southerners socialized and worshipped also fostered a sense of community. They allowed blacks a forum within which to deal with issues relating to domination. Churches, fraternal groups, and women's clubs reinforced and nurtured racial solidarity (Allen, Dawson, and Brown 1989; Dawson 1994; Harris 1999; Skocpol, Liazos, and Ganz 2006).

[14] Recent scholarship in political theory by Markell (2008) and Rogers (2008), however, interrogates the explanatory power of domination.

[15] Matthews and Prothro indicate that more often than not the targets of violence were institutions, such as churches, schools, and temples. In terms of personal violence, twenty-nine people were shot—including white sympathizers. Areas in which "old-style" racial violence (i.e., lynchings) occurred between 1900 and 1931 accounted for only 7 percent of the "new-style" racial violence. They conclude, however, that the absence of violence did not indicate the disappearance of the threat. On the contrary, it was indicative of white strength.

One of the areas in which black republicanism and the more conventional version of republicanism part company, then, is in the notion of allegiance. Conventional republicanism in the United States presumes the presence of a singular political community, one in which whiteness was the standard (Smith 1988). African Americans were excluded. The solidification of white domination in the late nineteenth and early twentieth centuries drove blacks to develop a separate, parallel society to which they felt a particular allegiance. Blacks were nevertheless committed to the political values on which the national community rested, if not to their white conationals. In short, they were drawn at once to national political values and to the black political community (Myrdal 1944;).

Domination and its consequences also interfered with the ability of blacks to participate in self-governance, the key to the maintenance of a free and equal republic. Effective participation in self-governance, according to republican ideology, requires individuals to have equal access to the political process (political equality) and the deliberative process, as well as the ability to discipline representatives through the use of the ballot (Sunstein 1988). But these mechanisms are only meaningful for full members of the political community. Black Southerners were not granted equal access to the political process, nor were they permitted to participate in meaningful deliberation beyond their indigenous institutions. They were also barred from choosing representatives, much less disciplining them. Equally devastating was the fact that domination prevented black Southerners from fully developing their democratic capacities. This is not to say that blacks did not have the opportunity to do so at all, for as Hahn (2003) illustrates, slaves formed deliberative bodies for the purpose of adjudicating disputes among themselves and meting out punishment for slaves in violation of community norms.[16] But this is not the same as taking part in the collective decision making of a diverse polity in which one is forced one to consider one's needs in light of the needs of others, and how both relate to social institutions. Participation in self-

---

[16] After the Civil War, former slaves acquitted themselves well in democratic politics. It is well known that black representation exploded during Reconstruction. Less well known is the extent to which freedmen participated in the deliberative process, with whites, in the Union League, the political arm of the radical Republicans. There they discussed and debated pressing issues such as the national debt, the proposed impeachment of President Johnson, and supporting one or another candidate for office. Members also discussed local issues such as school and church construction as well as drafting petitions decrying the continued exclusion of blacks from juries (Foner 1988; Franklin 1961). Black delegates' contribution to the deliberative process in both Louisiana's and South Carolina's constitutional conventions resulted in equal education in some parts of the South (Franklin 1961, chap. 7). Finally, in South Carolina's state house, black representatives eventually maneuvered to wrest power from their white counterparts (Holt 1977).

governance, in the context of diversity, also forces one to develop the ability to convey one's ideas and sentiments to others, a requirement of a healthy democracy (Young 1990).

The experience of domination, moreover, affected how black Southerners perceived the balance between rights and duties. Were it not for a combination of amendments and acts spaced a century apart, black Americans would have remained outside the political community, unable to participate in self-governance. Black republicanism departs from the more mainstream version, consequently, in its conception of rights. Some may object to my characterization of African Americans as republicans on the grounds that black republicanism's preference for rights is not prioritized in republican discourse. This is true, but only insofar as liberals insist on identifying the origin of rights in some prepolitical, natural source. In the absence of laws and customs to sustain them, rights are nothing more than moral claims. In this way, as Marizio Viroli (2002) argues, rights are historical rather than natural and inalienable. A more pragmatic view of republicanism understands it to include rights as long as they contribute to the democratic process. "What is distinctive about the republican view," Cass Sunstein writes, "is that it understands most rights as either preconditions or the outcome of an undistorted deliberative process . . . [including] the right to vote" (1998, 1551). Black republicanism's emphasis on the importance of rights is, in this sense, in keeping with the republican tradition. Few would disagree that the right to vote and equal access to the political system—both of which were secured by the Voting Rights Act—contributed to the democratization of the South.

Domination also affects how individuals view corruption. Republicans define corruption as anything that poses a threat to liberty and equality. Mainstream republicans saw corruption in the formation of factions, in the use of patronage, and in the machinations of interest groups, among other places (Pocock 1975). Black Southerners, by contrast, should have located corruption in the white domination that impeded liberty and equality in the South.

A final contrast between mainstream and black republicanism lies in their conceptions of the relationship between military service and liberty. Conventional republicanism calls for the military to defend liberty from external threats of domination, which, in the most extreme case, could ultimately result in slavery. To black Southerners, military service presented an opportunity for emancipation, a means of securing liberty from an internal enemy that robbed them of their liberty and dominated them in increasingly creative ways. Even when society failed to reward black Southerners for their service, black veterans drew on their military experience to contribute to social reform in the South.

Identifying Black Republicanism: Sources of Criticism and Activism

Now that we are familiar with some of the contradictions between black veterans' hypothesized belief system and republicanism as it is conventionally understood, we may sketch the analytical framework of black republicanism. As long as it is modified to account for the effects of domination, as it was experienced by black Southerners, republican ideology can explain the prevailing attitudes and behavior of black veterans. (While it is certainly possible that black republicanism as an ideology extends beyond black veterans, I believe they are its most faithful adherents, because they were forced to sacrifice the most on behalf of the black community.) Like mainstream republicanism, black republicanism calls upon individuals to criticize the state and its agents, be active in civic life, and embrace the values and institutions of the republic. As later chapters will show, however, black veterans' criticism, activism, and attachment to the nation were all stimulated by their respective military experiences.

Black veterans, I believe, were motivated by their military experiences and the meaning they attached to them. These experiences produced a relatively organic (as opposed to instrumental) connection between black veterans and the nation of the sort described by Snyder (1999). Since black veterans had been willing to perform the most demanding duty required by the state under less-than-ideal circumstances, they developed an emotional bond to their military service and what it meant to them. Black republicans' criticism of white domination turns on this connection to the nation and its values. More concretely, the paradox inherent to fighting for democracy within a military establishment in which one remained a second-class citizen highlighted the division between the professed American creed and white domination.

This experience activated something akin to what sociologist Morris Janowitz has called "civic consciousness." Civic consciousness, he argues, "refers to positive and meaningful attachment a person develops to the nation state," an attachment that involves "elements of reason . . . [and] personal commitment" (1983, x–xi). The military promotes in soldiers an attachment to America and a commitment to its principles. This understanding of the effect of military service on soldiers' political ideology is commensurate with an interpretation of a symbolic orientation in which strong positive affect coupled with a well-defined meaning results in an ideological symbolic attachment (Elder and Cobb 1983). Among other things, this type of symbolic attachment tends toward stability, promoting the meanings associated with the symbol. In time, individuals holding this symbolic attachment "may initiate actions in the name of the symbol or use it to challenge the actions of others" (Elder and Cobb 1983, 59). As we shall see, an attachment of this sort characterizes the meaning of military service embedded in black republicanism.

Through military service, black veterans came to identify more strongly than they had initially with the nation's values and institutions, if not with white conationals. Their commitment to national values, also known as patriotism, went beyond the reactionary, jingoistic disposition with which patriotism is sometimes confused (Adorno et al. 1950). True (or genuine) patriotism, they suggest, defines one's commitment to and critical understanding of a set of political principles and ideals, not simple conformity.[17] Political philosopher Viroli agrees, adding that patriotism is "critical inasmuch as it is dedicated to making sure that one's polity lives up to its highest traditions and ideals" (2002, 14).

In the American historical context, patriots were critical of the corruption, tyranny, and oppression associated with English rule. Theirs was a patriotism based upon criticism and dissent. Liberty and equality, therefore, are among the cornerstones of *American* patriotism (Dietz 2002). American political philosophers, like their European counterparts, recognize the need for a critical definition of patriotism. Walter Berns, for instance, believes it to be a mistake to assume that citizens understand what is required of patriots. He explains, "Devotion to a principle requires an understanding of its terms, and, especially in the case of an abstract philosophical principle, that understanding cannot be taken for granted. Most people can enjoy liberty, but not everyone understands its foundation in principle" (Berns 2001, 83).

Of course, the ideology to which one subscribes informs how one interprets certain principles. Consider the Jim Crow South. The "separate but equal doctrine" was a white supremacist interpretation of equality, but, as the Supreme Court's ruling in *Brown* suggested—and supporting the NAACP's interpretation of equality—separate was *inherently* unequal. Moreover, to the extent that American patriotism requires citizens to oppose domination and oppression (Viroli 1995), the court's decision was in keeping with the American patriotic tradition. Black veterans' patriotism, which took African American history into account, harmonized well with the patriotism described by Theodor Adorno, Walter Berns, Mary Dietz, Alasdair MacIntyre, and Maurizio Viroli. Indeed, in the service of social and political reform, patriotic appeals to the universal application of democratic ideals are capable of animating "different forms of emancipatory collective action" (Viroli 1995, 16).

---

[17] Genuine patriotism is in opposition to pseudopatriotism, which, according to Adorno et al. (1950), is consonant with blind, uncritical attachment to national values and folkways.

Frederick Douglass's interrogation of the Declaration of Independence during his famous address at Corinthian Hall provides an excellent example of the sort of critical patriotism to which I refer:"Pardon me, and allow me to ask, why I am called to speak here today? What have I or those I represent to do with your national independence? Are the great principles of political freedom and justice, embodied in the Declaration of Independence, extended to us? . . . The rich inheritance of justice, liberty, prosperity, and independence . . . is shared by you, not me. . . . This Fourth of July is yours, not mine. You may rejoice, I must mourn" (Douglass 1852, n.p.). This address, in which Douglass went on to call the Fourth of July celebration a "sham" and American liberty and equality a "hollow mockery" in the context of slavery, was delivered in 1852. Criticism like Douglass's is republican in the sense that the pursuit of the common good requires citizens to criticize the state and its agents (Sunstein 1988; Williams 1991). The maintenance of white supremacy impeded the spread of democracy throughout the South. In this context, white domination was the corruption that black Southerners battled. The commitment to American national ideals, represented by military service, was the bedrock upon which veterans rested their criticism of the racial status quo.

Republicans, moreover, are duty-bound to remain actively engaged in the maintenance of liberty. In republican thought, political activism ensures the pursuit of the common good, acting as a bulwark against corruption. In a republic, citizens are obliged to participate in the political process, serve on juries, and serve in the military, among other things. Such obligations, as we have seen, imply correlative rights, such as the right to hold public office, the right to a fair trial, and the right to the protection of the state (Kerber 1997). Black Americans' commitment to political activism was aimed at their *achievement* of the basic rights that whites were simply attempting to maintain.

Black republicanism is not without its flaws, perhaps the most important of which is the position it takes toward women. In this regard, it is similar to mainstream republicanism, in which women are effectively excluded from citizenship (Elshtain 1987; Kerber 1998). There are two reasons for this exclusion. First, military service—which in the mid-nineteenth century was virtually completely restricted to men—was institutionally connected to citizenship. Second, the military constructed and reinforced the importance of *manhood* through ritual.[18] Consequently, the institutional and experiential exclusion of women suggests that black

---

[18] We must also consider the black men who, for various reasons, failed to serve. For the most part, they were most often deemed unfit for military service due to educational deficiencies.

republicanism is a gender-specific ideology. I remain mindful of this fact.[19]

• • •

In this chapter I have proposed a framework for understanding black soldiers' and veterans' resistance to white domination as a product of an ideology—black republicanism—that these men developed as an outcome of their military service. Since the Civil War, some black veterans have sought to assert their perceived right to equal treatment and respect, a perception ultimately fueled by the American politicocultural belief in the importance of the citizen-soldier to the health of the polity. Veterans were transformed by their military service on a number of levels. First, service had normative symbolic effects: fighting for democracy and wearing the uniform symbolized black veterans' political equality and suggested the potential for African Americans' eventual liberation from domination.

Military experience, I argue, also had institutional symbolic effects, reinforcing soldiers' manhood, teaching them discipline and self-reliance, and giving them greater confidence. Among African Americans, especially black Southerners, exposure to military education and occupational skills furnished a new perspective on the world and their own capabilities. The military also allowed black GIs the chance to travel, which exposed them to alternative models of race relations and more tolerant cultures. The sum of these experiences encouraged black veterans to adopt a worldview commensurate with their military service. This worldview of black republicanism accounts for the criticism and activism of many black veterans in the civil rights era. Of course, other ideologies available to black citizens also encouraged criticism and activism, radical egalitarianism among them. Military experience, and the sacrifice entailed by it, however, separates black republicans from radical egalitarians.

It would be either a gross overstatement on the influence of black republicanism or the height of naïveté to suggest that all black veterans subscribed to black republicanism, using republican rhetoric to justify their actions. Like any social group, some members of the group would gravitate to alternative ways of perceiving and reacting to social and political life. Nevertheless, I contend that many black veterans drew on republican rhetoric to frame their discontent in the postwar South. Such discontent and the courage to act on it, at least among black veterans, was underwritten by their military experience, a subject to which I will turn in chapter 3.

---

[19] For a critique of republicanism, see Herzog (1986). For another critique of republicanism by way of comparison with liberalism, see Patten (1996).

Taking the Crooked with the Straight

THE PROS AND CONS OF AFRICAN AMERICAN MILITARY
EXPERIENCE DURING THE 1940s AND '50s

> For once let the black man get upon his person the brass letters,
> U.S., let him get an eagle on his button, and a musket on his
> shoulder and bullets in his pocket; and there is no power on
> earth which can deny that he has earned the right
> to citizenship in the United States.
> —Douglass, 1863, quoted in Benjamin Quarles,
> *Frederick Douglass*

In chapter 2, I defined black republicanism and suggested how it drew on the symbolic meaning of military service. In this chapter I will take the first empirical step toward confirming the influence of black republican ideology among black veterans of World War II and the Korean War by investigating the military experiences of a group of black veterans. The epigraph, one of Douglass's many trenchant observations, captures the essence of black republicanism. The overarching idea begins with the uniform and the suggestion that donning it should transform one into a member of the national political community. It's a public declaration that these black soldiers are committed to the defense of American ideals. More important, however, the uniform carries with it the expectation that these soldiers are to be recognized by the political community as American citizens. Of course, the uniform's principal accessory, the weapon, also symbolizes citizenship; so says the Second Amendment and Supreme Court Chief Justice Roger B. Taney's reliance upon it to deny Dred Scott's petition for citizenship. However, Douglass's prose suggests another use for the weapon: it is also a potential tool for securing, by force if necessary, the freedom and equality for which black veterans fought.

This chapter and chapter 4 will apply this portrait of black veterans of the Civil War to their mid-twentieth-century successors. The confidence and righteousness of purpose that Douglass illustrates finds its ideological expression in black republicanism. Like other ideologies, black republicanism is rooted in shared experience. In this case, that experience is constituted by the sacrifice associated with military life that promised to provide service members with relatively unique group experiences. Beginning with basic training, individuals who join the military are encouraged to leave their old selves behind and to think in terms of the unit. In the context of a total institution (Goffman 1974), they are taught to practice martial virtues of discipline and courage, pushing themselves to accomplish new and difficult tasks. Service during time of war, especially for those who participate in combat, is even more intense.

When we consider the effects of black veterans' race on their experiences, as I touched on in chapter 2, we must expand these parameters. As the literature makes clear, black servicemen made sacrifices beyond those required of whites. Initially they were forced to endure discrimination as a matter of policy; later it lingered as a matter of custom. Much of the scholarship on the military experience of African Americans correctly concentrates upon the consequences of the mistreatment of black servicemen and the ensuing racial conflict. More specifically, it documents how discrimination and segregation affected the morale of black troops, making some reluctant to do battle with the foreign enemy. This body of work also highlights black troops' willingness to contest domination in the military and suggests that their aversion to fighting had more to do with their mistreatment in the military and in society than it did to any innate fear of dying (Barbeau and Henri 1974; Binkin 1993; Dalfiume 1969; Fletcher 1974; Foner 1974; Kryder 2000; McGuire 1983; Nalty 1986; Stouffer et al. 1949).

This chapter takes a more comprehensive approach to the military experience of black veterans of World War II and the Korean War, examining both the good and the bad experiences associated with their military service. The chapter's title, "Taking the Crooked with the Straight," is drawn from a line in August Wilson's play *Fences* (1985) that suggests that in life one must take the bad with the good. The black veterans I interviewed seem to have done just that. To be sure, they have memories associated with segregation and discrimination, which are bitter to this day; but encountering different cultures, contributing to the nation's defense, and developing more confidence helped black soldiers to develop a unique perspective on racial domination. Even a symbol as seemingly minor as wearing the uniform helped to reshape how veterans viewed themselves: it symbolized personal and racial pride as well as confidence.

As this chapter illustrates, their military experience was on balance a positive one for many black veterans and something on which many of them continue to draw as a source of motivation and inspiration. More important, understanding the positive and negative aspects of black veterans' military experience and how they departed from the Southern norm lays the foundation for understanding the behavior of black veterans as a social group. Resisting the discrimination to which they were exposed in the military made black servicemen more willing to oppose it once they departed the military and returned to the South. As we shall see in a subsequent chapter, this willingness depended in no small part upon the increased self-confidence, racial awareness, and courage that came from bearing arms and fighting to defend the nation.

A Description of the Data

For the investigation in this chapter and chapter 4, I draw on seventeen of the twenty-five interviews I completed with veterans who were born in the South and continue to live there. Each served in either World War II or the Korean War; some interviewees served in both. Of the seventeen subjects, six were officers; the rest were enlisted men; twelve were combat veterans. A total of nine were drafted; eight volunteered. Volunteers generally either joined for socioeconomic reasons—that is, they served to escape crushing poverty in the South—or they sought to have more control over the branch of the military in which they would serve. Either way, under these circumstances, one may argue that these men didn't really volunteer, especially if doing so implies joining the military out of a sense of patriotism. Signing up to join the military in order avoid undesirable assignments, or to escape poverty, some argue, amounts to conscription (Leal 1999).

The interviews varied in duration from 35 to 150 minutes. To account for interregional variation between the Deep South and the Border South, I conducted interviews in Houston, Texas, during the summer of 2003 and in New Orleans, Louisiana, during the winter of 2004. While the interviews were conducted in metropolitan areas, many of the veterans came from the small towns and rural areas of the South. (See appendix C for details.)

By virtue of surviving (in some cases thriving) in a Jim Crow military establishment, especially during wartime, these are exceptional individuals. Yet, as individuals, there are stark differences among them. The men varied in age from sixty-nine to ninety years of age at the time of the interview. The educational achievement among them ranged from high school dropout to doctoral degree holder. Among them were a retired university president, a retired professor, and a retired principal; the group also included a retired firefighter and a retired state police officer. There was also a handful who made a career of the military, serving twenty years or more. The working class is also represented, with a painter, a photographer, and a cook among the interviewees. Both for the sake of brevity and privacy, I use only the veterans' last names to identify them.

The central purposes of this book are to (1) demonstrate that military service contributed to insurgency among black Southern veterans, and (2) to explain *why* this was the case. To the extent that interviews reveal processes, they are ideal for the second purpose, more so than survey research, which is better suited to the first task. In survey-based research, "the researcher infers the links between the variables," whereas "in intensive interviewing, the researcher induces the respondent to create links between the variables" (Hochschild 1981, 24). Furthermore, interviews, unlike surveys, force the respondent to articulate meaning. In the absence of qualitative information of how culture informs agency, we only know what the coefficients (based on survey data) tell us. The interview assists us with placing the numbers in the broader social and cultural context, aiding with their interpretation (McCracken 1988). In short, these interviews highlight a path through which military experience leads to subscription to black republicanism, and how black republicanism in turn sparked resistance.

Every methodological approach has its disadvantages, and the in-depth interview is no exception. It lacks the *statistical* precision associated with survey-based evidence, and representative samples are difficult to secure. In the absence of a representative sample, and given the relatively small number of observations that are typical of in-depth interviews, it's difficult to claim that interview findings are generalizable to the population at large. Obviously, external validity is important. Having said that, theory demands that I first establish a mechanism by which military experience connects with insurgency—something that, I contend, is ultimately explained by black republicanism. Upon establishing these relationships, such as why military service tended to spur resistance on the part of black Southerners, I attend to the issue of external validity. Ultimately I will turn to survey-based evidence in chapters 5 and 6 as a means of testing propositions based upon the claims I make in which military experience spurred challenges to white supremacy.

In this particular study, moreover, I had to contend with the passage of time. In some cases, I asked veterans to recall episodes that occurred sixty years earlier. Critics may, therefore, credibly charge that the passing years may have distorted the memory of the veterans I interviewed. While I cannot dismiss this possibility, it is also true that life-altering events in the lives of individuals tend to be recalled with a good deal of precision (Reisberg and Heuer 1992; Schuman and Scott 1989; Tourangeau, Rips, and Rasinski 2000). Moreover, the use of closed questions, ones that form the basis of survey-based research, isn't the best way to capture responses beyond the discrete, easily accessed answers on which quantitative research depends (McCracken 1988). For this reason,

I submit that requesting respondents to recall the meaning of their military service, in the context of white supremacy—in some cases sixty years ago—lies beyond the reach of quantitative research. In this case, an approach more conducive to recalling as well as interpreting the meaning of events—especially those that are important life events—is warranted (Lee 2002, chap. 5; McCracken 1988; Schuman 2008). Hence, we must use something other than closed-ended responses when questions require the respondent to go beyond the typical, on-the-spot, top-of-the-head assessment on which most survey research is based (Zaller 1992). In sum, since I rely on this set of interviews as an initial but not a definitive test of the validity of my argument about black republicanism, and since I am more interested in what military experience *meant* to veterans in the context of the postwar South than in precisely what it contained, concerns about the distortions of memory or inability to generalize beyond the following interviews do not diminish the validity of my conclusions.

The Crooked: Negative Aspects of Black Veterans' Military Experiences

Perhaps the most frustrating part of the black military experience was the prejudice and discrimination to which black servicemen were subjected. Even as the military took them to places far beyond Dixie and put them in the same uniform as whites, black Southerners continued to be dogged by racial oppression. Whether it was segregation during the Second World War or racism in the ranks as American forces helped prosecute the Korean War, black servicemen were forced to engage in conflicts that had nothing to do with the battlefield. On many occasions they faced open hostility in the Southern towns in which they were stationed stateside. They sometimes also faced it overseas, where white soldiers taught locals the finer points of Jim Crow. In this section, I identify the portion of blacks veterans' military experience that both alerted them to the stubbornness of white supremacy and created space for directly confronting it, both of which were critical to the formation of black republicanism. The interviews that follow represent the general sentiment of other veterans. The selections herein are simply the best articulations of each point, not the only ones.

Discrimination, Conflict, and Disaffection

In the mid-twentieth-century United States, almost all of the military bases were located in the South, and many in the officer corps were Southerners. Discrimination at these bases was rampant, and black soldiers were often the targets of verbal and physical abuse. Not even black officers were exempt. Dr. Bashful's experience is an example of black officers' experience and their reaction to mistreatment. Born in Louisiana, Bashful, now the retired chancellor of a historically black university, was drafted, serving in the army from 1942 to 1946. For two of those years he was an artillery officer in Italy attached to the all-black—and, as we've seen in chapter 1, much maligned—Ninety-Second Division. Before shipping over to the European theater, his unit prepared for deployment by going on various field exercises. On one occasion, while bivouacking in the states, his commanding officer, a white colonel, gathered the officers and instructed them on the upcoming exercise. Prior to dismissal, the colonel designated the areas in which the officers were allowed to relieve themselves: "This trench is for the white officers; this other trench is for the black officers," Bashful recalls the colonel saying in a rather matter-of-fact tone. When the meeting was over, he remembers with a mix of glee and pride that "almost every black officer there went to the white trench and urinated. That told them in a nice way to go to hell."

While he and some of his fellow black officers felt good about taking action to register their protest, Bashful ultimately became disillusioned with the ways in which black officers and soldiers were allowed to be mistreated: "I was very disappointed in some of the experiences which were allowed to take place while I was in the service . . . some of the riots that took place . . . some of the experiences which the [black] soldiers in uniform had happen to them." He places the blame not so much on army policy as on the federal government, which allowed black soldiers to be treated poorly and thereby enabled some of the racial incidents that such disrespect precipitated. "The fact that the government did not stop them, investigate them, issue reports . . . the fact that the government allowed these things to happen," he protests, "was very disappointing to me."

Perhaps because Bashful and his colleagues were officers, they dealt with mistreatment and their attendant disappointment in a relatively peaceful, genteel way. This, after all, is how officers are supposed to conduct themselves—as gentlemen. Enlisted men are not bound by the same code of conduct. Two Purple Heart awardees, both of whom were among the first to serve in as integrated units during the Korean War and were enlisted men, recall dealing with racism in the ranks more aggressively. The first, Mr. Thornton, was born in Giddings, Texas, and raised in Le Grange, Texas, where his father tended farm and worked in a chicken hatchery. His father went no farther in school than the fifth grade, while his mother completed the tenth grade. Thornton finished high school and, after leaving the military, attended some college. He was drafted in 1950, after which he spent a short stint at Fort Ord, California, shipping over to Korea in 1951. Thornton remembers that the treatment to which he was subjected by whites in his unit caused him to be "very bitter about white people." "Some of the things you read, some of things you heard . . . were messed up," he comments. "I didn't particularly enjoy some of the remarks that they [whites] would make." On occasion he confronted his tormentors, to no good result: "That got me in trouble, because I resented it, and I would let the white boys know I resented *them*," he says with a trace of anger.

A second veteran of the Korean conflict, Mr. Baines, has similar memories, though he recalls black soldiers taking action. Some white soldiers, it seems, enjoyed mocking blacks in his unit, questioning their intellectual capabilities among other things. Black soldiers, he chuckles, "were not too keen on being mocked by whites." Since they were in Korea and not the South, Baines recalls, they felt free to retaliate when they were accused of being dumb or their manhood was challenged. As a result, "there was a lot of fistfights going on with the white boys," he says. In the Twenty-Fifth Division in which Baines served "there was a fight every day." With some amusement, he recalls, "Every day some white boy was getting the mess beat out of him—*every day*." He laughs, "I mean, it got to be so bad, and the funny thing about it is that it wasn't even necessary. It would be because of a corny remark. But it was fun to see them [blacks] make some of them [whites] apologize, you know?"

Sometimes, though, the degradation to which black GIs were subjected was so stunning and complete it was difficult to digest, much less counter. Perhaps the most devastating blow to African American morale occurred stateside when German and Japanese prisoners of war (POWs)— the battlefield enemy—were accorded better treatment than black troops. Volunteering to serve upon finishing high school, and returning to the United States after serving in the Pacific theater during the Second World War, Mr. McWilliams, a seventy-six-year-old veteran of World War II and Korea who was raised in New Orleans, was assigned to a base in the South. There he discovered that "the Japanese soldiers and . . . the German soldiers had privileges that we [African American GIs] did not have." The German prisoners of war "had some privileges of war here—in *America*," McWilliams screamed in lingering disbelief. "They could go into the officer clubs—white officer clubs—and we could not go into them. We used to pay German and Japanese prisoners of war to go into the service club or PXs to get items for us. They could go to the social clubs and to the officer's club, these enlisted clubs, and we could not go!" McWilliams was upset as he recalled this, and for good reason: the *enemy* had received more respect than he and his fellow black soldiers had.

This type of mistreatment also extended to off-base ventures. Black military police officers routinely took German POWs out on work detail, during which they needed to be fed. The retired colonel recalls instances during World War II at a POW camp in New Orleans when "white officers, during lunchtime, would bring meal tickets to them [the POWs] and take the Germans to certain restaurants to eat." The black MPs were not allowed to enter these restaurants. "They had to stay outside or go to the back! Local whites was also inviting German—German *POWs*—to their home! But at the same time, they were still kicking blacks' butts down here!" As the colonel's comments suggest, instances of such unfair treatment were extremely insulting to black servicemen.

Discrimination and Third Parties

Serving overseas introduced third parties into an already volatile, if familiar, situation. Overseas, white servicemen often tried to convince locals to behave according to the tenets of white supremacy. Sometimes this strategy worked; sometimes it failed. Among black soldiers, the outcome mattered less than did their exposure to a racial dynamic to which they were not accustomed.

In general, exposing people to new patterns of social relations and cultural norms tends to expand their worldview by enlarging their perceptions of what is possible (Grasmick 1973; Inkeles 1969). In the context of the military, Glenn Elder and his colleagues have found that military service increases one's self-awareness by experiencing new places and interacting with new people (Elder, Gimble, and Ivie 1991). Employing this logic we should expect black Southerners who were exposed to different, more egalitarian cultures to have begun an aggressive interrogation of white supremacy.

In Europe during the Second World War, white troops attempted to upset the relatively amicable social relationships that had developed between some of the locals and black GIs. Mr. Baskin is one soldier who became annoyed with this interference. Born in 1919 in the city of Houston, Mississippi, he was familiar with the ways of Jim Crow. After volunteering for service in January 1941, he served in Scotland, England, France, and Germany during the war. After transferring from Scotland, Baskin reported to an airbase in England. "The English were very receptive to us for a while," he recalls, until "a lot of the white GIs came and kind of stirred things up and caused some problems." In France and Germany, by contrast, "there was no problem; the attitudes were so different from what it was in the South." Baskin felt more at ease in Europe than he did in the South. After suggesting that Europeans did not subscribe to group-based stereotypes, Baskin clarified, "They received you as a person, as an individual. There weren't any hang-ups about the color of your skin; they were much more receptive there than they were in the States at the time."

Serving overseas, in other words, was a refuge for Baskin, and it changed his attitudes toward race relations. He remembers, "There were periods of time when it [the racism on Southern bases] affected me very negatively, but after . . . I guess after I went overseas I began to see things differently. I began to realize that things weren't as bad as they sometimes seemed, because I came in contact with a lot of people who were very nice and very helpful. . . . Then later on, during the time I was in Europe, they began integration, and I was able to get different views and different feelings about the races."

Mr. Thomas had a similar experience during the Second World War. He was born in 1917 to a housewife and a railroad brakeman. Drafted in 1942, he entered the army air corps after two years of college, eventually earning a master's degree from Oxford University. The English, according to Thomas, treated him simply as a foreigner—not as a *black* GI. "When you are in a foreign country and you mingle and mix with foreign people," he says, "they treat you just like another foreigner." Serving overseas in a segregated air corps, he remembers saying to himself, "It's regrettable that I have to be three to four thousand miles away from home to experience what freedom really feels like." Europeans do not see color, according to Thomas; instead, "they just see another American in a uniform," adding, "But they become disillusioned when they are compelled to realize that all Americans don't think the same thing about Americans." The discrimination on the part of white GIs against black GIs confused some of the Europeans with whom Thomas came into contact. Britons in particular questioned why white GIs spoke so horribly about blacks. Were they not all Americans? The Britons in his social circle used to ask, "What's the matter? Why do they say these things about you? Why do they identify you as people with tails and all those kind of things?" It bothered him when his English buddies brought these remarks to his attention. These interrogations "raised serious questions in the mind" about white Americans. In his opinion, "Whites [soldiers] didn't feel bad about doing what that did to us."

Even so, for Thomas, the policy of segregation and the discrimination it bred were even more infuriating than the insensitivity of white servicemen. Thomas believed that the armed services could have served as a model for race relations in America. He felt that if blacks were going to serve, "at least it would mean that blacks and whites would be in the same organizations [and that] they'd have the same barracks in the same company, and all that sort of thing—doing the same things." Had that happened, Thomas believes, it "would have had a [positive] impact on the attitude of blacks returning to America." When the army insisted upon maintaining its policy of segregation, however, it all but guaranteed that black soldiers would remain embittered about it as they separated from the army. With a hint of lingering disappointment, Thomas flatly states that "when the practice of segregation is not only practiced, but reinforced in the services, [the black soldier] comes back with anything but a positive attitude."

Attempts to export the racial mores of the South were not confined to the European theater of operations; white GIs aimed to export Jim Crow to the Far East, too. Colonel McWilliams's experience in the Far East is a classic case. Reflecting on a stint in the Philippines in the latter stages of the Second World War, when he was an enlisted man, and on his time spent in Korea, where he was an officer, he recalls how white GIs made "it a Jim Crow society [over there]," explaining, "The American whites overseas tried to put the *'for white only'* sign up." Sometimes white supremacists convinced locals to adopt their belief in black inferiority. According to McWilliams, more than a few Koreans "catered to" Jim Crow—actions that he and other soldiers found hard to believe. For the most part, black GIs "were treated okay," he concedes, "but it [white supremacy] was so embedded . . . it was so indoctrinated that blacks were inferior to whites." "The whites," he protests, "preached this. And they [the locals] believed it! That's all they [the locals] could see, was white!"

Baskin's, Thomas's, and McWilliams's experiences with racism overseas showed them just how determined some white servicemen were to maintain the racial status quo, increasing the men's racial awareness. All of these encounters, however, happened in town or on post. Other, more disturbing incidents occurred in a different context, one in which the battlefield enemy made black soldiers aware of the unjust conditions under which they served. Perhaps the most painful and ironic way in which black GIs became more racially aware was through the eyes of the enemy. While serving overseas, some black GIs were propagandized directly by the enemy, who made them aware of their second-class status in the United States. Mr. Baines had such an experience during the Korean War.

Sometime after reporting for duty in Korea in August 1950, Baines's company captured a few North Korean soldiers. To his surprise, some of the prisoners spoke broken English. "Some of those Koreans," he remembers, "asked me some questions that really stung." While he was on guard duty, he says, he and a prisoner "got into a conversation." Baines recounts, "He asked me, 'Why are you over here fighting against us? We haven't done anything to you. You're not even free in your own country, man!'" Upon reflection, he says, "That hurt me, because it was true." With palpable sense of continuing outrage, Baines explains, "It had never dawned on me that that I'm over here fighting these people and I'm not even free in my own country."

•   •   •

Just as earlier studies have concluded (Dalfiume 1969; Foner 1974; McGuire 1983; Nalty 1986), my interviews demonstrate that black soldiers resented the mistreatment to which were subjected and that this resentment sometimes affected their morale. My findings also confirm historical accounts in which black servicemen actively resisted affronts to their dignity and manhood. Yet the men I interviewed discussed, in addition to these subjects, the range of strategies black troops used to deal with discrimination and mistreatment. From the more veiled efforts of the officers to the more brazen modes employed by enlisted troops, black servicemen often fought back.

These interviews also validate the scholarly consensus that the experiences associated with travel, such as contact with new cultures and people, promoted a more cosmopolitan, progressive outlook so that veterans who served overseas tended to return home more mature (Elder et al. 1991; Mettler 2005b). But the interviews also reveal that black veterans, like other black Southerners who became increasingly militant as they moved beyond their Southern roots (Marx 1967), were frequently radicalized by the military experience. The interviews suggest a mechanism through which service overseas stimulated a racial awareness that peeled away the veil of white supremacy that many black Southerners had reluctantly come to accept as a fact of life. Coming into contact with more tolerant cultures and observing the tenacity of white supremacy among some white troops pushed black GIs to question the legitimacy of Jim Crow more than they would have had they remained in the South.

I'm not suggesting that service overseas was necessary for the interrogation of Jim Crow. As I have shown in chapter 1, history is replete with examples of soldiers who bucked white supremacy, soldiers who never served a day outside of the United States. Nevertheless, when one compares the modicum of equality to which black troops were exposed overseas to the white supremacy with which all blacks had to deal, it became increasingly likely that black veterans would be radicalized. Indeed, the attempted transplantation of Jim Crow showed black servicemen that no matter what their contributions to the war effort, the inferiority associated with their race would always outweigh their sacrifices in the eyes of mainstream American society.

Serving overseas also lit the path to racial awareness in another way. By facilitating friendships with locals, through which black servicemen became increasingly aware of alternative patterns of race relations, the illegitimacy of white supremacy was laid bare. Again, this is not to suggest that all Europeans were opposed to a racial order in which whites were perceived as unambiguously superior, as some certainly were not (Carby 1999; Gilroy 1991; Small 1994; Winant 2001). For the most part, however, black servicemen had positive experiences with individuals associated with the dominant culture overseas. Perhaps it's also the case that equal treatment by Europeans caused them to imagine themselves part of the broader American political community. After all, many of the French and English, among others, had accepted them, had they not? Based on this, it wasn't unreasonable to think it possible that American whites would also accept them on their return. Consequently, as we shall see in chapter 4, they had a hard time returning to the racial status quo in the South upon separating from the military.

The Straight: Positive Aspects of Black Veterans' Military Experiences

Generally, military service represents a turning point in the lives of veterans insofar as travel and overcoming the challenges associated with military life contribute to veterans' self-assurance (Elder, Gimble, and Ivie 1986). Moreover, military service expanded many black servicemen's educational and occupational opportunities, from which they subsequently benefited (Mettler 2005a, 2005b; cf. Katznelson 2005). Indeed, by any objective criteria, black veterans were better off for their military service during the Second World War and the Korean War. On average, their educational and occupational achievements were superior to those of black nonveterans (Cohen, Warner, and Segal 1995; Kasarda 1976; Little and Friedland 1979; Lopreato and Poston 1977; Moskos and Butler 1996; Phillips and Gilroy 1992).

Beyond these objective measures, however, we know very little about how black veterans of World War II and Korea view their service. Did military service increase the self-confidence of black veterans, or did the disrespect that they endured in uniform and upon their return to the South dampen any positive feelings they may have otherwise had about their achievements? If military service is indeed foundational to black republicanism, as I claim, we should expect veterans to take pride in their service and to have gained confidence from their military experiences. In addition, if their positive associations with the military contributed to the formation of republican attitudes, we should also expect at least some of the veterans to emphasize the importance of sacrificing for the good of the black community. In short, black veterans should express their positive feelings about their military experience in the language of republicanism.

Because I examine veterans who served during the Second World War *and* the Korean War, I must entertain the possibility that black veterans' military experience may have been affected by the period in which they served. This is relevant because there was a change in the manpower policy between the wars, one that went from an official policy of segregation during World War II to one of integration—albeit limited—during the Korean War. It is possible that veterans of the latter war had a better overall experience than World War II veterans because they were allowed to fight and serve on a more equal basis. On the other hand, World War II was considered a "good war" (Gerstle 2001), one that continues to capture the American imagination. Though costly in terms of blood and treasure, the Korean War has not attained the same level of social and political significance (Ducksworth 1994). Veterans of the Second World War may consequently perceive their military experience in a more positive light than their counterparts who served during the Korean War.

As it turns out, the veterans with whom I spoke, from both eras, take great pride in their military accomplishments. Several indicated, moreover, that military service furnished them with a sense of achievement and confidence they had never felt before serving. While others were not happy that they were drafted and therefore viewed military service as a duty or burden, even these veterans were ultimately glad they complied with the law.

Mr. Thomas, a World War II army air corps veteran, is a case in point. For him, the military was an important turning point. Beaming with lingering satisfaction, Thomas says that military service "was the cornerstone of my life." Thomas views military service as both a duty and a privilege: "By virtue of your citizenship, it was a duty to serve, and in the service, you could be happy with it or unhappy with it." But he balances duty and obligations against the "privileges and opportunities that you wouldn't get otherwise," concluding, "A lot depended on what your attitude was." Thomas chose to make the best of the situation, matriculating at Oxford University after the war. "The air force made it possible for me to attend the world's most famous—or one of the world's most famous—universities," he says. "Had I not been in the air force, I don't think that that would've happened. So, I can be very grateful to the air force for the opportunity."

Another veteran of World War II, Mr. Grant, uses the language of republicanism to express similar gratitude for the lessons he learned in the military. Born in 1918, he served in the Ninth Calvary, one of the four black regiments created in 1866 by order of Congress. Drafted in 1942, Grant saw extensive duty in North Africa and southern France, landing a month after D-Day. Of the 227 men with whom he departed the United States in 1943, only 27 returned. His feelings about serving are a bit mixed. He surrendered himself to military service for the good of the country. Sighing, he adds, "There was no need of registering any animosity . . . you tried to make the best of it . . . you had to go. There was no value in going along with a chip on your shoulder . . . because your life depended on your ability as well as the next guy. So you were part of the puzzle and you adhered accordingly." Despite his initial reluctance to serve, Grant takes pride in having done so, admitting, "I'm proud, I'll start right off on that. It was something that had to be done and I made the most of it." As for what the service did for him, he comments, "I had confidence, but it [military service] kept it boosted." Military service was "a duty to society," and he is glad to have done it, regardless of how he felt about being called up at the time. He explains, "I don't regret the fact that I went into the service . . . as a result of going into the service it was very beneficial when we came out. They had the GI Bill of Rights so you could go to school—job openings and things of that sort."

For others, military service represented a means of seeing the world and gaining access to opportunity. Mr. Moret, a seventy-nine-year-old native of Louisiana, is one example. As one of the celebrated Tuskegee Airmen, he volunteered to join the army as a means of realizing a lifelong dream of flying. He departed New Orleans in 1943 for flight training in Alabama. Moret has fond memories and takes pride in what he did. "I'm proud to have done what I did," he says, "and evidently, masses of people think the same way, because I am so often called on to give talks about my experiences, and not just to blacks, but more often by whites." Thus, military service was "certainly not a burden" for him. Though Moret "was fulfilling an obligation at the time," flying was also "something that [I had] wanted to do since [I] was a little boy." He also mentions how the military exposed him to people with different backgrounds, something that probably would not have happened had he not served. As the Tuskegee airman tells it, "[the service] put me in with other guys from all over the country" and "gave me an opportunity to hear stories of life from other parts of the country."

Like Thomas and Grant, Moret also conceives of his military service in terms of sacrifice and the common good, the essence of republicanism. "In the period that I came up in, the nation was at war," he says, "[and] everybody should have served, you understand?" For him it mattered not whether one was drafted or one volunteered because "the need was there at the time." Moret sees the need for the draft's return today because he feels that contemporary Americans are selfish. In his estimation, more universal military service has the potential to bring the country closer together, because "the conditions in the military [make] one consider other people." With equal parts urgency and irritability, Moret cautions, "We can't be on our own and don't worry about the other guy, you understand?" To illustrate his point, he describes his first rendezvous training mission at Tuskegee, flying an AT-6 in the fall of 1944:

> I was to be at a certain point at a certain time to meet up with certain other airplanes. I had flown a three-legged triangle before getting to this point, so my navigation skills were being tested. It was kind of misty that particular day, hazy, and when I got up to my point, there were the other planes that I was to meet up with. I said, "These guys are the ones I'm going to depend on to go and fight. They are determined to be as skillful and accurate as I'm trying to be"; and this is a good feeling. This is a protection, like a backup that you have standing right beside you, you know, and that's what the military was a molding factor at.

In this regard Moret believes that military service taught him the value of teamwork: "Yeah, the military definitely molded me . . . the military gave me a sense that everything I did was a team effort."

When interviewing veterans, I also asked them whether they saw their military service as a privilege or a duty—as something they gladly performed or something into which they had to be coerced. According to Mr. Baskin, a veteran of World War II, military service was a privilege, not a duty. He wanted to reenlist. Upon the birth of his son back in the United States, however, his wife "enticed [him] to get out and come back home." Baskin remained long enough for the service to change the way he viewed himself. "I have a much higher opinion of myself and my lifestyle," he says, "than I did prior to [serving]." As a result of his stint in the military, Baskin feels more confident and self-assured. He also takes great pride in his having served because it enabled him to assist other soldiers and rise through the ranks. "I felt that I accomplished something, and I felt that I helped a lot of people when I was in the service. . . . I felt that I was in a good position to do some things and in many cases I did. . . . I was able to get promoted and I rose through the ranks fairly rapidly, and so I felt very fortunate," he says with obvious satisfaction.

A similar theme emerges from Mr. Pete's perspective. A Korean War veteran who hails from Nacodoches, Texas, Pete is the son of a sharecropper and housewife who volunteered to join the military to take advantage of the educational opportunities offered in the service. He reported to the Korean Peninsula just prior to the commencement of hostilities in 1950 and was attached to the all-black Twenty-Fourth Infantry Regiment. Overall, Pete describes his service as a privilege: "I'm glad I went in for the experience, adventures, and that's some experience that you get. You don't get it out here. I enjoyed that portion of it." For him, the principal drawback of serving in the military was that one's tour of duty interrupts one's life. "I was kind of slowed down a little bit when I got out. I mean, I was behind because when I went to college I had to go there and start with younger students, and that really had a burden on me and had an effect." Since he was so much older than the other students, he found returning to school difficult. Pete considered quitting but ultimately decided against it. "It was a struggle," he says, "but I'm glad I got through it."

Pete credits his military experience with allowing him to get through the rough patch he faced upon separating from the military. It gave him the courage and confidence to get on with his life: "I mean, number one, I was more matured. See when I went in I was green and crazed, and I didn't know anything. Never had been away from home and I was just glad, you know, to go in and get that experience. I had a chance to grow up. . . . I had a chance to travel and get some experience." Compared to other things he did prior to enlisting, the military served as an invaluable growth opportunity: "I mean, it helped me go to through life better out here and to pursue better things out here in civilian life." In sum, Pete says, "It gave me more confidence. It made a man out of me."

Others share the view that the military boosted their confidence, helping them to overcome a rough start in life. Mr. Baines's story represents this perspective. Born in 1928 in Wharton, Texas, Baines lost his father early in his life. His mother, who had a fifth-grade education, was left to fend for seven children. Life was "very, very tough" for his family, he recalls, "We had very little money." Coming from such a tough upbringing, the military allowed him to feel good about himself. Indeed, Baines views his performance in the military as a source of confidence; it was a chance for him to prove himself. With great pride, he says that his military experience "made me feel that the jobs that I accomplished in the military . . . the training that I received and the awards that I received . . . proved that I'm the equal to any other man." In a rather wistful tone, he goes on to catalog what else he gained from his experience in the military. For instance, the military also taught him discipline and broadened his horizons: "It gave me some stick-to-it-ness; it taught me about things that I would never have seen before, had I not gone into the military. The travel that I saw, the people that I met . . . it has changed my life. It made me a better person." While Baines saw military service as a duty citizens must perform, he was glad to do so. "This country's been good to me and my family," he says, "despite all of this prejudice and discrimination. I think it's the greatest country in the world."

Baines's positive view of the military is augmented by what serving did for him personally and professionally. During his initial run at college, he dropped out. "I just wasn't ready for college," he says. "Then I went into the United States Army. That was the smartest move I ever made was to go into the United States Army, because then I had the chance to travel. I didn't realize I would end up in a war, though." Nonetheless, as he sees it, "the military was a turning point, because after I came back from the war, I had the chance to go back to college and get my education and [buy] my home and so forth, and do both my bachelor's and master's degree on the GI Bill, otherwise I probably wouldn't have had the money to do it. That was a significant turning point in my life."

Many of the men I interviewed, then, viewed their time in the military in a positive light; it was challenging but worth it. The military helped build a foundation for success in their postservice lives. I failed to encounter a consensus on this point, however. Some of the veterans I spoke to had reservations about the sacrifices they made, including the lifelong injuries they sustained in the service. Mr. Thornton is one of them. He feels that to a certain extent he and other young men of his generation were duped into service: "I guess because I was kind of, I guess, brainwashed to feel that as a young man that we were . . . that I was obligated to serve my country, and this was a duty that I had to do." Still, Thornton says that serving "wasn't a burden," and that in fact he considered it to be a noble act: "I also saw it as, not prestige, but . . . I thought it was a good thing to do, you know? To be honest with you, once I had gone through my basic and realized it was a job, I said, 'Well, hell, I'll make the best of it and enjoy it,' you know?"

Thornton's cheerful disposition changed shortly after he arrived in Korea, where he suffered from frostbite and head injuries. He was angry at the military for failing to adequately prepare him for the conditions he would encounter: "I was angry at, uh, I was angry at the army I guess because I felt that I wasn't protected enough." He was also upset by what he believed to be inadequate training for the mission:

> I felt that the basic [training] I received did not forewarn me about what I was going into. I really didn't know what I was going into. Hell, I didn't know what was in Korea. I didn't realize it was that cold in Korea, you know? I felt as though our clothing was inadequate because of that climate that we were in. I had no idea that it was that type of weather over there. Of course, I kept wondering, "What the hell am I doing here? Why? What for? Why do we want these hills and these mountains? What for? What's over here for us?"

After sustaining his injuries, Thornton recalls, it was not clear whether he would recover; his condition was touch and go for quite some time. "I stayed unconscious for about six months and my wife had been told and my mother had been told that if I lived I would be a vegetable, and that I'd never walk again." In the end, however, surviving the war improved his self-image and allowed him to better appreciate life. As he reflects on it now, Thornton says that the service made him stronger: "It made me realize that I developed a will to live and to live a strong life and a beautiful life, and I think it helped me there."

Mr. McWilliams's experience is a slight departure from the others; he was initially indifferent about going to war. He has no recollection of what motivated him to fight, though he suspects that his motives were instrumental rather than sentimental. "I think I went (to the Korean War) because of the opportunity to be promoted to lieutenant," he guesses. Even though he is not quite sure why he did not resist going to war, he is clear about what did *not* motivate him: "It was not fighting the communists. It was not for freedom. No, you were ordered to go into combat. You didn't question it. It may sound silly, you know, as I look at it now. Flag waving? Fighting for the flag? God, no! Defending democracy? No, it wasn't that, either. You were just told to go and you went. You got orders and went."

Even so, McWilliams believed it important that blacks be allowed to fight. Black Americans, in his estimation, have always been stigmatized by what he perceived as an unfair assessment of their fighting ability. McWilliams drew on history to illustrate his point: "You go all the way back to the Spanish-American War, you had [a] very limited number of black combat units. And especially during World War I the black units were sent over to France to fight, but didn't get the chance." Turning to the Second World War, he makes the following observation regarding black military service. "It was so stigmatized," he says indignantly, "that you had a couple of black combat units that they shipped them to a place away from combat areas. They said they didn't have the backbone, or they couldn't fight under stress or they—they just couldn't, or were not—good combat people." The "they" to which the colonel refers are "the Southern senators and generals and everybody else—because they didn't give them [blacks] a chance to prove themselves—the 371st Tank Battalion and the Triple Nickel Airborne Battalion."

It was only during the Korean War, the colonel argues, that the military establishment acceded to political pressure applied by the black community: "Now, come the Korean War, the pressure was on for black combat [men]. They [blacks] demand, 'Let's have some black infantry units. Let's have some black tankers. Let's have some black artillerymen, airborne units.'" Recalling his own experience in Korea with the Twenty-Fifth Regiment of the Twenty-Fifth Division, he remembers the unit "do[ing] an outstanding job in Korea, but because of the overwhelming forces of the North Korean and Chinese, they ran a bunch of people—including whites—back. But because it was the Twenty-Fifth, a black unit, it was broadcast that we ran."

In the end, though, McWilliams is glad that he served—glad that he had the opportunity to engage in combat. He believes that fighting made blacks "more of an American than this picture they portrayed of us." Combat experience allowed him and fellow black servicemen to say, with a sense of gratification, "Hey, I served, and served in a combat unit. They didn't just throw me in the military to clean the latrines or drive a truck, or to do some of this manual labor." The actions of black servicemen in World War II and Korea, he believes, corrected the misperception that they were incapable of fighting. McWilliams also clamored to fight in order to prove a point. He says that he was determined "to prove that [black soldiers] could do the same as anyone else, because they said blacks were not good enough or capable of fighting in combat against an enemy." He admitted one final reason for fighting: it was a means of proving his manhood to whites. "It was very important," McWilliams explains, "to say that I'm a man also."

• • •

If we look beyond the negative effects of segregation and discrimination, military service was a positive experience for many of the black veterans I interviewed. This confirms McMillen's (1997) and Moore's (1996) findings that black veterans of the Second World War took pride in their service, as well as their conclusion that military service was a turning point in the lives of black veterans. My findings extend these results to veterans of the Korean War as well. In other words, it didn't matter *when* one served; all are proud of what they accomplished and learned in the military. Even for Thornton and McWilliams, both of whom were ambivalent about their experiences in the military, military service was, overall, a positive experience. Their opinions regarding the *conditions* under which they joined the military, however, are mixed: some saw it as a duty to fight for their country, something they were compelled to do. Others considered it a privilege, something they were glad to undertake. This split seems to correspond to how much veterans believed they had benefited from their service. Those who perceived military service as an opportunity for advancement, whether personal or racial, tended to call service as a privilege. Those who believed that nothing in the way of tangible advancement would result from their service, on the other hand, appear to have perceived it as a duty or burden. This is a slight departure from Mettler's (2005b) findings as they pertain to white veterans in that almost all of her subjects believed their military service to have been an obligation they were happy to fulfill. It is safe to say that race has something to do with the difference between white veterans who were happy to fulfill their obligations and some of the black veterans who were less than enthusiastic about doing so.

In the end, though, each of the men I interviewed believes his military service was worthwhile and that it contributed to the greater good, be it national security or dispelling the notion that blacks are not effective fighters. The experience associated with military service, as predicted, gave the veterans confidence and taught them teamwork and discipline. The finding that military service produces confidence is in keeping with prior research (Elder and Clipp 1989). My findings differ, however, in the sense that black veterans emphasize the *opportunities* provided by the military as a source of their confidence. Indeed, that several mentioned the opportunities for which they were grateful affirms that the military gave them a chance to excel, convincing them that they were capable of exceeding the low expectations imposed by racism. Black veterans, furthermore, tended to use whites as a benchmark for measuring their successes: their ability to compete with whites in the military made them feel successful. Finally, serving in the military affirmed veterans' masculinity, especially for those who saw combat. Proving their mettle on the battlefield, as Samuel Stouffer and colleagues (1949) have suggested, gave black servicemen an opportunity to refute racist claims that they were too cowardly or too dumb to serve on par with whites.

DONNING THE UNIFORM

Many veterans spoke of the uniform as a symbol of the pride they felt in their service. Sometimes, a uniform transcends mere association with the group in that it represents group attributes, ultimately coming to represent the group, and becomes the focus of attention (Joseph and Alex 1972). Put differently, the uniform becomes a means by which individuals identify with the core values of the organization it represents (Pratt and Rafaeli 1997). In the case of the American military, the uniform represents the martial virtues of discipline, courage, and sacrifice, the last of which is indispensable to the practice of republicanism: without sacrifice, there is no civic virtue.

Perhaps more important, at least for black Southerners, the uniform symbolized their equality, their membership in the political community. It also embodied these service members' sense of accomplishment and their commitment to American ideals. For these reasons we should expect black veterans to express pride in having donned the uniform, some of which they derived from how they were received in the black community.

I can find no better example than Dr. Carey's experience. Born and raised in rural Florida, Carey moved to Louisiana to take a faculty position at a historically black university in the 1960s. His father, who had only a second-grade education, was a fruit grower, and his mother, a housewife, had a seventh-grade education. As much as he admired his father's work ethic, Carey didn't wish to follow in his footsteps; he wanted something more. He wanted to attend college, and he knew his parents didn't have the resources to send him. After listening to a recruiting pitch in which the recruiter apprised him of the educational opportunities that accompanied military service through the GI Bill, he was persuaded to join, enlisting on June 12, 1950—thirteen days prior to the commencement of the Korean War. Nonetheless, for a young man from such humble beginnings, military service and the uniform that symbolized it were a means of elevating his status. Carey felt "pretty damn proud" of his uniform. "In the rural South," he says, "the military is viewed with a bit more respect than, say, in the Northern inner city." Once reports from the Korean War began to trickle back to America, black Southerners gained an even greater appreciation of the sacrifices made by black soldiers. (See appendix C for content analysis.) Because Carey was wounded, he returned home early on a medical furlough. Consequently, there were few black servicemen around when he returned home. On the occasions when he decided to wear his uniform in public, it "gave me a measure of respect," he says with unabashed pride, "especially among blacks and my peers. Whites also respected it."

Carey is not the only veteran to feel this way about the uniform. Thornton also derived great pride from wearing his uniform, especially off-post, around family and friends: "When I wore my uniform I felt proud. I really did. I felt proud." He elaborates, "I was especially proud of wearing it if I went to church. You know, with members of my family. I also discovered there was a lot of sympathy with it." The uniform, according to Thornton, had cachet beyond the black community. "If you had your uniform on," he declares, "you were allowed to do almost anything. Without it, you didn't." According to Carey and Thornton, black soldiers in uniform commanded a grudging respect from white Southerners. Thornton remembers that "they [whites] wouldn't bother you. They were normal, you would hear it [the racist talk], but they wouldn't challenge you."

Veterans also internalized how the uniform, which symbolized desert and achievement, made them feel. Mr. Carter, a career army man who volunteered in 1940, declares, "[Wearing the uniform] made me feel as though I was a true American—that I merited everything that I received." For Williams, the uniform represented much more. "I know that once I got in that uniform, I was somebody; I stood for something," he says.

"The uniform showed me what discipline was . . . it told me how to receive and accept responsibility." Before he volunteered to join the army at the age of seventeen in 1952, Williams was illiterate. He did not remain that way, he says, because "the uniform of the United States Army helped educate me when I probably never would be educated." Baines, too, was "proud, very proud" to wear the uniform. "By going into the military," he recalls, "I not only traveled but I had the opportunity to really meet people, to engage in war, fight for this country, and make me proud of what I've done."

Not all of the veterans I interviewed hold the uniform in such high regard. For Mr. Stewart, drafted in 1945, wearing the uniform changed nothing. Even after the war, he recalls with some bitterness, "they [whites] looked at you . . . you're just another nigger, you know?" He recalls an experience he had while he was on leave. En route from California to Texas, he stopped at a gas station. "I needed to use the bathroom," he remembers. "I had my wife, and we stopped there, and I said we'll stop at the service station and get some gas. So I asked the attendant, did they have a restroom? He said, 'Not for colored.' I said, 'Well, don't put no gas in the car.'" Stewart was in uniform when this exchange took place.

The uniform, it seems, meant something different to each veteran. Some emphasized how it made them feel. To others, it brought a measure of respect from the black community and from some whites. Why did the uniform mean so much? Like the right to vote and the right to work (Shklar 1991), being permitted to wear the uniform represented an elevation in social standing. The uniform at once conveys the depth of one's commitment to America and the reality of one's membership in the national community. This is why the black community took pride in the servicemen's achievements: they represented blacks' commitment to the nation's ideals. White Southerners respected the uniform, if not the individual, for similar reasons. Of course, as Stewart's example indicates, affinity for the uniform was not universal. If the other veterans' sentiments are even remotely representative of black Southerners who served during the Second World War and the Korean War, however, we may conclude that many veterans drew positive meaning from donning the uniform.

• • •

This chapter explored the military experiences of black servicemen from the South during the Second World War and the Korean War. Most accounts of black veterans' experience in the military centers on the egregious policies and practices to which they were exposed, and rightfully so. The positive aspects of military service, however, are often buried under the debris of segregation and discrimination. The veterans I interviewed appreciate the opportunities military service provided them. Many take pride in their service; overcoming the challenges they encountered in the military filled them with confidence. These sentiments were not unanimous, of course. On more than one occasion I spoke to veterans who were angry at the persistence of racism in the military and at being forced by the draft to serve a country that allowed the military to export its racist practices overseas. Overall, though, the veterans I talked to seem to have made the most of their experiences, and these experiences shaped their lives and laid the foundations of a black republican worldview.

From a theoretical perspective, we can also observe the ways in which the military, as an institution, shaped the behavior of black servicemen. Both race-neutral and racialized effects of military service are apparent in the testimonies of the veterans I interviewed. On the one hand, the policy of segregation institutionalized racism in the military. Even though desegregation eventually eliminated the institutionalization of racism in the military, it remained intact as a practice, infecting the chain of command from top to bottom during the Korean War. On the other hand, military culture is also responsible for institutionalizing courage, pride, discipline, and the confidence that comes from bearing arms. Racialized effects, including the racial awareness gained from serving overseas and exposure to educational as well as vocational experiences, also served veterans well upon their departure from the military. In the absence of these experiences it is difficult to imagine that black servicemen would have taken on white supremacy in the way that they did. All of these experiences contributed to the development of veterans' worldview of black republicanism and thereby helped to sustain their resistance to domination.

The bittersweet experience of serving overseas—the feeling of at once being liberated by one's encounters with foreigners and oppressed by one's own countrymen—is something that black veterans did not soon forget. Together, the negative and the positive aspects of their military experiences came to represent their ability to overcome adversity, their courage, their sense of self-worth, their sense of equality, and their sense of manhood. As a result, veterans returned to the South with a new sense of self and their ability to change things. They returned with a new set of expectations, confident of their ability to achieve them. There is no doubt that serving in a Jim Crow military curbed the potential of some soldiers, sailors, and airmen. But the educational opportunities, travel, sense of purpose, and—for some—leadership that were also part of military experience ensured an upward trajectory for many of these men for the rest of their lives.

These experiences set black veterans apart from other black Southerners, laying the groundwork for the formation of a group. As we shall see, the members of this group had an attachment to America, its ideals and institutions, but not the type of blind attachment often confused with patriotism. Instead, theirs was a critical attachment. Black veterans returned home determined to secure the rights to which they, and the community they represented, were entitled. After all, if they were willing to die to preserve freedom overseas—a freedom they had failed to enjoy prior to their departure—why should they not have been willing to die for it when they returned?

CHAPTER 4

When Jim Crow Meets Uncle Sam

THE VETERAN RETURNS TO DIXIE

> I went to World [War] II. I helped train a thousand men to kill . . . and I didn't know what the hell I was teaching 'em for. Went in behind the Civil Rights Act, I know what the hell I was fightin'; I was fightin' for equal rights that Roosevelt promised us before he died. Didn't do a damn thing about it. . . . He didn't do a damn thing.
>
> —Charlie Sims, World War II veteran,
> quoted in George Lipsitz, *A Life in the Struggle:*
> *Ivory Perry and the Culture of Opposition*

In chapter 3, I showed how military experience confirmed the illegitimacy of white supremacy for the black veterans I interviewed, and how it furnished them with the confidence to confront it upon their return to the South. In this chapter I will complete the theoretical framework begun in chapter 2 by illustrating how, for black Southerners who served in the military, the experience produced a belief system that affected their attitudes and behavior on returning home. By way of example, I turn briefly to two of the leaders of the Southern freedom struggle, both of whom donned the uniform during the Second World War before returning to the South to face off with Jim Crow.

Aaron Henry was born in 1922 into a family of sharecroppers. A native of Dublin, Mississippi, Henry was educated in segregated schools before being drafted in 1943. In the army, he was assigned to a segregated quartermaster unit during the Second World War. Disturbed by the irony of fighting for democracy in a Jim Crow army, Henry returned to Mississippi, where he became the first African American to register to vote in the Democratic Party primary in the county of Coahoma. Thanks to the GI Bill, Henry obtained a degree in pharmacology from Xavier University in Louisiana. In 1950, he returned to his native Mississippi, settling in Clarksdale, where he opened his own pharmacy.

From his Fourth Street Drugstore, Henry began his assault upon segregation. In 1954, he joined the local NAACP, becoming the president of the statewide branch in 1959. In 1962, he was a key member of the

Council of Federated Organizations, the umbrella organization charged with coordinating the activities of the Congress of Racial Equality (CORE), the Student Nonviolent Coordinating Committee (SNCC), the Southern Christian Leadership Conference (SCLC), and the NAACP in Mississippi. Two years later, Henry became a founding member of the Mississippi Freedom Democratic Party, an organization that challenged the dominance of Mississippi's Democratic Party at the 1964 Democratic National Convention. In 1982, Henry ran for and won a seat in Mississippi's House of Representatives, an office he held for twenty-four years. Henry's civil rights advocacy caused him to be jailed thirty-three times, his business to be firebombed, and his wife to lose her job as a teacher.

What was the source of Henry's determination to challenge domination? Perhaps the epigraph above provides a clue. Charlie Sims, also a veteran of the Second World War, was frustrated with the pace of state-sponsored change. He was under the impression—apparently mistaken—that his willingness to fight would produce equal rights for African Americans. But when he perceived that the state had reneged on the republican compact to reward his military service with rights, Sims felt that he was forced to take matters into his own hands—to supplement his critical view of the state with activism. He became a member of Deacons for Defense and Justice, the organization in which many black veterans protected CORE workers from the Ku Klux Klan in Louisiana.

At issue in this study is whether or not Sims's and Henry's critical and activist reactions to their frustrations with the refusal of Southern state and local authorities, as well as Southern society, to honor the republican compact—where the burden of military service is associated with first-class citizenship—was common among veterans. Thus, this chapter builds on the preceding chapter, in which the experiential foundations of black republicanism were revealed, by fleshing out this system of belief in full by considering the enduring meaning of military service to black veterans.

After sketching a portrait of the unforgiving South to which black veterans returned, I examine the extent to which they used the language of republicanism to organize their political and social views. Upon establishing the tenability of black republicanism as set of organizing principles, finally, I illustrate some of its practical implications. Here I will argue that veterans' postwar criticism and activism—the attitudinal and behavioral consequences of black republicanism—were motivated by the sacrifices undertaken in service to the country. As in the preceding chapter, interviews will provide the evidentiary basis for the aforementioned claims. As we shall soon see, black veterans used republican rhetoric to frame postwar claims on the state and society for equality, the basis of which was their military service. Finally, the interviews on which I draw for evidence in the present chapter reflect the most clearly articulated views of particular points of view. If I draw on a particular veteran to illustrate a point, be assured that he isn't the only one with that general opinion.

WHITE DOMINATION IN THE 1950s

As the South emerged from the Korean War, there were at least three reasons for black Southerners to be optimistic. First, the demise of the white primary in 1944 promised to restore the relevance of black voters once again after a half-century hiatus. Second, blacks were now serving in a desegregated military in which they saw plenty of combat. And finally, the recent victory in the *Brown v. Board of Education of Topeka* case, many believed, promised to end segregation once and for all. With the benefit of time and exceptional scholarship, we know that these events set the stage for the insurgent movement that would eventually produce lasting change in the South (Andrews 2004; Button 1989; Jenkins and Argonne 2003; McAdam 1999; Morris 1984). Of the aforementioned reforms, the order to desegregate the military enjoyed the most immediate and tangible impact. But as I have already noted, it took three years, exigent circumstances during war, and a commander committed more to moral principle than army culture to realize the spirit of President Harry S. Truman's executive order. While many of the white officer elite in the armed forces lost their battle to maintain segregation, their counterparts in civil society continued to fight desegregation and the political representation of blacks in the South.

White Southerners conjured myriad reasons to resist social change. The need to fight communism, the belief in states' rights, and the ascription of communist motives to civil rights activists, among other things, were all offered as excuses to impede—if not crush—the civil rights movement (Lee 2002).[1] "Negroes" and "Whites Only" signs haunted restrooms, water fountains, and various modes of public transportation, as public accommodations remained segregated. The better schools remained off-limits to black children, thanks to "massive resistance" in which Southern state houses "interposed" themselves between the federal government and its citizens (McMillen 1994), devising a cascade of laws

Circumstances in the South

---

[1] For alternative explanations for white Southerners' reaction to racial reform, see Frederickson (1981) and Kruse (2005) for ideological accounts. See Cash (1941) for a psychocultural explanation, and Franklin (2002) for a more cultural explanation; for a point of view in which politics, personal ambition, and Southern elites explain Southern recalcitrance, see Bartley (1969) and Mickey (forthcoming).

to avoid desegregation. It was a smashing success for white supremacists: ten years after the *Brown* decision, 99 percent of schools in the South remained segregated (Orfield 2000). It took the educational provision of the Civil Rights Act (1964) to remove the remaining barriers to school integration. As of 1960, moreover, only 28 percent of black Southerners who were eligible to vote were actually registered (Matthews and Prothro 1966).

The continued oppression of black Southerners rested upon a foundation of terror and coercion. Black veterans returned to a South in which the murder of blacks went for the most part unpunished.[2] From 1941 through 1955, ninety-two black Southerners were murdered by whites,[3] including fourteen-year-old Emmett Till, who was killed for *whistling* at a white woman. In most of these cases that were brought to trial in the South, the accused escaped conviction. Moreover, the threat posed by *Brown* to the Southern social order stimulated a revival of the Klan in at least one state and the creation of a second white supremacist organization in another. In 1954 and 1955, the Georgia-based Klan embarked upon a membership drive that produced approximately fifteen thousand recruits (Robinson 1997). In October 1954, mainly to resist conforming to the ruling in *Brown*, white Mississippians formed the Citizens' Council (McMillen 1994). "Pursuing the agenda of the Klan, with the demeanor of the Rotary," as sociologist Charles Payne puts it (1995, 34–35), the council was constituted by "professionals, businessmen, and planters." It accumulated a membership of 80,000 by 1956 in Mississippi alone, and eventually spread to six other states. These councils, assisted by state and local authorities, often targeted members or sympathizers of the NAACP, threatening (and using) economic sanctions such as employment termination and the denial of credit to achieve the desired result: impeding school integration by weakening the organizational power of the NAACP (McMillen 1994; Payne 1995).

Beyond the terror, segregation, and discrimination to which all blacks in the South were subjected, black veterans as a group were singled out for discriminatory treatment. The GI Bill of Rights, conceived in part to reward veterans for their sacrifices, remains the most ambitious social welfare program ever offered by the government (Katznelson 2005). It ushered in unprecedented social mobility by giving veterans access to home and business loans, educational assistance, and employment services. Even though the Selective Service Readjustment Act of 1944 did

[2] For an account in which socioeconomic mobility dampened whites' desire to engage in postwar violence, see O'Brien (1999).

[3] Data compiled by the author from the Espy File, part of the National Archive of Criminal Justice Data, deposited at the Inter-university Consortium for Political and Social Research.

not contain language restricting the benefits of the act to whites, politics affected the distribution of benefits. To guarantee the support of Southern legislators, the bill was structured to ensure that program administration would devolve to state-level bureaucrats, who in turn undermined the social mobility promised by the program by depriving black veterans of access to resources to which they were entitled, thereby maintaining the social status quo.

Only on rare occasions were black veterans in the South allowed to redeem the educational provision of the GI Bill at predominantly white colleges and universities; otherwise, they were forced to attend black colleges (Onkst 1998). These institutions were often overcrowded, making it difficult for some veterans to gain admission. Fair access to housing was also restricted, as redlining prevented all blacks, including veterans, from purchasing homes in more desirable white neighborhoods where homes accumulated equity at much faster rates (Katznelson 2005; Oliver and Shapiro 1995). Black veterans, furthermore, were often forced to accept employment in occupations for which they were overqualified. Jobs in many of the professional, skilled, and semiskilled occupations were reserved for white veterans, leaving only menial, dirty jobs for black veterans (Onkst 1998).

This is not to say that the GI Bill did not benefit black Southerners; it did. To the extent possible, black Southerners took advantage of the program, and society was the better for it because program participants were more likely than nonparticipants to undertake political activism (Metter 2005a). Nevertheless, frustration with not receiving the benefits they were due may partly explain why black veterans fled the South in greater numbers than blacks who did not serve (Modell, Goulden, and Magnussen 1989). By 1950, 50 percent of all black veterans who joined the armed forces from Southern states had relocated to a different region. By contrast, two-thirds of nonveteran black men remained in Dixie (Modell et al. 1989, 839).[4] Veteran or not, those who remained faced the same restrictions on their liberties.

Framing the Meaning of Military Service and Black Republicanism

Veterans returned to a hostile South, a place that refused to appreciate, much less honor, their sacrifices. How did they make sense of this mis-

---

[4] Veterans, through exposure to other ways of life, were a bit more mobile than nonveterans. In any case, by 1970, the number of veterans living beyond the region of their birth declined to 41 percent (Gregory 2004).

treatment? How, if at all, did their experiences shape their view of the South? I gain analytical traction on these questions by turning to framing. Interpretive frames, according to David Snow and his colleagues, "ren[der] events and occurrences meaningful [by] organiz[ing] experience and guid[ing] action, whether individual or collective" (Snow et al. 1986, 464). As interpretive devices, frames guide how people think about their social and political world by "selectively punctuating and encoding objects, situations, events, experiences, and sequences of actions, within one's present or past environment" (Snow and Benford 1992, 137). Frames assist collective action in manifold ways. Their ability to identify injustice, attribute blame to a group or an individual, and prescribe a means of corrective action is essential for mobilization (Gamson 1992; Snow and Benford 1992).

I am less interested in the ways in which frames were constructed by movement entrepreneurs than I am in exploring how veterans made sense of their world upon returning to the South. Accordingly, I aim to use insights from framing as an analytical tool to illustrate how veterans' ideological proclivities, derived from their military experience(s), informed their views of the postwar South. To do so, I follow Taeku Lee's (2002) example, which examines constituency mail from the period of the civil rights movement. To make sense of the ways in which individuals articulated their appeals to the president, Lee drew on interpretive frames, explaining that "citizens frame an argument when they put their *personal* 'spin' on a particular matter" (2002, 156; emphasis added). Similarly, my goal is to examine black veterans' *personal* versions of events, not the framing process per se.

I use frames to capture how veterans' military experience structured their perceptions of the postwar South. Frames use culture in creative ways to generate ideological perspectives that identify injustice and prescribe corrective action, among other things. More to the point, culture informs both frames and the ideologies in which they're embedded (Tarrow 1992; Zald 1996). Frames are also relevant to their users' life experiences (Snow et al. 1986; Snow and Benford 1988, 2000). Individuals must feel that a frame speaks to their life history before they accept it and act.

Below, I draw on frames to illuminate the process through which black republicanism animated the insurgent attitudes and behavior of black veterans during the Jim Crow era. If black republicanism has any explanatory power, we should expect veterans to have framed their discontent with social conditions in the South and their resistance to domination in terms consistent with their military experience. If I am correct, the meaning of military service functioned as a prism through which veterans viewed white domination and their reaction to it. It was by means of their perceived full membership in the political community, in concert with the confidence they accrued in the service, that black veterans interrogated and challenged white supremacy.

Before I examine some of the consequences of black republicanism, however, I must first consider its constitution and whether or not black veterans used it to organize their thinking. One way to assess this latter question is to ask veterans to consider their relationship with the nation-state. In doing so, I hope to shed light on two questions. First, if we know how veterans conceive of the relationship between the individual and the nation-state, we should gain at least a partial understanding of why the militant black veterans, mentioned in the introduction to this volume, acted as they did. And second, to the extent that ideologies assist individuals and groups to navigate the political world, veterans' beliefs about the relationship between the individual and the nation-state should help adjudicate differences between black republicanism and competing ideologies.

BLACK REPUBLICANISM AND NATIONAL IDENTIFICATION

One way in which individuals relate to the nation-state is through their attachment to it. There are at least three ways to explain blacks' attachment to the nation. One, based on radical egalitarianism, represents the black liberal position, and is the black ideology most similar, in my estimation, to black republicanism. An approach that used radical egalitarianism to explain black attachment to the nation would suggest that African Americans identify with the nation and its values as a means of securing progress—that their attachment is a strategy by which they interrogate American social practices in order to advance the race by forcing whites to observe the founding values of the nation (Dawson 2001). In other words, for radical egalitarians, national attachment is relatively instrumental. An approach that uses conventional republicanism to explain black attachment to the nation, alternatively, would suggest that national identification is not instrumental but fundamentally primordial and emotional, guided by affective attachment to the nation's institutions and conationals.

My approach is firmly planted in the middle of these two. Black republicanism, unlike radical egalitarianism, links black veterans' attachment to the nation explicitly to their military service. It departs from conventional republicanism insofar as national identification, according to black republicanism, is complicated by race and a history of domination. Thus, for those veterans who adhere to black republicanism, we expect them to allude to systemic, race-based discrimination even as they declare their allegiance to the nation. To examine these competing hypotheses, I asked the veterans I interviewed to choose whether they identify themselves as Americans or African Americans. I deliberately chose the term *African American* instead of *black* simply because the latter would pose too stark a contrast with identification as *American*.

Some veterans, as one may imagine, feel closer to the nation as a result of their service. Mr. Shaw typifies this sentiment. An awardee of the Silver Star, one of the nation's highest military honors, he feels that he has earned right to be called American because, as he puts it, "I served my country in war." The son of a farmer and a housewife, he was born on a farm in Terrell, Texas, in 1929. Initially educated at Tuskegee Institute, he eventually received a master's degree in agronomy from Rutgers University. Shaw served in World War II as an enlisted man, and as an officer who commanded white troops during the Korean War. As a result of his military service he feels that he should be afforded "any rights that any other American is exposed to." Shaw's rationale for demanding recognition as an American is understandable and straightforward. After all, he fought for the country, and did so gallantly; the citation for Shaw's medal, the Silver Star, says as much. Shaw recognizes himself as an American and feels that whites should follow suit and acknowledge him as an equal.

Veterans also tie their military service to identification with the nation by means of references to patriotism. Dr. Bashful, who was an artillery officer during the Second World War, is a good example. His is not a blind "my country right or wrong" patriotism; Bashful's patriotism reflects the tension between his commitment to America and his commitment to his race. For instance, the 351st Field Artillery Battalion, in which he served, held an annual reunion. He recalls one meeting in particular at which, he says, "it was the feeling of all of our members that the whole system in the army—and that was a segregated army by the way—was meant to crush you."

Nevertheless, Bashful maintained his allegiance to the nation—albeit a critical allegiance. When he was chancellor of a historically black university, an aide alerted him to a problem one afternoon. A group of students attempted to remove the American flag and replace it with the now familiar red, black, and green "black flag of liberation." Bashful recalls that there were approximately fifty students around the flagpole. He advised the students that continuing with this action would "invite a lot of problems." When they were slow to respond, he qualified his position to the students, explaining, "I am a veteran of World War II, and I fought for that flag, so I have some allegiance to it. But I also have allegiance to the black flag of liberation in terms of what we're [black people] trying to do. I don't think that one flag is more important than the other."

Given his experience in a segregated army, it is no surprise that the chancellor sympathized with the students.

The incident was reported in the local news. Bashful received a phone call from a school trustee, who asked him what exactly was happening at the school. The official questioned the chancellor's patriotism, something that Bashful failed to appreciate. He recalls "setting the official straight." He did so by citing his military service: "I'm a veteran of World War II." Bashful continued dressing down the man on the other line: "I was an artillery officer, so don't tell me about patriotism. I think I have at least as much patriotism as you." The chancellor indicated that despite his negative experiences in the army, he could not let the American flag be disrespected. To him, the flag "is a symbol of the nation." Like Shaw's, his respect for the flag is rooted in his military service. "As a former officer in the army," he says with a blend of amusement and pride, "I just didn't see how I could allow the flag to be disrespected." Bashful's actions are consistent with the critical attachment to nation that I argue is characteristic of black republicanism.

It is no surprise that military service affects the extent to which veterans identify with the nation and its symbols. After all, they were willing to put their lives on the line for both. There are, however, other reasons that these black veterans identify with the nation. Mr. Pete, a veteran of the Korean War, provides us with one: a desire to belong. He reported to Korea just prior to the commencement of hostilities in 1950 and was a member of the all-black Twenty-Fourth Infantry Regiment. Despite his experiences with segregation in the military, he absolutely insists that he is first and foremost an American because, he proclaims, "I was born here as an American. . . . I am American!" While Pete's identification with America is primarily tethered to his birthright, his insistence that he is American is also rooted in his fear of being singled out: "I mean, leave the 'African' off and just say I'm American. When you say 'African American,' you want to say 'Alaskan American' or 'Hispanic American'; I mean, it's really pointing you out, I mean as far as race. Just say, 'I'm American!' "

Pete's view is exceptional in that his desire to identify with the national community is driven mostly by a wish to belong. Shaw's position is that his service entitles him to call himself American. Both are firm in their declarations. Neither, though, can match Mr. Stewart's determination to identify with the nation. He resents the mere implication that he is anything but American, pure and simple. Drafted in 1945, Stewart shipped out to Korea in 1948, where he served during the occupation of South Korea prior to the war's commencement in 1950. When asked what he identifies as—African American or simply American—he comments, "I think of myself [as] an American." He completely rejects the currently favored term used to identify Americans of African descent. "I've never been to Africa; I wasn't born in Africa. I am American," he insists. "And I resent it [being categorized as African American], myself. Now I don't know about the other fellow, but I resent it." Asked why he resents it, Stewart carefully weighs the question before offering an answer. "Well, I resent it because I was born here in the United States and in Texas, and I don't like it [being called African American]. Period. It's like on an application and they have 'African American' on it, I draw a line. I'm serious. I draw a line through 'Africa[n]' and I leave the 'American.'"

For other veterans, identification as an American has less to do with how they see themselves than how they wish whites to see them. Mr. Williams's view is illustrative in this regard. He feels that the term *African American* qualifies his membership in the national community: "I'm no Afro-American, and I don't like to be called one," he maintains. A former member of an elite Ranger unit who'd risen to the highest enlisted rank (E-9), he insists that *Afro-American* is another way for whites to avoid recognizing black Southerners as equals. In other words, he says, "it's a polite way for a white man, in an intelligent way, to still call you a nigger." Williams's membership in the political community, in his estimation, is guaranteed by the Constitution. "It states it real well," he says, "that any man that is born in the United States of America, regardless of race, creed, or color—is an American citizen. I'm an American citizen. I'm not no Afro-American!" For him it's important that blacks claim their birthright; otherwise, as he sees it, whites may decide to declare them unfit for citizenship and return them to a status of servitude. "I didn't come from Africa to stay in America for a number of years to sit under American rule to gain and prepare myself for citizenship and still might not make it if they see fit to that they didn't want me; that 'We got enough niggers in here already, why bring some more in?'"

It's one thing to refer oneself as an African American, but Williams shudders at the thought of a *white man* calling him Afro-American. Indeed, for a white man to call him anything but American is an insult. "No! Anytime a white man call[s] me Afro-American, I correct him real quick and tell him, 'You quit using that polite way of calling me a nigger,'" he emphasizes, illustrating how he would handle a situation in which a white person referred to him as anything but American. Williams's identification with the nation is tethered in chief to the Constitution. Without it, he suggests, whites would attempt to force blacks to accept second-class citizenship. Thus, his identification with America is linked to his belief of how whites perceive him. He refuses to allow whites to strip him of his claim to first-class membership in the political community. His insistence upon identifying with the nation, it seems, is a radical egalitarian one. But the fact that Williams emphasizes how whites—if they wished—could invalidate blacks' citizenship is a direct reference to the domination referenced by republicans: the arbitrariness with which the dominant party can impinge upon a subordinate's liberty.

There is evidence that some of the veterans with whom I spoke subscribe to conventional republican thought. In short, their identity is framed to coincide with a primordial view of national identification: they were born in America, so as they see it they are American; it is an insult to suggest otherwise. However, these veterans were in the minority. Most of the veterans I interviewed were firmly rooted in the radical egalitarian or black republican camp. Williams, for instance, is a clear case in which identification is guided by the former. By framing his identification with America as a constitutional guarantee, Williams indicates that white America need only act in accordance with its most sacred document to ensure his membership in the national community. This claim, shared by other veterans, is consistent with radical egalitarianism insofar as they also reference the Constitution as the basis for their identification as an American. We also see veterans identifying themselves as American because of their service to the country—an allegiance that has more to do with their sacrifices than with any primordial or strategic identification. This approach, as we see with Shaw, is both critical and organic (i.e., as opposed to instrumental), both of which are constitutive of black republicanism. We should note that, regardless of one's ideological proclivities, each of these perspectives is complicated by race. Invoking race raises the specter of the domination to which black republicanism responds, resulting in a more critical attachment to the nation. Such an attachment is not part of mainstream republicanism, which promotes an allegiance that is unencumbered.

BLACK REPUBLICANISM AND CITIZENSHIP

Analyzing responses to a question about identification is one way to assess attachment to the nation. But I can think of at least two reasons why it may be necessary to draw on additional evidence to make the case for black republicanism. First, it remains possible that one's identity preference may have just as much to do with one's generation as it has to do with military experience. Since age tends to breed conservatism, and the labels *Afro-American* and *African American* were militant responses to the baggage attached to the term *Negro*, it's possible that these veterans rejected the former terms because of their association with militancy. Second, as we have witnessed, black veterans' responses on this matter revealed their affiliations with a range of ideological positions. Though black republicanism was clearly one option, more evidence is needed to confirm its conceptual validity. Thus, we must move beyond the affect associated with national attachment and toward the associated cognitions (Citrin, Wong, and Duff 2001). I choose to do so by examining veterans' beliefs about citizenship.

Citizenship functions as the institutional nexus between the individual and the political community (Conover 1995). To the extent that a political community consists of both members and formal institutions, furthermore, "citizenship shapes how individuals relate to both" (Conover 1995, 134). Ultimately, the content of these relationships is part of a larger cognitive framework in which individuals consider the proper role of the state in society as well as their rights and duties within the political community. This framework has been shown to promote at least two basic interpretations of citizenship: liberal and republican (Conover, Crewe, and Searing 1991). The former, of course, emphasizes rights over duties; republicanism represents the inverse of these priorities. For this reason, a discussion with veterans about their understanding of citizenship should therefore function as a rough litmus test of the presence or absence of black republicanism. If they conceive of citizenship in a way that consistently prioritizes rights over obligations, this would suggest that they subscribe to a black liberal ideology, most likely radical egalitarianism. If, however, veterans have a mixed view of citizenship in which rights are combined with obligations, the case for black republicanism is strengthened.

To explore the veterans' conceptions of citizenship, I asked three open-ended questions. Drawing on Mettler's (2005b) survey instrument, the first question required interviewees to discuss the meaning of citizenship. I then asked them to define good citizenship. I concluded by asking them to assess the importance of citizenship in their lives. Almost invariably, they framed their responses to the first question in liberal terms. The language of rights, in other words, dominated the discourse. Good citizenship, on the other hand, was clearly a matter of duty. In response to the third question, many of the veterans expressed their appreciation of citizenship as an institution.

Mr. Thomas, an army air corps veteran of the Second World War, is a prime example. To him, "citizenship means everything." He qualifies his affection for the institution, however, on the basis of his memories of the Jim Crow South where he was raised, explaining, "I've been in situations where American citizenship became questionable." "There were periods in . . . my lifetime," Thomas explains, "when that general type of freedom that we construe as freedom wasn't available." Ultimately, though, he is satisfied with the institution of citizenship. From his perspective, citizenship "means that you have considerable rights and freedoms." For these reasons, he declares, "I don't think I would be willing to trade it for another country." Thomas defines citizenship in liberal terms—that is, our "rights and freedoms." Yet his view of *good* citizenship is more consistent with republicanism, emphasizing citizens' duties. Thomas believes, for instance, that good citizens "honor the flag, respect other people, respect property, obey the laws of the land, defend [their] country, and represent [their] country in a commendable way locally, nationally, and internationally." He has some doubts about American citizenship, but he ultimately believes in the institution.

Pete shares several of Thomas's views. He also associates citizenship with freedom, and argues that citizenship is commensurate with "a certain freedom that's due you," elaborating, "I mean, you can act upon and receive those things as rights, privileges, and so forth." Neither of his parents was educated beyond the seventh grade. Perhaps this is why, for Pete, good citizenship depends upon civic education, without which individuals do not know how to serve the wider political community. His conception of good citizenship requires individual citizens to be educated in the habits of service to the country. "Oh, I think a good citizen should come through training," he says; "they [citizens] should come through elementary through high school, and go to college." Pete includes the military as a source of civic education. He believes that a good citizen also "serve[s] his country . . . through the military."

Just as his life circumstances seem to have affected Pete's view of citizenship, Mr. Baines's history of growing up in poverty in a farming community shaped his perception of the institution. His family was very poor. "Except for living on a farm, we probably wouldn't have survived," he says. Reflecting on the poverty in which he was raised and his ability to rise beyond his humble beginnings, he voices his appreciation of American citizenship, which provides people "with so many different rights and privileges." While Baines, like the others, believes good citizenship should promote the common good, he interprets the mechanism by which it does so differently. Baines implies that good citizenship, among other things, means meeting "certain responsibilities" that citizens have, including "getting yourself a job and support[ing] your family." He also departs from his contemporaries in insisting that unconditional support for the nation-state is a requirement of good citizenship. He believes it essential that citizens "support the ideals of this country, support our government in time of peace or war."

Citizenship, Baines says, has played an important role in his life. Had he not been a U.S. citizen, his opportunities for personal development would have suffered. Like Thomas, Baines associates the military with the performance of citizenship. In particular, he mentions that his citizenship furnished him with the opportunity to serve in the military, for which he is grateful. "Had I not been a citizen, they [the armed forces] wouldn't have accepted me," he explains, "and that was one of my greatest experiences [serving in the military]." Given Baines's affinity for the military, it is not surprising that his definition of citizenship requires the citizen to support the nation and its government, regardless of the citizen's feelings about particular policies.

While there is some disagreement among the veterans I interviewed about the precise meaning and nature of citizenship, each of the men mentioned thus far recognizes its importance and seems grateful for the opportunities his own citizenship has provided. Generally, these men, and the many for whom their opinions are representative, stress the rights *and* duties associated with citizenship. This was not, however, the consensus among all the veterans. Upon witnessing the conditions of blacks in the South after returning from war, some were disappointed and frustrated with American society. We should not be surprised, then, that some of the black veterans I interviewed were skeptical about the ability of citizenship to have a meaningful impact on their lives.

Mr. Womack is one such individual. Womack, a decorated veteran of Korea and Vietnam who retired as a sergeant major (E-9) after thirty-four years in the army, joined the armed forces in 1946, volunteering in order to escape a bad relationship. Despite all that he has done for America and accomplished in his life, he bitterly refers to himself as "retired sergeant major, second-class citizen." Unlike his contemporaries who define citizenship in terms of rights and privileges, the sergeant major believes that citizenship represents opportunity. But his race, he says, cuts him off from this opportunity. "I don't have an opportunity to do a damn thing first class," Womack sighs, referring particularly to his lack of employment opportunities. "I don't have the opportunity to walk in an office and be hired based on my credentials," he explains. Instead, "you are judged on your complexion," and this limits black Americans' life chances.

Womack also questions the presumption of equality associated with citizenship. He believes that people of color have always been the dupes of whites. To illustrate, he mentions a chapter in history in which blacks were pitted against Native Americans: "You had Buffalo Soldiers fighting . . . Native Americans. So you had two minorities fighting for the benefit of whom? Whites. It [the whites pitting minorities against one another] hasn't changed." Womack then cut to the heart of the matter: his contempt for the phrase "level playing field." It is often used by those on the right who seek to thwart a fair distribution of opportunity, he says. "Don't tell me 'level playing field,'" Womack fumes. Speaking from whites' perspective, he points out, "If I own the playing field, can I determine who goes on it? You're damn right [I can]." He suggests that whites have reduced the equality of opportunity to an illusion, and the futility of it all frustrates Womack. "Don't give me a level playing field," he repeats, "it doesn't mean shit!"

To the extent that American citizenship is defined in terms of opportunity, Womack is not terribly impressed with it. That said, it is not altogether clear that he disapproves of the ideal of citizenship either. Indeed, Womack sees himself as a good, if frustrated, citizen. He remains angry that American society fails to see him the same way. From his perspective as a career military man, "a good citizen does what he is told." Military service is clearly part of his definition of good citizenship when he says, "I'm a good citizen. I put thirty-something years in the military." In the end, Womack seems torn about American citizenship. On the one hand, he sees a problem with the lack of opportunity and the treatment that black Southerners have been forced to tolerate. On the other hand, he believes that he is a good citizen, largely because of his many years of military service. The problem, as far as he is concerned, is that whites fail to see him as an equal.

If possible, other veterans were even more pessimistic about citizenship. Veterans like Dr. Carey see little value in the institution. He agrees with Womack's definition of citizenship as opportunity, though his pessimism about the institution exceeds the sergeant major's. "I won't say [that citizenship means] *complete* opportunity," Carey states matter-of-factly, "because I'm a black male living in the South, [and] I have been relegated to a second-class citizenship." *Second-class citizenship* is a term often bandied about in academic discourse, but Carey defines what it means to him in concrete terms: "I was not accorded all of the rights and privileges and opportunities that my fellow white people had. I was mistreated. I was brutalized. I lived in the segregated South . . . that sort of tells the story by itself. You go in the back door. You [sit] in the back of the bus. You use worn-out books that had been used by white children."

Carey is nevertheless cognizant of what constitutes a good citizen, though his cynicism is difficult to miss. For him, good citizenship is defined by the "proverbial things such as obeying the laws, paying your taxes, and serving in the military if you're called or want to. Just generally being civic-minded, work[ing] with your community." He certainly knows what is expected of citizens. I suspect, however, that this is more a matter of his education and occupation than a reflection of his own beliefs and values: as a retired professor of political science, he is well aware of the normative duties of citizens. His childhood experiences with segregation, coupled with his use of the word *proverbial* to describe a good citizen, indicate his skepticism about the institution—at least as it pertains to black Southerners.

With the notable exceptions of Womack and Carey, citizenship as an institution is held in high regard by the veterans I interviewed. But even Womack and Carey do not so much reject the ideal of republican citizenship as much as they question the extent to which the benefits of such citizenship have applied to them. Consistent with my understanding of black republicanism, nearly all of the veterans with whom I spoke framed citizenship as a mixture of rights and duties. In addition to military service and compliance with the law, the veterans also cited several types of civic-minded behavior that are identified with republicanism. They also often invoked the values commensurate with liberal democratic citizenship. Each man in his own way mentioned freedom and equality, both of which are central to republican thought. Americans commonly conceive of citizenship as combining rights with duties in some manner (Conover et al. 1991; Conover, Searing, and Crewe 2004). What makes the veterans' vision of citizenship commensurate with black republicanism is the way in which it reflects the history of internal domination—by an enemy at home, rather than an enemy abroad—that impeded their ability to enjoy the freedom for which they fought. Almost without fail, each of the veterans qualified his appraisal of the institution of citizenship by noting the ways in which racial prejudice affected his ability to reap the benefits of full membership in the political community.

EXPECTATIONS OF RACIAL PROGRESS: SERVICE AND SACRIFICE

The black veterans I interviewed were committed to the idea that they had earned full membership in the political community through their military service. In this section we gain a sense of why black veterans felt that they and other black Americans would be treated as equal citizens following World War II or the Korean War. My understanding of black republicanism predicts that veterans would have cited their sacrifices in the military to justify their expectations of change in the South and thus that they would have framed their postwar expectations in the context of the understanding that they went to war to ameliorate the oppressive conditions under which black Southerners lived. (See appendix B for an example of the public discourse on this issue.) Alternatively, a radical egalitarian account predicts that veterans would have tied their postwar expectations to their belief (or hope) that America would act in accordance with its founding values. Military service during wartime, to be sure, is *part* of the radical egalitarian account of racial reform. But it remains only part of the recipe for radical egalitarians. For those who use the language of republicanism, military service was the *centerpiece* of postwar reform. To assess which was in fact the case, I asked the veterans I interviewed about their postwar expectations, after which I asked them to explain why they harbored such expectations.

Notwithstanding minor differences in the way in which they expressed themselves, the veterans framed responses to my questions in similar ways. To the extent that each thought his military service would help spur change, moreover, their responses are consistent with my understanding of black republicanism. Pete's conception of the relationship between participation in war and racial progress is a fine illustration. He is quick to equate military service with first-class citizenship. In his estimation, African Americans "had this expectation . . . if you were good enough, and your skin was dark and you were good enough to go to the military, I mean you should be treated, you know, as a first-class citizen when you got back here." For him, "things should [have] be[en] changed on that basis." That is, the postwar condition of black Southerners should have improved based upon their fitness to serve as first-class citizens. Pete's is a roundly republican view of citizenship, in which service to the state and equality march in lockstep.

Other veterans with whom I spoke shared Pete's view, including Mr. Carter, a veteran of World War II and the Korean War. Carter served from 1940 through 1965, retiring from the army as a lieutenant colonel. Raised by his physician father in rural North Carolina, Carter settled in New Orleans after retiring from the army. Referring to what he thought would be the result of the wars in which he fought, Carter asserts, "I expected them [black citizens] to obtain better treatment in many respects than they had and to be respected much more than they had been." This expectation rested upon a republican understanding of citizenship. "If you didn't hesitate to serve your country," he observes, "your country had no right to hesitate to serve you or give you what you were due." Carter continues, emphasizing reciprocity: "For me, it's always been a matter of I've tried to do that which is right or which I'm supposed to do. But if I'm going to do that, then I expect you to do the same damn thing." He also subscribed to the belief that, as citizen-soldiers, black veterans were entitled to just treatment; they had earned it. Elaborating on this point, he flatly asserts, "We have to look at it from the point of view that we are serving as citizens, and as citizens, you expect to be treated accordingly. Don't give me a damn thing. If I don't deserve it, don't give it to me. But if I deserve it, don't take it away from me."

On the subject of war and the desire for change, the colonel indicates that his own desire for better treatment was always present. However, as groups go, he recalls distinct differences between veterans and nonveterans. Black nonveterans, in his estimation, simply failed to insist upon full equality; but veterans, having gone to war, became more resolute in their demands for change, Carter says, "because people felt as though 'I went to war for my country; now it's time for my country to do for me.'" Carter's expectations, as I read them, were tied more to the relationship between the individual and the state than to that between the individual and American society writ large.

Carter and Pete are joined in their view that military sacrifice should be rewarded with postwar rights and privileges commensurate with full citizenship by another Korean War veteran. Dr. Carey, mustering out of the army in March of 1953 after serving with the Fifteenth Regiment of the 3rd Infantry Division, returned to the Jim Crow South. Like the other veterans, Carey voiced his disappointment at the stubbornness of Jim Crow. With palpable anger, he says that, "I expected the barriers of segregation to come tumbling down. When I came back, they were not down. And I had some problems because of it."

Carey's displeasure with Jim Crow differed from that of the other veterans, however, in at least one way: he was prepared to take by force the respect he felt he had earned by fighting for the country. He was ready to do harm to whites who denied him the dignity to which he perceived himself entitled. "It was just by the grace of God that I didn't kill somebody and end up in the penitentiary, because I made an attempt a couple of times," he recalls. Elaborating on the source of his anger, he cites a now familiar formula—military service merits a measure of respect: "I sort of felt like that if a young person puts his life on the line for his country, there ought to be some kind of respect for that, and some allowances made for it." Although Carey was the first veteran I spoke to who openly mentioned killing whites who did not recognize the sacrifice he had made, his rage was driven by the same thing mentioned by other veterans: America's refusal to recognize their sacrifices.

Another group of veterans referred to tangible instances of discrimination to make the connection between their military service and postwar expectations more concrete. In this regard, Stewart's experience after the Korean War is illustrative. Upon returning to Texas in 1953, he was disappointed at the conditions under which African Americans lived in the South. "I was hoping it [change] would've occurred," he recalls. "I was disappointed that it really hadn't to an extent, and of course that little remark I heard about niggers at the bus station sure didn't help me none, you know? That let me know that at least down there, they hadn't changed." Stewart illustrates his point: "For instance, they still had the sign 'colored' up; I guess that was probably one of my biggest disappointments, especially at the bus stations and at the train stations."

Black veterans' postwar expectations need not have been great to result in anger when they were not met. Some of the veterans with whom I spoke were pragmatic, even pessimistic, about change. They had no faith that war or military service would change the ways in which whites viewed them. Mr. Fuller's feeling about race, war, and change illustrates this line of thought. Born and raised in Camden, Alabama, to parents who both had a sixth grade education, he was drafted in 1951, served in the army air corps during the Korean War, and eventually earned a master's degree. Because of his experiences with white domination, he had no expectation when he returned from overseas that war would change anything. With a hint of resignation, he recalls, "I did not expect [social conditions] to be different. I knew I was going back to where I was going before, and I knew that the laws of the land had not changed. I knew I was going back to . . . the same house I was living in, right? . . . so I didn't expect a difference." Nevertheless, Fuller felt entitled to better treatment than he received. He recalls "a couple incidents" that "irritated" him when he returned: "One was having to go before a voter registration poll, or whatever, to take a test in order to get the right to vote. . . . A guy asked me three or four questions to determine whether or not I would be given the right to vote. I remember that very distinctly, and I felt really angry about that particular thing, especially after having served in the military." Fuller was angered by the indignity of sitting in the room with someone who was "Caucasian" who had the power to determine whether or not he would be able to vote. In a rather dejected tone, Fuller asked, "He didn't have to ask me questions, right?"

Another incident occurred during a trip to the Department of Motor Vehicles to apply for a driver's license. "I remember this so well," Fuller says. "I think it was around one o' clock or something like that, and the policy at that point in time was they took Caucasians before they took adjunct [i.e., black] Americans." He waited patiently until approximately three fifteen. At that moment, he recalls, "several Caucasian high school students came in to take their tests, after which someone came over and told me that they wouldn't be able to take me that day." Such incidents "stick out in your mind," he says. To have endured these racial slights "after serving in the military" made them particularly difficult to bear: "So then you get a flashback to having been in the military, and then you have to live with that [discrimination]!" While he did not expect much improvement in race relations upon his return, Fuller nonetheless viewed his military service in terms commensurate with republicanism. In his estimation, military service entitled him to the right to vote and to obtain a driver's license without a hassle. He concluded from these experiences, "I thought at that point, after serving in the military, I was more of an American than, apparently, the system thought I was."

Some of the veterans who believed that their demonstration of national loyalty through military service entitled them to better treatment upon their return to America were sorely disappointed; others were downright angry. Shaw felt rather differently. Unlike his contemporaries, who observed no progress in the wake of war, Shaw declares that "things had changed" when he returned home. He explains, "African Americans were being assimilated into more respectful positions rather than just shining shoes or being hose boys or carrying out typical old-school slavery kinds of behavior. They were being integrated into vocational skills and things of that type."

Change, however, was not confined to how whites viewed blacks and their contribution to war. In Shaw's estimation, black Southerners began to exercise more agency, becoming more assertive in the wake of both wars. According to Shaw, something changed within the black community in the South: "They realized that they could change things—the black man should not and would not accept what we had accepted before the war." Black Southerners became more "conscious," he says, in the 1940s and early '50s. Shaw suggests that progress was gradual and difficult: "I think it got continuously better . . . but having to push it . . . it didn't happen naturally. I think every progress we've made, we had to pay a fee for it. You know what I'm talking about; nothing is just a given."

In this regard, Shaw's sentiments are similar to Carter's: both men saw the need for black Southerners to actively seek change. Also like Carter, Shaw believes the return of veterans to the South had a catalytic effect. He recalls that "when . . . veterans demonstrated beyond reasonable doubt that we had the same respect for the flag, and ability, you know, they decided, 'Well, these folk are no different than anyone else.'" At this point, he suggests, whites began to treat blacks with a little more humanity—especially black men who were known to have served in the military.

With the notable exception of Shaw, then, the veterans I interviewed were less than satisfied with the speed of change. Even Shaw, however, mentioned that change did not come without activism. They anticipated that the country would recognize these sacrifices and reward them. When this did not happen, the veterans were disappointed. Some placed part of the blame on black Southerners for not demanding change. Others were more angry than disappointed. While the veterans' reactions to the postwar status of black Southerners differed, they shared the same source: a moral claim to equality based upon their service. In other words, they felt entitled to more equal treatment. In this sense, the sentiments of the veterans are in keeping with the republican narrative. Their disappointment and experiences of ongoing domination, though, transformed these sentiments into black republicanism.

A Source of Republican Criticism: Military Service and Entitlement

Strictly speaking, being entitled to something means having a right to it because of one's acts or qualities. The republican social contract, which is emphasized during and shortly after war (Krebs 2006), is the contract that black veterans used to determine their entitlements. Every society rests on a set of ideological norms that serve as a benchmark against which entitlement is assessed (Deutsch 1985). In American society, in which merit-based individualism is indigenous to national politicocultural beliefs, one's entitlements are proportionate to one's investment in society (Deutsch 1985; Hochschild 1981; Sampson 1975). Thus, it is easy to see why entitlement is invested with moral force (Major 1994), and why it is therefore affectively experienced and motivationally important. For justice to obtain, the actor's outcomes must be commensurate with the act (Lerner 1975).

Veterans, as we have seen, believe that military service reflects good citizenship and conclude that they are full members of the political community because of their service.[5] If veterans subscribe to a black republican worldview, we ought to expect their critiques of the postwar South to be motivated by their sense of entitlement borne of their military service. A radical egalitarian critique, by contrast, should be tethered to the feeling that America was failing to live up to its founding values absent references to military service.[6]

In some cases, the veterans I spoke to drew on history to illustrate their anger and to generate criticism. Mr. Williams, for instance, suggests that America has never paid its debt in full to its black veterans. He laments that "this country refused to know that black units such as the Ninth and Tenth Cavalry . . . was taking care of the police force of the Western Frontier and what troops have done throughout the history of this United States . . . that blacks have [been] charged [with] the hardest fighting position out there and never got the recognition for it." For Williams, the failure of America, and particularly the American South, to recognize the contributions of black soldiers during war is a symptom of a larger

---

[5] Of course, this view may seem a bit self-serving—perhaps a means of elevating their contributions to society. But it is not only veterans who feel this way; members of the wider political community also see military service as indicative of good citizenship (Conover et al. 1991).

[6] Criticism enjoys a long and venerable tradition in black political thought. But what separates criticism generated by black republicanism from, say, the Jeremiadic tradition, identified by Howard-Pitney (2005), is that the fact that black republican criticism is based upon the need for America to realize its values based upon black military service. Criticism in the Jeremiadic tradition, by contrast, is rooted in religion.

trend. Black Southerners, he believes, will never receive their just due because of the inability of whites to see them as equals. "What is wrong with this country," he protests, "is that they cannot recognize what the black man do for this country, period. Job-wise, teaching-wise, military-wise, because they still look at him like he's still a slave."

Lack of recognition was a recurring theme in my conversations with veterans. Mr. Baines also feels as though black soldiers deserved more recognition than they received after the war. His view, however, is based upon his personal experiences rather than on American history. "Well," he says, "when I came back in 1953, after I'd been there [in Korea] for three years, I was thinking that things would have been better after I'd fought that war." He thought that when he and other black soldiers returned that their service would be appreciated by all. He recalls, "I felt like while I was looking at some movies before I went in the army, I used to see the whites coming in here with the stripes [on uniforms] and with the bands playing, the awards they were given. They just gave them more recognition. And I thought that maybe we should get the same thing. We were a part of the war; we'd given our best. We lost a lot of people, and we didn't get the recognition that we should have gotten."

Beyond his disappointment with the reception he and other black servicemen received on their return to the South from Korea, Baines was concerned that his efforts in Korea failed to benefit the black community at large. His dismay is apparent upon recalling his return to the postwar South, and the disparity he observed. "It gave me a bitter taste in my mouth because here I am, way overseas fighting, and my people, African American and black, they are not even free, they can't even vote." Indeed, Baines becomes visibly agitated when he considers the educational and economic disparities black Southerners faced in the aftermath of the Korean War, especially given the sacrifices made by black veterans, himself included. He remembers, "They still had all the segregated schools, and we had poor, menial paying jobs . . . so it kind of makes you a little angry when you're over there dodging those bullets and things just trying to keep your life, and you think about what you're going back to, you know?" Some soldiers were more than discouraged with the news from home—they were devastated, so much so that Baines notes, "A lot of those guys stayed over there, overseas, they wouldn't come back."

Baines's criticism focuses upon the immediate aftermath of the Korean War, a time during which he and other veterans were in a state of disbelief at the relentless oppression to which black Southerners were subjected. His criticism was motivated by the juxtaposition between the notions of equality for which he fought and the conditions to which he returned. Likewise, Mr. Womack's criticism is anchored to his normative expectations about America, but his angst is tethered to more recent events; these drive his pessimism concerning equality. "Equality means I don't have a flag. This [the American flag] ain't my flag." "It ain't yours either," he says, nodding in my direction. He continues, "If you go somewhere to this day, you'd be better treated in a foreign country than you would be here. I'm not a racist, and I'm not upset. This is the best country that I could say I had the opportunity of thirty-four years in the military that I have been in. But I'm in Texas right now. This is one of the [most] racist states there is." As proof, he cites the murder of James Byrd, observing, "If a man gets drug behind an automobile, a truck, and people say it's not racist, there's something wrong."

Eventually Womack focuses upon his personal torment. He is angry that whites fail to see him as a civic equal. He is even more troubled, though, when he contemplates how his military service failed to afford him better treatment:

> I've been to almost every country in the world, so I have to say if I had to pick a place to live, this is the place to live. And I'm still living as a second-class citizen, because there are places I can't go. I was a citizen in the United States Army in uniform, [and] we got put off the bus in St. Petersburg, Virginia, and I had already been in combat. So you're telling me what it takes to be equal? I got on a uniform! I fought for my country! Yet I can't sit on the bus? That's some bullshit!"

Mr. McWilliams sees things slightly differently. Unlike Womack, whose criticism was laced with international comparisons and passion, McWilliams is initially more measured, due in part, I believe, to his modest expectations for postwar change: "I couldn't say that I was fighting for freedom, because at the same time I was in Korea, they was lynching blacks, killing blacks . . . blacks was having a helluva time here in the United States. So it was not for freedom, because we were not free over here." On further reflection, he recalls, "Segregation was very . . . Jim Crow was very embedded in the United States. It wasn't freedom. You know, once you came from Korea, it was 'Black go this way, white go that way'—as soon as you got back to the United States."

In McWilliams's mind, black people in America were having a rough time of it even as black men were fighting and dying overseas. When he and other black servicemen returned, they returned to the status quo; nothing had changed. Eventually, however, this arrangement proved insufficient. "Soldiers," he recalls, "expected to go back and be treated fairly, be able to equally apply for jobs, or the same thing, that they'd be able to travel or go places or buy a home where they wanted to." His military service—especially his experience serving in integrated units in Korea—had a lot to do with his insistence that he be treated equally:

"You seen what was happening on the other side of the fence, how green those other people's pastures or backyards were, and you wanted yours to be green, too. In essence, you wanted to be treated the same as your neighbor who was white. You cut his grass, cut mine, too. You know, pick up his garbage, pick mine up, too." Why did he insist on this? "Sacrifice," he maintains, "has quite a bit to do with the equation. Quite a bit. You figure that, shit, I done this here for you, at least you could pick up my garbage—just using these terms like that—pick up my garbage same as you pick up theirs."

Mr. Williams's story is similar. A veteran of the Korean War, he was born in Louisiana but raised in Houston, Texas. His mother had a fourth-grade education; he never knew his father. Williams served for ten years, mostly with the 101st Airborne division as a Ranger. He recalls very clearly an encounter that occurred in 1957 upon his return home. In fact, according to him, it was "the worst thing that ever hurt me in my life." Williams was ordered to report to Fort Chaffey, Arkansas, for a short time, after which he would be honorably discharged. He and a white buddy with whom he had served departed Arkansas, taking a flight to Dallas. Williams had been gone so long from the South that he had become unfamiliar with its ways. He recalls "forgetting about the signs that said 'Colored go in here, white go there.'" Williams and his buddy had to make a pit stop. Thinking nothing of it, he remembers "walk[ing] into the white restroom with a uniform on and ribbons on my chest." "A white man walked in with short sleeves and necktie and a white shirt," he recalls with increasing anger. After the white man relieved himself, Williams reports, "he turned and zipped up his pants . . . and he looked at me, and he said, 'Huh! Because a nigger gets his uniform on and a couple of ribbons on his chest, he still think he could do what a white man can do.'"

After a short pause he continued, saying that "it took me five years to get over what that man done said to me." Stunned, his initial reaction was to want to "hurt that man." After all, "he going to call me a nigger while [during the war] he had heat while I was freezing [in Korea]?" Williams, however, realizes the larger commitment he and other veterans made to democracy: "As much as I got shot up for him. . . . But I realized that he had the right to call me anything or say anything he wanted to say to me, because when I fought for this country, I fought for the right of freedom and free speech." Putting it all into perspective, Williams discusses why he was able to put such personal insults behind him: "So, from that day to this day, nothing bothered me, because whatever happened in this country, whether I disliked it or not, I fought for the right for people to do as they please."

Mr. Stewart's view is very similar. A native of Beaumont, Texas, Stewart grew up in a single-parent home where his mother, a cook, raised four children. After separating from the service, Stewart went on to earn a general equivalency diploma and eventually became a chef, retiring after thirty years in that occupation. Stewart recalls that he "was expecting big change" after the war. "When I went over and served the country and a lot of blacks died, and it looked like things should've got loose, been more prestigious for us back home," he muses. "But things didn't really change until I'm gonna say after 1966 or '65, because I got out in '62, you see, and they hadn't changed by then."

Stewart believed that his service and the sacrifices of other black veterans should have resulted in better postwar treatment for black Southerners. He was particularly alarmed by the manner in which whites continued to observe racial conventions after the war. He became frustrated upon his return to the South "because they were still calling you those words and you still had to go to the back door." Stewart explained, "You were looking for all that to be changed after you'd been over there and come back." He compared the plight of African Americans to immigrants: "People come from a foreign country and get a better break. They do," he stresses in continuing disbelief.

Other veterans tied their expectations of better treatment more directly to sacrifices they made on the battlefield. Mr. Baines, a Korean War veteran, locates his frustration with the postwar treatment of black Southerners in what he perceives as breach of the compact made between the nation-state and the individual: "I put my life on the line; I'm talking about when you're over there in that foxhole and you see your buddies and everybody get shot and [there is] blood everywhere and you realize that man, these peoples [the enemy] here are real. I mean I may not make it back, and in hindsight, I didn't think I was going to make it many a day." After surviving one battle after another, Baines says that he thought, "When I get back to America, things ought to be better for us." When he returned and found the South "still the same," his reaction was, "Man, that hurts."

One interpretation of the veterans' perception that whites failed to acknowledge their contributions to the nation's security is that black veterans simply desired recognition, but a second and probably more likely interpretation is that they hoped that recognition would set the stage for racial reform. This better explains the anger the veterans expressed in their criticism of the postwar South. These criticisms were based on the veterans' perception of injustice—the unjust ignoring of their wartime sacrifice and suffering, as well as the injustice of the dismal social conditions to which they returned.

FROM CRITICISM TO ACTIVISM

Naturally, the depth and conviction of the criticism leveled by black veterans against America begs the question whether they moved beyond voicing their grievances to act. We already know that famous veterans such as Medgar Evers and Hosea Williams contested domination. We know less, though, about the willingness of so-called ordinary veterans to challenge racial conventions. As it turns out, the veterans I interviewed were eager to challenge white authority. The interviews reveal two modes of resistance: one personal, the other collective. To the extent that entitlement provides an impetus for action (Major 1994; Shaver et al. 1987), I argue that black veterans drew on republican rhetoric as motivation for resistance against internal domination. Thus, their resistance was tied to their military service. To investigate these claims, I asked veterans how, if at all, military service changed them and whether or not they acted on this perceived change.

Although interracial contact was limited, taking place mainly during garrison duty and in transit during the Second World War, it was sometimes an occasion on which black servicemen realized the illegitimacy of Jim Crow policies. This situation triggered Mr. Shaw's racial awareness. In 1945, he was in transit to the Philippines on a ship in which he "was in the very hole of that ship, you know, about four [people] deep," he says referring to the crowded conditions aboard ship. Upon earning the rank of E-5 in the Philippines, he was allowed to roam the top deck of the ship in transit back to America. There, he says, "we [black and white noncommissioned officers] were also intermixed as opposed to all being separate." Once he reached the United States and had to travel from California to Colorado, the black and white officers were again segregated. At that time, he says, he "became aware of the difference" he had experienced while overseas. Shaw says: "It was . . . an indescribable thing. . . . I was not happy to continue anymore with the status quo."

Apparently, facing racism overseas and in transit was difficult, if barely tolerable, but Shaw's experience on a bus in Dallas cemented, for him, the militant disposition that he carries to this day. "When I came back to Dallas where I was spending quite a bit of time," he says, "I got on the front of the bus with my three stripes on my flight jacket, and I was indirectly told to get off of the bus." Elaborating on this, he recalls that "some maids got on the same bus going across town to work and he [the driver] directed his comments to them, but he implied it to me, you know, 'You have to sit in the back.'" The bus driver told the maids to "get in the back of the bus, and they did." Shaw refused to comply with the driver. He concludes, "I don't think I've been on a bus since. I knew

that I had changed [during his service] . . . and I'm sure I was not alone."
Shaw searches to summarize what he took away from experiencing discrimination in post–World War II America: "We just kept looking for an
opportunity that would not associate with being discriminated against."
Enduring discrimination in the postwar South, in other words, ceased to
be an option for Shaw and many other black veterans.

A bus also served as a locus of confrontation for Mr. Thornton. After
the war, he split his time between Texas and Louisiana. Though Thornton says that whites chose not to openly challenge black GIs in uniform
who rode the bus, he remembers that they were uncomfortable with the
manner in which black soldiers ignored Southern convention. "It wasn't
hostility," he says, "but, 'Should we ask him to move?' is what was on
their minds." He remembers one incident while traveling in Louisiana.
He sensed the displeasure of the bus driver when he decided to ignore
social custom and remained seated in the "white" section of the bus,
something the white driver failed to appreciate. "I guess I was about the
third seat back, and I was sitting next to the window, and I didn't get off,
and some people got on. This white boy got on and sat next to me and he
spoke. . . . I could see the bus driver looking at us through the mirror.
The bus driver looked like he wanted to come and ask me to move.
That's the impression I got, but I had something for him, and I was not
going to move!"

Thornton indicated that prior to spending time in the military he
would have simply moved or not sat in the restricted section in the first
place. Like Shaw, however, something about him had changed: "I guess
the fact that I had gone and served, I felt that I was entitled to sit where I
wanted to. I felt that I had the right to do it, and this is one of the things
that we went to the military for." He was inspired in part by the man
who was his drill sergeant during basic training, a black Alabamian who,
as he recalls, "was mean as hell." The sergeant instilled within his charges
the feeling that their service counted for something. Thornton then repeats what his drill instructor told them: "The sergeant used to tell us all
the time, 'Remember that you will really have changed your country to
make it better for those that are at home. So when you get out, you go
home and you help make it better, 'cause it's not going to get better un-
less you help to make it better.'"

Shaw's and Thornton's recollections describe militancy at the individual level; in the absence of group-based support, they resisted white
supremacy. There were others, however, who participated in more collective efforts, including Dr. Bashful. When he returned to Louisiana in
1946, Bashful says, he "expected at least . . . there would be change . . .
[and] the veterans and other people would be given the rights of citizenship. Voting and maybe jobs would be given to people who qualified. I

expected better to take place. . . . In other words, I expected people to be treated properly and fairly." Because Bashful "was not satisfied with what happened in the South," he went to graduate school in order to "get equal rights" for himself and others. A math major as an undergraduate, Bashful switched to political science because he wanted to both learn about and teach a subject that would help him better understand the political reasons for the continued oppression of black Southerners. Military service increased his desire for equal rights, as he says, "beyond doubt." Bashful remembers being "dead set on getting the rights that I should have, by whatever means within the law." While he disapproved of the idea of using firearms for anything but self-defense, he was so frustrated with the condition of black Southerners that he "sometimes felt like putting [his] shotgun on the corner and blowing down people."

As a graduate student at the University of Illinois, Bashful encountered some of the same social practices that caused him to leave the South for a short time. He involved himself in the campus movement to resist segregation: "When I came back in 1948, I went to Champaign, Illinois. That's almost the South; it has many ways of the South." The restaurants across the street from the university, for instance, refused to serve African Americans. In response, Bashful remembers, he and other black students "drew a picket line around one of 'em" in 1946." After the students protested for a few days, he reports, the local owners of segregated restaurants and movie theaters "all capitulated." Bashful was the leader of the protest, involving other students and members of the track team. His experience at leadership in the military as an officer and his determination to achieve equality convinced him to take the initiative. "I'll put it this way," Bashful said. "Somebody had to do it, and I just said, 'I'm going to have to.'"

Carey, a veteran of the Korean War, had a similar reaction upon returning to the South on medical leave. He had sustained an injury to his leg during combat after he was shot four times. Carey often frequented a service station not far from his home, where he fueled his car and spoke with the relatively young manager. Though the fellow was white, he and Carey had something in common: both had served in Korea. Carey recalls hobbling up to the water fountain and taking a sip from it. "That was a no-no," he sighs, "but I drank anyway." One day when he did this, an old white man was present who had just concluded filling up his truck and was preparing to leave. He said something to Carey, but Carey did not hear what it was because they were too far away from each other. So Carey hobbled over to him and asked him to repeat what he said. At that point, Carey recalls, "he called me a nig—the magic name—and said I shouldn't be drinking from the white folks' fountain." The white man then began to drive away. "I was on crutches," Carey remembers, "and I tried to get him as he pulled away from me. My full intention was to kill him." After mulling the confrontation over, Carey concluded, "The Good Lord was looking out for me, because I was angry enough several times to just kill somebody."

The military had a significant impact on his bearing after the war. "Having been exposed to other . . . cultures, having had the military training," Carey explains, "I would not have had that reaction had I not left home to go into the military. I probably would have submitted to the culture. . . . I probably would not have drunk from the fountain." He explained how his military service allowed him to resist Southern racial expectations: "The culture was [that] blacks were secondhand citizens. But having been in the military, I wasn't taking any of that. In the military," he says with pride, "you're trained to fight, and you're trained to die if you have to. That's the best I can explain it."

Carey's feelings about equality and respect motivated him to become a movement activist. Like Bashful, he, too, attended graduate school, enrolling at Florida A&M University. He was an active participant in the civil rights movement on and around campus. At the time, he saw participation in movement-based protest as a "duty to [himself] and to [his] race." Carey made it clear that, in his opinion, "Every person has a duty to make the situation better for his race." Apparently, the atmosphere around the university was conducive to protest activity, and as the sit-ins got underway in the late 1950s, Florida A&M served as one of the training centers for potential protesters. Carey remembers the training in nonviolent protest: "They sit you in a stool and then they come a-yelling at you, yelling in your face and spit on you." Carey had a difficult time adjusting to such treatment: "So when the guy spit on me, I drew back [to hit him]. They said, 'No, you won't. We can't use you for this.' So they put me on the strategy team." While a graduate student, Carey helped to organize the NAACP at Florida A&M and drove his car in the motor pool during the Tallahassee bus boycott in 1956. He channeled his frustration with the postwar social order into positive political action.

Finally, Thornton's activism was not confined to the episode on the bus. Apparently he accepted the challenge issued by above-mentioned drill instructor, because he also participated in some of the collective action associated with the movement. He did so because, he says, "Number one, I believe in it." Beset with familial and financial responsibilities, however, his participation was limited. As he tells it, "I felt it was the right thing to do, and yet I was cautious in that I didn't have the finances. I wanted to go to Selma . . . and join Dr. King's march, but I also had a family. I had small kids and my priority was with my family." However, when blacks undertook protest in Houston, where he lived, he joined in. So often were he and other protesters harassed that his wife got into the habit of asking whether or not he had been beaten that day. One such protest, during which they boycotted a Kress department store downtown for not allowing blacks to eat at the lunch counter, forced the store to change its policy. The next week, his son was able to have a hotdog at an integrated counter. Beyond his belief in the cause, Thornton was able to act on his convictions because of his military experience, reasoning that, "I didn't have any fear because I felt like I had already been through hell in Korea. It doesn't get any worse."

If this small sample of veterans is representative of larger patterns, then we can conclude that military service was a catalyst for change among black Americans in the 1940s and '50s. In addition to providing the normative impetus for change, it is clear that something about these veterans' military service braced them to challenge the racial order. From refusing to move to the back of the bus, to organizing insurgent activities, roughly two-thirds of the veterans I interviewed reported resisting white supremacy. What's more, all of the veterans interviewed who participated in activism of any kind cited their military service as a motivation for interrogating the status quo, a finding consistent with black republicanism. What they had seen overseas, the values for which they fought, and the confidence they gathered through arms bearing made it difficult for them to accede to white supremacy as they once had. Indeed, the conditions of life in the segregated South at times posed a challenge to their manhood. But the military had trained them to not to run from a fight.

• • •

The interviews I conducted illustrate veterans' critical commitment to America and their subscription to black republicanism. Using the language of republicanism, these black veterans identified with the nation and at least one of its political institutions, citizenship. Race, however, repeatedly came up in our discussions, making it clear that experiences with domination affected the veterans' thinking. Time and again these men drew on republican rhetoric, modified to fit their experience with white domination, and used it to frame their claims upon America for social justice. The normative meaning of military service guided their postwar expectations. By virtue of their sacrifice they believed that social conditions should have improved for the black community on their return. Criticism also highlighted their military service; the veterans expressed disappointment in the lack of appreciation for their sacrifices. Military experience served a practical purpose in these veterans' responses to the postwar situation, however; it prepared and motivated them to actively challenge domination. Furthermore, these sentiments may not be reduced to whether or not one volunteered or was drafted. Of the seventeen interviewees tapped for this book, eight had been drafted; the balance, for various reasons, had volunteered to serve. Generally, conscripts and volunteers differ in their views on the military and the meaning of military service with the latter taking a relatively dim view of both (Moskos 1970). Almost without exception, this was not the case among my respondents.

Veterans' attitudes about national identification shed new light upon how black Americans view their attachments. Consider identification with the nation. Relatively speaking, blacks are less likely than whites to identify with America (Citrin et al. 2001; Sidanius et al. 1997). But the veterans I interviewed insist upon identifying with the nation, even if their identification is somewhat critical. We may speculate that their attachment reflects a generational difference—that older blacks may feel more attached to the nation because they have grown more conservative with age. But we must also consider that these men were born and reared in the Jim Crow South. Why should they feel attached to a nation in which they were second-class citizens? The black veterans I interviewed identify with the nation because being American, for them, means being a first-class citizen of the nation—it is a right that they have earned. Their insistence upon identifying as American also appears to be tied to a sense of recognition, of membership in the wider political community.

Likewise, perceptions of the institution of citizenship are structured by race. For the most part, the men I interviewed recognized and appreciated the import of American citizenship. But none of this appreciation came without criticism. With few exceptions, each veteran qualified the importance of American citizenship, lamenting that America has far to go before it fulfills the promise of democracy. Several of the veterans felt that racism had affected their ability to take advantage of the rights and privileges associated with citizenship. Their critical attitudes toward citizenship were stimulated, at least in part, by the disappointment of their postwar expectations of a more racially equitable South.

Black republicanism appears to have structured the opinions and actions of these veterans once they returned to the South. Judging by the tone of their comments, military service symbolized their commitment to the common good, for which they expected to be rewarded. In the classical republican account, rewards are not necessary: citizens are willing to go to war to *preserve* freedom, among other things. Black Southerners, by contrast, agreed to fight because they expected to *gain* freedom— hence, *black* republicanism. Criticism, also central to classical republican thought, was similarly "raced" to the extent that it was fueled by references to military service. The veterans I interviewed criticized the state and society for failing to at least recognize their contributions to the war effort.

Traces of black republicanism were perhaps most visible when the veterans discussed various forms of activism, for it was in these situations that they drew upon both the normative meaning of their military service and what it symbolized as an experience. In general, they justified their activism by referring to the purpose for which they served: the *achievement* of equality. And if Carey is any indication, veterans drew on the military experience to sustain their efforts to do battle with Jim Crow. Trained to be fearless and in many cases accustomed to confronting racism overseas, these veterans saw no obstacle to confronting racism at home.

This chapter and the preceding chapter, then, have provided support for my theory of black republicanism. To a greater or lesser extent, black veterans feel an attachment to America, and they use their military service as a basis for criticism and activism. Still, a skeptic may pose at least three issues with which I must contend. First, I make much of the claim that military experience affected how black veterans viewed the South to which they returned, and ultimately guided the resistance of those who chose to do so. Since a principal purpose of the conversations we had was designed to assess the import of military service on their postwar views, it's natural that they'd emphasize how it affected their perception of the postwar South. Yet, as we have seen, the extent to which the military affected postwar attitudes and behavior isn't without some variation. For some, in other words, the military had no impact; for one or two, it may have even made things worse.

Second, one may credibly argue that it's not altogether clear for whom the veterans fought on their return. In other words, did the veterans who sought to resist Jim Crow on returning to the South do so on behalf of their fellow Southerners, the black community? Or, did their resistance amount to correcting a perceived *personal* wrong, slights and injustices that, in view of their sacrifice to the country, they felt they didn't deserve? For many of these veterans it's clear that they were upset their sacrifices failed to earn for the race the equality for which they were willing to pay the ultimate price. It's also true that some veterans used the first person to describe particular instance of discrimination or racism. On this basis, one might question whether or not activism was undertaken to correct a personal indignity in light of one's service, or whether resistance was undertaken on behalf of the community. I think it's both; they're not mutually exclusive.

It's certainly the case that some veterans drew on instances of personal discrimination and individual instances of resistance during the interviews. But this doesn't mean that the community wasn't also important to them. To me, as the person who conducted the interviews, it's clear that they used first-person narrative for merely illustrative purposes, an example of how they had *personally* experienced discrimination and racism. These experiences often triggered subsequent resistance and activism for themselves *and* for the community. But even if we take the extreme as truth, where some veterans may have resisted for purely personal reasons, I believe black republicanism remains largely intact, for regardless of whether or not veterans resisted on behalf of the community, or they did so because they felt personally offended, in the end it was their perception of the relationship between military service and citizenship that ultimately served as a motive to resist white supremacy. At least this much is clear from the interviews. What's most important, and what the following chapters will illustrate, is that, more often than not, veterans contested Jim Crow.

A final charge to which I must respond rests upon my ability to apply these findings to veterans as a group. In short, I have so far produced relatively few observations on which to base my findings, which hinders generalizing about black republicanism among veterans in the mass public. It is possible that the veterans with whom I came into contact were exceptional in some regard. Furthermore, it is not clear whether the use of republican rhetoric among black veterans enjoys any explanatory power. That is, when other sources of activism in the black community are taken into account, such as black civic organizations, black republicanism may turn out to be a red herring. Such a finding would strengthen the assertion that military service, on its own terms, fails to activate insurgency. Drawing on survey data, the next two chapters are dedicated to confirming and generalizing the explanatory power of black republicanism.

CHAPTER 5

Exploring the Attitudinal Consequences
of African American Military Experience

Black Southerners entered the turbulent 1960s with tremendous momentum. Only a few years removed from the Supreme Court's *Brown v. Board of Education of Topeka* decision, their hopes were further buoyed by the passage of the first civil rights legislation in over eighty years. The Civil Rights Acts of 1957 and 1960 sought to ease blacks' access to the polls in the South. While neither these acts nor the *Brown* decision had the immediate impact they were intended to have (Rosenberg 1991), one should not underestimate their symbolic value to black Southerners. Taken together, the *Brown* victory and the legislative enactments contributed to the perceived expansion of political opportunities (McAdam 1999).

Even so, many black Southerners failed to completely embrace change. In 1964, for instance, almost two-thirds of African Americans surveyed in Atlanta agreed with the proposition that blacks should first demonstrate their fitness for equal rights before they received them (Marx 1967). Black Southerners, moreover, were twice as likely as non-Southern blacks to believe that social change was happening too fast; and to the extent that they wished for change, they frowned on protest as a means of achieving it. Moreover, 58 percent of black Southerners versus 32 percent of blacks residing in cities beyond the South believed the "Negroes should spend more time praying and less time demonstrating." Black Southerners, in short, were more conservative and patient than blacks elsewhere in the country (Marx 1967, 44).[1] To be sure, the core of the civil rights movement was firmly established, with cadres of activists within churches, among university students, and in civil rights organizations (McAdam 1999; Morris 1984). Nevertheless, as late as 1964,

---

[1] According to Marx, a "conservative seems happy in his place or, rather, the place relegated to him by racism; he is not opposed to discrimination . . . is content with the speed of social change, feels that negroes must show they deserve rights before they are given them, desires fewer civil rights demonstrations and would not participate in such demonstrations, and thinks negroes should spend more time praying and less time demonstrating" (1967, 44). His survey included 1,119 interviews, 492 of which were samples in cities beyond the South. The balance of the cases were collected from Chicago, New York City, Birmingham, and Atlanta. For more details, see Marx (1967).

black Southerners as a whole were relatively reluctant to grant unqualified support to the movement.

How do black veterans fit into this picture of a largely, relatively conservative populace in the South? In the two preceding chapters, I illustrated how military experience transformed black veterans, providing a new perspective from which these black Southerners viewed white supremacy while giving them a new sense of agency with which to combat it. I indicated that this transformation informed the attitudes and behavior of these veterans on their return to the South, giving them a belief system in which criticism and activism were motivated by their military experience(s). But chapters 3 and 4 only dealt with a relatively small number of veterans. It remains possible that veterans in the mass public were more likely to adhere to the respect for authority and tradition that was also part of their military socialization.

In the present chapter I begin to explore how black republicanism structured the attitudes and behavior of Southern veterans in the mass public by examining hypotheses related to change in the South, comparing Southern black veterans' political attitudes to those of black Southerners generally. One claim that I test, to which I have already alluded, suggests that black Southerners were less inclined than blacks elsewhere to challenge white dominance. Attitudes in support of "business as usual" in the South impeded the realization of democracy, since the status quo affected the ability of black Southerners to effectively participate in self-governance. The issue is where black veterans stood. Were they more like fellow black Southerners who grudgingly accepted the Southern way of life in which blacks were second-class citizens? Or, were their attitudes more similar to blacks elsewhere? I also examine some of the general policy preferences of black Southerners, particularly those related to the role of the federal government, after which I explore more specific policy preferences, perhaps the most important of which were attitudes toward integration. How, if at all, did black veterans' attitudes on these issues depart from those of other black Southerners'?

Based upon my interpretation of the interviews, I make two claims. First, we should expect black veterans, more than black Southerners at large, to have embraced change, but to have shied away from liberal policies requiring state assistance. As the interviews indicate, it may be the case that their experience in the military with segregation and discrimination caused veterans to develop distrust for the state. In addition, we should expect black veterans, more than black Southerners generally, to have favored policies that promoted integration in principle and to have been even keener than their nonveteran peers to implement these policies. As we shall see, using the language of republicanism on the part of black veterans transcended the rhetoric used by the veterans I interviewed. It seems to have also shaped the attitudes of black veterans in the mass public, causing them to become relatively critical of white supremacy.

In the present chapter as well as chapter 6, in which I examine the behavior of veterans in the mass public, I draw on data collected in the early 1960s for the Negro Political Participation Study to test my claims. Donald Matthews and James Prothro served as the principal investigators for this study, which examined the social and political attitudes of blacks and whites in the eleven former Confederate states of the South. For immediate purposes, the study drew a representative sample of 168 black Southerners, augmented with another 450 interviews. All respondents were at least eighteen years old. Since the substantive focus of the present project is veterans, and because women serving in the military were few and far between in World War II and the Korean War, the following analyses include black men only, reducing the number of respondents to 246 black Southerners. (See appendix A for details.)

Ultimately, this book aims to capture the effect of military experience on black Southerners and resistance to Jim Crow. More to the point, and as I highlighted in the introduction, this study seeks to examine the political learning that took place among black Southerners thanks to the symbolism associated with serving in the military—that is, what it meant to them, as well as some of the institutional experiences conferred through serving. Of course, this includes the equal treatment to which many black Southerners were exposed overseas, and their experiences fighting racism in the ranks. Adherence to such criteria eliminates two groups that would otherwise serve as reasonable comparisons. The first is white men. After all, they, too, served, and were affected by their military experiences (Brooks 2004; MacLean 2006; Mettler 2005b). Nevertheless, the present study aims to assess the extent to which military service spurred black Southerners to resist white supremacy, something with which white veterans didn't have to contend.

Experiencing racial oppression wasn't the only problem for black women; they were also forced to endure sexism. In fact, it was the sexism to which most women were subjected that prevented black women from serving in the requisite numbers to include in the analysis. Until 1967, when the 2 percent cap on women's participation in the military was lifted, black women, like most women, didn't have much opportunity to serve in the military. Much of this may be traced to the early days of the republic when gender mores tethered arms bearing to masculinity, effectively gendering citizenship (Kerber 1998). Hence, even during the Second World War, the largest military mobilization in American history, black women represented roughly 4 percent (4,000) of the approximately

1 million blacks who served during the war. Such a low incidence rate suggests that very few black women were exposed to the type of political learning that accompanied military service.

Black Veterans' Attitudes toward Southern Traditionalism: Resisting the Status Quo

Why were black Southerners less likely than blacks in other parts of the country to challenge the status quo? We should start looking for an explanation in Southern culture, part of which was driven by social and economic considerations after Reconstruction. For the New South to thrive, both socially and economically, securing cheap labor was essential. Emancipation, however, dealt a serious blow to the plantation economy since the supply of free labor was no longer available. Another obstacle for the planter class was the extension of the franchise to the former slave population. To continue the stream of cheap labor desired by the planter class, Southerners replaced the "slave state" with the "racial state" to ensure the domination of blacks. The racial state, according to David James (1988), rested upon three pillars: racial segregation, laws defending the rights of landlords against those of sharecroppers, and black disenfranchisement. This third pillar was the linchpin (Key 1949).[2] Without political power, blacks were robbed of the punitive power of the ballot—the ability to fire officials who failed to represent their interests. Needless to say, these same officials defended the brutality of Jim Crow.

The planter class devised a dual-track strategy to protect their interests, one economic, the other physical. First, debt peonage exposed black sharecroppers and tenant farmers to exploitive financial arrangements with plantation owners. These arrangements almost always resulted with the black farmer further in debt than he was the previous year. Once again, the sharecropper/tenant farmer found himself in a familiar position: at the mercy of whites. Unbridled terror represented the second means of social control. Physical coercion and the ever-looming specter of lynching convinced rural blacks to honor their farm-related debt and discouraged political organization, the only legal means of redress. Together, these arrangements forced black Southerners into reluctant compliance with Jim Crow (McAdam 1999; Tolnay and Beck 1995). Violence, furthermore, was used as a tool to keep black Southerners in their place, subordinate to whites. From birth, African Americans in the New South were socialized to observe Jim Crow mores lest they court harass-

---

[2] Another compatible, more complex definition of the racial state is the version offered by Omi and Winant (1994). Theirs is more discursive, drawing on new institutionalism.

ment or even death. Leon Litwack summarizes this process, noting, "The New South into which a generation of African Americans would be born had clearly drawn racial boundaries and modes of behavior based on centuries of enforced custom and thought. Every black child would come to appreciate the terrible unfairness and narrowness of that world—the limited options, the need to curb ambitions, to contain feelings, and to weigh carefully every word, gesture, and movement when in the presence of whites. To learn to live with this kind of harsh reality became no less than a prerequisite of survival" (1998, 7).

The murder of fourteen-year-old Emmett Till, something on which I touched in chapter 4, is an example of this. Violence was also used to keep successful black Southerners in their place. Examples of those who "forgot their place" are many. Southern whites, like the Ku Klux Klan, whose members strongly opposed radical Reconstruction, resented black success. Fannie Lou Hammer, the civil rights activist from Mississippi, remembers when her father had finally saved enough money to buy mules and requisite supplies to work the land. Whites, however, took exception, exacting "revenge" by poisoning the family's mules. This, Ms. Hammer explains, "'killed everything we had. . . . We never did get back up again. That white man did it just because we were getting somewhere. White people never like to see Negroes get a little success'" (quoted in Litwack 1998, 154). Others were lynched for being "dangerous niggers." They were considered "dangerous" by white supremacists because they had achieved a measure of prominence and success.

The ever-present economic and physical threats under which Southern whites forced blacks to live no doubt caused long-lasting psychological scars. Under these circumstances, it is not difficult to understand why black Southerners were more hesitant than blacks living in other parts of the country to rock the boat (Marx 1967; Matthews and Prothro 1966, 298–300). Adopting a relatively conservative approach to change, there-fore, was one way of avoiding the wrath of the white supremacists who sought to maintain the status quo (Litwack 1998).

Another possible explanation for black Southerners' relatively conser-vative position on change may also rest upon regional factors that have given rise to a culture of traditionalism (Black and Black 1987). Indeed, the South possessed several of the markers indicative of traditional soci-ety, including an agrarian-based economy and rural residency. In the early 1960s, the South employed twice the number of people in the agri-cultural sector than the non-South, and whereas two-thirds of non-Southerners lived in urban areas, only half of the Southerners in 1960 called a big city home (Grasmick 1973). In his attempt to place the traditionalism-modernism paradigm in a sociostructural context, Gras-mick suggests that factors distinguishing traditional from modern societies do so through early and late socialization processes. In his scheme, education and father's occupation, for instance, contributed early on toward one's socialization. Later socialization factors include, among other things, size of current place of residence and travel experience.

Based upon these criteria, black Southerners were, at least in terms of social structural location, more traditional than whites. More important, these demographic characteristics are commensurate with attitudes and behavior that are the antithesis of modernism, militating against the possibility of change. For instance, in a modern society, innovation, ambition, independence, and social mobility are desirable, even encouraged (Inkeles 1969). Traditional societies, on the other hand, are the polar opposite in their basic orientation. Inhabitants of traditional societies emphasize kinship ties, wish to avoid change, and passively accept the hand dealt them by fate (Gillin 1955). Therefore, in the South, the ways of the past—or, "tradition," if you will—commanded reverence. This pattern of thinking, among Southerners, continued into the early 1960s (Matthews and Prothro 1966, 298).

Whether or not the relative patience of black Southerners had something to do with fear or the fact that the South as a region resisted change, both are part of Southern traditionalism, a belief system that favors stasis. Like any belief embedded within a culture, Southern tradition, at least among the general population, was beyond interrogation. Traditionalism derives its resilience from what sociologist Edward Shils (1971) calls "consensual reception." Adherence to beliefs inherited from the past, to a large extent, is based on their contemporaneous presence and the apparent consensus they achieve among one's peers and contemporaries. Resistance to change, for which the South is well known, has been a signature trait of the region from the very beginning (Franklin 2002). Perhaps this is why a preference for the status quo has achieved the sort of consensual reception to which Shils refers. By the time the 1960s had arrived, at least three generations had been raised in the midst of Southern traditionalism. For black Southerners, conditioned by physical and economic repression, and a culture in which change was typically interrogated, rejecting the traditionalism of Southern life required an enormous leap of imagination or faith, something on which traditional values foreclose (McMillen 1989; Shils 1971).

Black veterans, on the other hand, had experiences in the military that encouraged them to question and criticize the status quo. Moreover, they were afforded the opportunity to travel and experience foreign culture and customs during the Second World War and Korean War. As we observed in chapter 3, service overseas was a jarring experience for black Southerners. In many cases, it furnished a fresh perspective through which returning veterans assessed their home region. This exposure, I suggest, should have resulted in an increased desire for change, especially if we recall that such a desire for change was the product of black men's service in earlier wars. And indeed, we saw examples that this was the case in chapter 4. Mr. Thomas, a veteran of the Second World War, and Mr. Baines, a Korean War veteran, both stated that serving overseas made them realize the illegitimacy of Jim Crow policies and, by extension, of the system on which it rested.

Of course, for some veterans, traditionalism, and the racial status quo with which it had come to be associated, proved too difficult to overcome. Mr. Pete's experience offers an example. Prior to serving in the military, he had not had much contact with whites. Yet he knew what observing Jim Crow meant: "I worked part-time through high school and my dad was a sharecropper, and I hadn't worked too much in the public. I hadn't faced [whites], but I was always told, you know, when I was a teenager coming up, I couldn't go in a white restroom." Upon returning from war, he noticed that nothing had changed. "I saw the signs," he recalls, "that said colored here and white there, you know, the waiting rooms at the train station." Resigning himself to the seeming invincibility of Jim Crow, he says, "I knew I was still here; there weren't any changes, and so I just went on and accepted things the way they were."

The question is, How typical was Pete's experience? Did black veterans on the whole adhere to the tenets of black republicanism and reject the status quo—that is, Southern tradition—or did they accept it? The interviews suggest that they rejected the status quo, but these were only a handful of veterans. It remains unclear whether or not veterans' attitudes, in general, were of the insurgent type or were more in line with the status quo. To answer these questions, I draw upon a battery of five statements put to subjects of the Negro Political Participation Study that were designed to gauge the extent to which the respondents adhered to the status quo. The statements were as follows:

1. If you start trying to change things very much, you usually make them worse.
2. If something grows up over a long period of time, there will always be much wisdom in it.
3. It's better to stick by what you have than to be trying new things you don't really know about.
4. We must respect the work of our forefathers and not think that we know better than they did
5. A man doesn't really get to have much wisdom until he's well along in his years.[3]

[3] These items are based on some of McClosky's (1958) work.

Respondents were asked to indicate whether they agreed a little, agreed quite a bit, disagreed a little, or disagreed quite a bit with each statement. Agreement or strong agreement with the questions indicates that the individual preferred stasis over change. Table 5.1, which, for reasons discussed above includes only men, indicates how black Southerners responded to these questions and offers preliminary confirmation that military service promoted a desire for change.

As table 5.1 indicates, black veterans were far more likely than non-veterans to embrace change over the status quo associated with traditionalism. Even the most cursory glance at the distribution of responses reveals sharp differences between the groups. There were only two statements for which the gap between the groups dipped below 30 points, and both of these statements related to sources of wisdom: time and seasoning. Even more substantial group differences are apparent in responses to the statements about change. Here, veterans consistently favored change by at least 30 points more than other Southern black men.

So far, the preliminary results conform to expectations. Though they do not indicate that the vast majority of black veterans—or black Southerners generally—rejected the status quo, they do suggest that black veterans were considerably more likely to do so than nonveterans. To gain more traction on the relationship between military service and traditionalism, however, we must move beyond the individual questions to assess whether or not veteran/nonveteran differences are maintained as we imagine support for change as an index. I did so by constructing a composite index from the items in table 5.1.[4]

The results in figure 5.1 confirm that as we move from an item-by-item examination of the status quo to one in which we assess support for the concept, the effect of military service remains intact. Veterans, according to this test, were less inclined to embrace Southern culture than nonveterans. The magnitude of between-group differences (t=6.5, p<.01) underscores the extent to which veterans rejected the Southern mind-set. This is consistent with theoretical expectations that service permitted a new perspective on the South.

To certify that military service affected the extent to which change was embraced, however, we must account for competing explanations that bear upon the likelihood that one accepted or rejected traditionalism. For this I turn to multivariate regression, which allows me to isolate the effect of military service on the index representing support for traditionalism while accounting for competing explanations. The dependent

---

[4] I test the coherence of this index with confirmatory factor analysis. Table A.2 (see appendix A) displays the results of the corresponding measurement model. The data provide a good fit to the model.

TABLE 5.1
Comparison of Black Southern Nonveterans' and Veterans' Support
for Traditionalism

Item	Nonveterans (158)	Veterans (80)
A man doesn't really get to have much wisdom until he's well along in years.		
Disagree quite a bit	11.4	25.6
Disagree a little	13.4	17.9
Agree a little	24.8	21.8
Agree quite a bit	50.4	34.7*
We must respect the work of our forefathers and not think that we know better.		
Disagree quite a bit	19.4	46.8
Disagree a little	12.5	20.3
Agree a little	16.2	15.2
Agree quite a bit	51.9	17.7*
It's better to stick by what you have than to be trying new things you don't know about.		
Disagree quite a bit	16.9	40.5
Disagree a little	10.6	17.7
Agree a little	13.1	16.5
Agree quite a bit	59.4	25.3*
If something grows up over for a long time, there will always be much wisdom in it.		
Disagree quite a bit	15.8	24.0
Disagree a little	13.3	25.3
Agree a little	16.5	30.4
Agree quite a bit	54.4	20.3*
If you start trying to change things very much, you usually make them worse.		
Disagree quite a bit	16.4	44.3
Disagree a little	20.4	22.8
Agree a little	23.4	13.9
Agree quite a bit	39.8	19.0*

Source: Negro Political Participation Study 1961–62.
Note: All cross-tabulations significant (*) at p<.05 or lower.

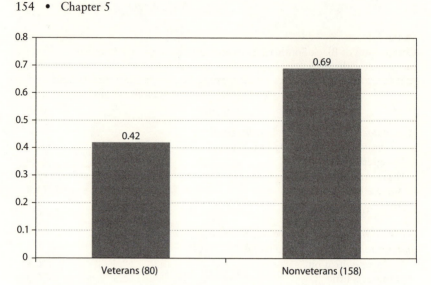

Figure 5.1. Mean support for traditionalism, by veteran status. *Source:* Negro Political Participation Study 1961–62. Support for traditionalism is an additive index rescaled from 0 to 1. Standard deviations: veterans (.28); nonveterans (.26).

variable, support for traditionalism, is represented by the index in figure 5.1. The model controls for key demographic and political variables. Beginning with the relevant demographic controls, we must, of course, account for age. Black Southerners who were socialized during Jim Crow were more likely than those who were born more recently to accept the Southern way of life, including the concession that white supremacy was a fact of life in the South (Litwack 1998; McMillen 1989). Education and urban residency, on the other hand, tend to undercut traditionalism (Grasmick 1973; Reed 1983). Rounding out the controls, I add party identification, since black Southerners saw the Democratic Party as an institutional means of redressing their grievances (Matthews and Prothro 1966), and thus Democratic Party members, among blacks, may have been associated with change.

Membership in churches or in black civic organizations, as well as identification with the race, represent alternative sources for Southerners' rejection of the status quo for which we must account. Historically, black churches served as a site through which the interests of the race were advanced (Dawson 1994; Harris 1999; Tate 1993). To the extent that embracing the status quo meant continued subordination, religiosity should have dampened support for it. Black secular organizations also promoted change and activism; the NAACP, as well as black fraternal groups, sought to upset the status quo in the South (Gurin, Hatchett, and

Jackson 1989; Skocpol, Liazos, and Ganz 2006). Finally, we must consider racial identification. The more attached one is to one's group, the more solidarity one feels with his group, the more likely he is to embrace the possibility of an improvement in the status of the group (Gurin et al. 1989; Tate 1993).

We must also account for the effects of residential context. For instance, rural versus urban areas tend to foster relatively traditional attitudes. Likewise, areas in which blacks were in the majority—that is, at least 50 percent of the population, often encouraged the adoption of attitudes more consistent with the status quo, for in these areas black Southerners were more likely than blacks in other areas of the South to be deprived of the opportunities to realize alternative life choices (Litwack 1998; McMillen 1989; see appendix A for measurement details.)[5]

Table 5.2 presents the results of the model in which positive coefficients indicate support for Southern tradition. Otherwise, we can infer that change is embraced. The results indicate that even when alternative explanations and possible confounds are taken into account, the conclusion that veterans as a group preferred change to the status quo remains. This confirms what the veterans I interviewed told me: military experience changed them, making it impossible for them to continue to respect and abide Southern convention. Military service isn't the only factor that affected support of the status quo. As predicted, increasing age promoted a preference for the way things were. This indicates that those who were exposed to Jim Crow for longer periods of time merely accepted it as a fact of life. On the other hand, youth promoted a desire for change. Furthermore, black Southerners who closely identified with the Democratic Party also favored change, consistent with their belief that the party would somehow ease their suffering. As we move to group-based factors, we observe that membership in secular civic organizations was conducive to support for change and rejection of "business as usual" in the South. We also discover an inverse relationship between racial identification and support for the status quo: as one moves from less to more affinity for other black Southerners, the likelihood that one will support the status quo decreases.

Apparently, there were many in the Jim Crow South who accepted the way things were, including black people.[6] Perhaps this had more to do the survival impulse than anything else, because blacks who challenged the status quo were often punished, either physically or economically— sometimes both. Maybe there were even some, especially among older black Southerners, who resigned themselves to believe that white

---

[5] I use Tate's model of ideological self-identification (1993, 32) as a proxy. She finds that racial identification is commensurate with liberal self-identification.

[6] This was not true for all blacks, however; see Kelley (1990, 1993, 1994) for exceptions.

TABLE 5.2
Determinants of Support for Traditionalism among
Black Southerners

Variables	b	β
Age	.243	.277*
	(.059)	
Income	.026	.024
	(.071)	
Education	−.101	−.102
	(.071)	
Urban=1	−.044	−.090
	(.038)	
Percent black≥50%	.090	.150*
	(.039)	
Strong Democrat=1	−.134	−.141*
	(.059)	
Veteran=1	−.123	−.199*
	(.040)	
Race organization=1	−.171	−.161*
	(.068)	
Racial identification	−.177	−.129*
	(.085)	
Church	.041	.041
	(.061)	
Constant	.734*	
	(.106)	
Adj. R^2	.334	
Root MSE	.246	
Cases	186	

Note: All cell entries are OLS estimates. All tests are one-tailed, where (*) indicates significance at $p<.05$ or better. All variables are scaled 0–1.

supremacy was the natural order of things. Because of their military experiences, however, many black veterans were more likely than others to wish for something different. Their desire to achieve republican aims of freedom and equality resulted in their rejection of the conditions that impeded their realization. Indeed, even as we considered other sources that fostered the pursuit of change, like black civic institutions and group solidarity, military experience enjoyed a unique contribution to black Southerners' wish for something different.

BLACK VETERANS AND THE ROLE OF THE STATE

While the general culture of the South was a great place to begin an inquiry into the attitudinal consequences of military experience, it is now time to add more specificity to the investigation. To do so, I turn to the political culture of the South—something that scholars tend to associate with conservatism (Black and Black 1987; Myrdal 1944)—and the role of the state. Few would dispute the cultural distinctiveness of the South. The evolution of its social, economic, and political institutions owes much to the establishment of the entity that served as the hub of Southern life: the plantation. Indeed, it was the development of the plantation as a freestanding socioeconomic unit that sowed the seeds for and helped sustain conservatism in the Old South as part of Southern tradition, one that preferred a minimalist state. Indeed, as Cash indicates in his seminal volume on the psychology of the South, Southerners "contained . . . an intense distrust of, and, indeed, downright aversion to, any actual exercise of authority beyond the barest minimum essential to the existence of the social organism" (1941, 33). Disdain for a strong central government, fueled in part by a desire among Redeemers to reverse reforms undertaken during Reconstruction, also carried over to the so-called New South (Foner 1988; Franklin 1961).

We should not, therefore, be surprised to find that the South, as a region, held relatively conservative policy preferences even in the midtwentieth century, especially as those policy preferences relate to the role of the central government. To this day, Southerners remain staunch believers in limited government (Black and Black 1987; Hurlbert 1989); white Southerners were particularly militant on this point during the 1940s, '50s, and '60s.[7] Race, as one may imagine, also contributed to conservatism. Proposed reforms designed to improve the condition of whites were sometimes rejected because they also stood to benefit blacks and would ultimately work to undermine white supremacy (Myrdal 1944).[8]

---

[7] For more on the genesis of Southern militancy, see Franklin (2002).

[8] The Southern conservative tradition is alive and well in the modern South. Indeed, Southerners are more likely than residents of other regions to identify as conservative (Hurlbert 1989) or to view themselves as having "very traditional and old fashioned values" (Page and Shapiro 1992). Leaving aside the well-known Southern proclivity for

Southern blacks tended to have a different view of government, for only a strong central state could protect their rights (Dawson 1994, 2001). Perhaps this is why, in general, blacks tend to support a more activist state in the area of policy than do whites (Dawson 1994; Kinder and Sanders 1996; Tate 1993). Race-based cleavages have also partitioned opinion on the place of government in the South. Black Southerners, it seems, have historically been more likely than the whites with whom they share the region to support a strong central government as a matter of principle (Bass and DeVries 1976; Black and Black 1987).

How, if at all, did military service affect the preferred role of the state as indexed by policy preferences? Based upon black veterans' criticism of the postwar conditions of the South, we might expect them to have endorsed liberal policies for the sake of reform. Yet because the state would be responsible for implementing such reforms, we might conversely predict that black veterans would fail to support liberal policy—that due to their experiences with discrimination in the military they would have distrusted the state, perhaps affecting their support for liberal policy. To examine support for liberal policy preferences, I turn to another battery of items from the Negro Political Participation Study. Designed to measure the extent of the respondents' support for liberal policy, they are as follows:

1. The government in Washington ought to see to it that everyone who wants to work can find a job.
2. If cities and towns around the country need help to build more schools, the government in Washington ought to give them the money they need.
3. The government ought to help people get doctors and hospital care at low cost.

Table 5.3 reports on how those interviewed responded to the three statements.

As table 5.3 indicates, black Southerners generally were extraordinarily supportive of political liberalism, a more activist central state.

---

states' rights, Southern tradition has also maintained its affinity for individualism over governmental responsibility (Black and Black 1987). Southern antistatism and individualism crop up on the issues of redistribution, gun control, and tax increases; as a region, the South squarely opposes all three (Glenn and Simmons 1967; Hurlbert 1989). If Southern blacks and whites share a common culture in which conservatism holds sway, we should see few, if any, differences in the attitudes of the two groups. It is not at all clear, however, that the Southern status quo affects the races in a similar fashion. For instance, Bass and DeVries report large racial differences in attitudes toward busing and the question of whether to grant amnesty to those who refused to fight in Vietnam. Nonetheless, blacks' and whites' views are roughly similar regarding their support for governmental institutions and the extent of their political disaffection (Bass and Devries 1976, 490–91).

TABLE 5.3
Comparison of Black Southern Nonveterans' and Veterans' Support for Liberal Policy

Item	Nonveterans (158)	Veterans (80)
The government in Washington ought to see to it that everybody who wants to work can find a job.		
Disagree quite a bit	1.3	8.7
Disagree a little	5.0	10.0
Agree a little	9.5	12.5
Agree quite a bit	81.2	68.8*
If cities and towns around the country need help to build more schools, the government in Washington ought to give them the money they need.		
Disagree quite a bit	3.8	10.0
Disagree a little	5.0	15.0
Agree a little	9.2	15.0
Agree quite a bit	82.0	60.0*
The government ought to help people get doctors and hospital care at low cost.		
Disagree quite a bit	.6	5.0
Disagree a little	2.5	6.2
Agree a little	10.7	20.0
Agree quite a bit	86.1	68.8*

Source: Negro Political Participation Study 1961–62.

Note: Cell entries represent percentages. All comparisons significant (*) at p<.01 or less.

Across the board, however, veterans were less supportive of liberal policy than were nonveterans. Compared to the difference in attitudes toward the maintenance of the status quo, the gap in opinion between veterans and nonveterans was relatively small—as small as 8 points, and never greater than 16 points. More than 90 percent of nonveterans favored governmental assistance for jobs, schools, and medical care. Veterans' approval of liberal policy did not reach 90 percent in any of these three categories, but it was above 75 percent in each case.

Black veterans appear, then, to have been less liberal than nonveterans. But given the high levels of support for liberal policy from each group, it is not at all clear that the group-based differences that seem to exist here will hold up to further scrutiny once policy liberalism is

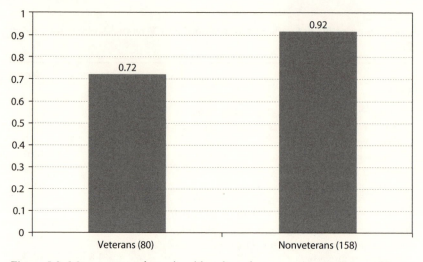

Figure 5.2. Mean support for policy liberalism, by veteran status. *Source:* Negro Political Participation Study 1961–62. Support for policy liberalism is an additive index, rescaled 0–1. Standard deviations: veterans (.16); nonveterans (.27).

measured as an index. To examine group-based differences a little further, I have created an index of the items from table 5.3, assigning complete support for political conservatism the value of 0 and complete support for political liberalism the value of 1.[9] Figure 5.2 reports the results.

The results confirm the presence of group differences between veterans and nonveterans on the matter of policy preferences and the role of the state. As figure 5.2 illustrates, black veterans were considerably less liberal than those who never served. While the item-by-item comparisons point to a relatively small gap in opinion, this gap widens when we examine policy liberalism as an index rather than responses to individual policy options (t=4.3; p<.001).

Controlling for the influence of other factors should add more clarity to the picture. To assess whether or not military service genuinely depressed policy liberalism, I deployed the index used in figure 5.2 to gauge political conservatism. I used the same set of controls as I did for the test of support for the status quo in table 5.2: sociodemographic controls for age, education, and income are included, and racial identi-

[9] I test the coherence of this scale with confirmatory factor analysis. Table A.3 (see appendix A) displays the results of the corresponding measurement model. The model provides a good fit to the data.

fication, church attendance, and membership in racial organizations are retained as psychological determinants. Party identification is also retained.[10]

As table 5.4 indicates, the veteran/nonveteran distinction in preferences for policy liberalism among black Southerners remained intact. Even controlling for sociodemographic and group-based factors, military service clearly dampened the preference for policy liberalism among black Southern males, indicating a lack of trust toward the central state. Among the sociodemographic factors, education is the only one to register a clear influence on policy preferences; it did so, like veteran status, by working *against* policy liberalism. From the perspective of the least well educated, the desire for liberal social policy is not difficult to understand, for they were (and are) the ones who are the most deprived. Since more educated blacks were (and are) less deprived, they may have felt moved by the Protestant ethic, something that discourages state intervention. Beyond that, neither increasing age nor income, nor racial context nor group-based resources, affected black Southerners' view of the state, hinting at a rough consensus around a more interventionist state, at least as redistribution goes.

The results confirm the antistatist orientation of black veterans relative to black Southerners in general (though we should keep in mind that this antistatism affected only a small proportion of veterans, most of whom were squarely liberal in their political preferences) and tell us that at least some of this antistatism is attributable to their status as veterans—and thus, most likely, to their mistreatment in the military. This result offers some support for Cynthia Enloe's (1980) assertion that many minority group members who have served develop contempt and distrust for the state based in part upon the circumstances under which they served. It is also possible that military socialization affected the work ethic and the notion of individual merit instilled by the military. In other words, relative to other black Southerners, some veterans may have viewed governmental help of any kind as a handout. While they were trained to act as members of a team, military culture also emphasizes individual merit (Laufer 1989; Moskos and Butler 1996). Mr. Carter expressed his military-driven view of merit in this way: "My philosophy has always been, the world doesn't owe me a damn thing, but it's up to me to obtain anything which I desire or feel as though I should be entitled to. And if I don't merit it, I don't expect it. . . . Now, I didn't expect anybody to give me anything. Don't *give* me a damn thing!"

---

[10] In another specification, I also included a predictor for traditionalism; there were no substantive differences in the remaining coefficients.

Table 5.4
Determinants of Policy Liberalism among Black Southerners

Variables	b	ß
Age	.010 (.049)	.016
Income	−.071 (.061)	−.084
Education	−.142 (.061)	−.187*
Urban=1	.023 (.032)	.052
Percent black≥50%	.046 (.033)	.099
Strong Democrat=1	−.057 (.050)	−.080
Veteran=1	−.088 (.034)	−.189*
Race organization=1	−.012 (.058)	−.015
Racial identification	.089 (.068)	.092
Church	.033 (.052)	.044
Constant	.824* (.088)	
Adj. R²	.154	
Root MSE	.212	
Cases	195	

Note: All cell entries are OLS estimates. All tests are one-tailed, where (*) indicates significance at p<.05 or less. All variables are scaled 0–1.

A HARD CASE: BLACK VETERANS' ATTITUDES
TOWARD SEGREGATION

So far, black veterans' attitudes conform to expectations. We have yet, however, to consider what was perhaps the single most important policy goal of the early civil rights movement: integration (McAdam 1999).

Because segregation signified their inferiority (Higginbotham 1996), black Southerners viewed integration as consonant with the equality to which they were entitled. Beyond the symbolism associated with it, moreover, there were very real things, relating to the practice of democracy, that were driving the push for integration. First, as many scholars illustrate, education is absolutely necessary for the practice of democratic citizenship (Nie, Junn, and Stehlik-Barry 1996; Verba and Nie 1972). As the Supreme Court recognized in the *Brown* case, school-based segregation degraded the educational experience of black children, affecting their ability to discharge the duties of citizens in a liberal democracy. Second, segregation impinges upon the democratic process by effectively isolating the voices of marginalized groups from wider political discourse and deliberation (Young 2000). Third, under segregation, black Southerners were effectively denied agency. Dr. Martin Luther King Jr. articulated this point quite well when he said, " 'I can never know what my total capacity is until I live in an integrated society. . . . I cannot be free until I have had the opportunity to fulfill my total capacity untrammeled by any artificial hindrance or barrier' " (quoted in Washington 1986, 121). For both sociopsychological and democratic reasons, then, integration was important to black Southerners, something that was generally favored, and as such it might prove difficult to find much cleavage, by veteran status, on this issue; hence the "hard case" reference in this section's title.

As we have seen, serving their country forced black servicemen to confront the illegitimacy of segregation and convinced them that they had earned the right to return to American society as full, equal partners in American democracy. Hence, black republicanism derived through military service is one potential source of support for integration. Another way to explain black Southerners' support for integration, however, is through their connection with black civic organizations, which made integration a priority (McAdam 1999; Morris 1984; Skocpol et al. 2006). Thus, we might also expect the survey respondents' church membership or their membership in, say, the NAACP or a fraternal organization, to have supplied the principal basis of their support for integration.

To examine the impact of military service upon attitudes toward integration, I draw on two questions from the Negro Political Participation Study. The first, "Are you in favor of integration, strict segregation, or something in between?" addresses integration in the abstract, as a matter of principle. As Howard Schuman and colleagues (1997) illustrate, people are more comfortable with principle than they are with concrete policy: the former is an ideal to be worked toward, whereas in the latter case people must come to grips with the difficulties entailed in its implementation. Thus, we might expect to see a difference

TABLE 5.5

Comparison of Black Southern Nonveterans' and Veterans' Support for Integration in Principle

Item	Nonveterans (148)	Veterans (79)
There's quite a bit of talk these days about segregation and integration, and it is important to know how Negroes <White people> really feel about these questions. Are you in favor of integration, strict segregation, or something in between?		
Segregation	14.9	6.3
Something in between	13.5	10.2
Integration	71.6	83.5*

Source: Negro Political Participation Study 1961–62.
Note: Cell entries represent percentages, where (*)$p < .10$.

in responses to the second question, which places the matter of integration in a more concrete context, gauging responses to the issue of school desegregation. Black Southerners were asked, "Suppose that you are married and have small children. Then you decided that the white school closest to where you live is much better than the Negro school. Would you want your children to go there, even if they were among the first few Negroes to attend the school?"

Table 5.5 tabulates how the respondents answered the first question. It's no great shock that black Southerners overwhelmingly preferred integration, at least in principle. Approximately 72 percent of nonveterans favored integration over either segregation (15 percent) or something in between (13.5 percent). As expected, a great many of the veterans also preferred integration. Over four-fifths (83 percent) preferred integration over the alternatives. Hence, the gap in opinion is noticeable, if not necessarily overwhelming.

This result begs the question of whether it represents a real difference of opinion. A simple statistical test should provide the answer. Figure 5.3 displays the results of this test, in which support for the principle of integration is assigned a value of 1.

As we can see, the gap between the groups is real ($t = 2.1$, $p < .05$), if somewhat narrow. Both groups, to be sure, score fairly high, indicating widespread support for the principle of integration. Nonetheless, the veterans embraced the principle of integration with more resolution than did black men who had not served.

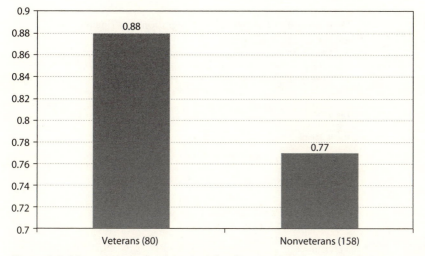

Figure 5.3. Mean support for the principle of integration, by veteran status. *Source:* Negro Political Participation Study 1961–62. The item was rescaled to a 0–1 interval. Standard deviations: veterans (.30); nonveterans (.41).

That said, it's quite possible that once we account for the respondents' education, income, and age, the apparent group distinctions will disappear. It is also reasonable to assume that political orientation is relevant to evaluations of integration. Therefore, party identification and ideological orientation were both included as controls. Since the Negro Political Participation Study did not ask respondents to identify themselves as liberal, moderate, or conservative, as many surveys do, I used the respondents' positions on policy (employing the policy liberalism scale) as a proxy for their political ideology. Further, racial identification and church membership have proven powerful predictors on issues of race and race policy (Dawson 1994; Harris 1999; Tate 1993). We should also expect membership in secular black civic organizations to have promoted support for the principle of integration. Finally, we must entertain the possibility the how one felt about the status quo affected one's support for integration: if one embraced change, it's likely that one supported the principle of integration. Table 5.6 displays the results.

Perhaps the most arresting facet of the model is the near unanimity with which the principle of integration is received. Differences in sociodemographics, political orientation, and context all fail to index support for integration in the abstract among black Southerners. Even varying levels of traditionalism, a factor that should have driven something as important as one's view of integration—especially at the time—failed to affect black

TABLE 5.6
Determinants of Support for Integration in Principle
among Black Southerners

Variables	Coefficient	Standard error
Age	−.153	.643
Income	.558	.996
Education	1.17	1.06
Strong Democrat=1	.142	.631
Policy liberalism	.453	1.22
Urban=1	.629	.419
Percent black≥50%	.343	.430
Veteran=1	.674	.493
Race organization=1	2.69	1.55*
Racial identification	1.61	.920*
Church	1.64	.674*
Traditionalism	−.868	.844
μ_1	.378	1.51
μ_2	1.50	1.53
Pseudo R^2	.158	
χ^2	37.59	
−2 Log likelihood	−100.11	
Cases	189	

Note: All cell entries are ordered logistic coefficients and
standard errors where (*) indicates significance at $p<.05$ or
less. All variables are scaled 0–1.

Southerners' opinion on the issue. Only variation in the extent to which
black Southerners took advantage of group-based resources offers any
traction. Having said that, the remaining estimates in table 5.6 preclude
clear, intuitive, substantive interpretation. In the interest of clarity, I have
converted the estimates in the table into predicted probabilities. Figure 5.4
illustrates the results.

Once controls are introduced and competing explanations are taken
into account, the already slight differences between veterans' and nonveterans' views of the principle of integration vanish altogether. This

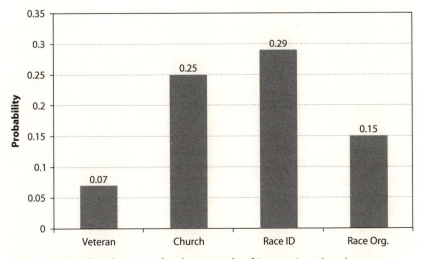

Figure 5.4. Predicted support for the principle of integration. Age, income, education, party identification, and support for the status quo are set to their respective means.

result is not too troubling in terms of the theory of black republicanism because support for the principle of integration was overwhelming. While military service seems not to have made it more likely that a black Southern man would endorse the principle of integration, the respondents' relationships with what Gurin and colleagues (1989) dub "group-based resources" succeeded in doing so. Membership in black civic organizations, both religious and secular, increased the probability that individuals supported integration in principle by 25 and 15 percent, respectively. Moreover, holding other variables at their respective means, those who identified with other black Southerners were 29 percent more likely to embrace integration in principle than those who felt less solidarity with other black Southerners.[11] The entire set of sociodemographic and political controls, on the other hand, failed to affect preferences for the principle of integration in any meaningful way, proving the depth of consensus for it. Black Southerners, regardless of age or class, embraced it equally. Finally, those who preferred the status quo seem to have been no different in their preference for integration than those who preferred change.

It was relatively cost free to embrace the *principle* of integration. Principles are relatively remote and abstract. What happened, though, when

[11] All of the predicted probabilities were calculated with the statistical software programs STATA.

TABLE 5.7
Comparison of Black Southern Nonveterans' and Veterans' Support for Integration in Practice

Item	Nonveterans (158)	Veterans (80)
Suppose that you are married and have small children. Then you decided that the white school closest to where you live is much better than the Negro school. Would you want your children to go there, even if they were among the first few Negroes to attend the school?		
Child currently attends integrated school	.6	3.7
Definitely would want children to go	31.6	56.2
Probably would want children to go	15.8	17.5
It makes no difference	5.0	1.2
Probably would not want children to go	9.5	6.2
Definitely would not want children to go	37.5	15.2*

Source: Negro Political Participation Study 1961–62.
Note: Cell entries represent percentages. Differences are significant (*) at $p < .01$ or less.

the respondents were asked to react to a question about the more tangible implications of integration? One might predict altogether different results, particularly in response to a question about school integration. After all, it was the Supreme Court's decision in the *Brown* case that stimulated "massive resistance" among many white Southerners (Bartley 1969; McMillen 1994). In 1957 at the Little Rock, Arkansas, Central High School, nine students were escorted onto campus shielded by the 101st Airborne *and* the Arkansas National Guard, the latter of which had been federalized by President Dwight Eisenhower as a means of preventing violence on the part of whites. All black Southerners were familiar with the hostility surrounding this event, and thus the issue of school integration made the principle of integration more concrete, with very real consequences. Did military service, under these circumstances, affect black Southerners' responses? Table 5.7 indicates that military experience mattered.

When the issue of integration shifted from abstract principle to more concrete policy, a sizable gap between veterans and nonveterans emerged. Table 5.7 reveals that approximately 77 percent of those who served were determined to send their children to an integrated school "even if they were among the first few negroes to attend the school." This response suggests that many of these individuals were willing to deal with the hostilities associated with school integration. By contrast, only roughly 47 per-

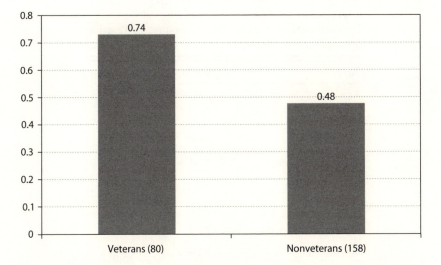

Figure 5.5. Mean support for school-based integration in practice, by veteran status. *Source:* Negro Political Participation Study 1961–62. The item is rescaled to a 0–1 interval. Standard deviations: veterans (.38); nonveterans (.43).

cent of black nonveterans were open to the idea of integration under these circumstances. Thirty percentage points separate the groups.

Figure 5.5 displays the result of a more rigorous test of this disparity, where strong support for sending one's own children to an integrated school is assigned a value of 1.

This second test seems to confirm that veterans were considerably more likely than nonveterans to support a policy of integration in which their children were involved (t=4.6, p<.01). Without accounting for group-based resources, however, we cannot be sure that this result is truly attributable to the veteran/nonveteran difference. As was the case for the assessment of the determinants of integration as a principle, it is likely that black civic organizational membership and racial solidarity strongly influenced individuals' desire to make a move toward more substantive equality. Moreover, we need to control for the possibility of confounding effects of sociodemographics, political orientation, and preference for the status quo. Table 5.8 displays the results of a third, more restrictive test of the influence of these variables on the respondents' support for school integration.[12]

---

[12] Since relatively few actually had kids enrolled in white schools, for estimation purposes, I collapsed this category into the "Definitely would want kids to attend" category.

TABLE 5.8
Determinants of Support for Integration in Practice among Black Southerners

Variables	Coefficient	Standard error
Age	.190	.459
Income	.257	.599
Education	.608	.631
Strong Democrat=1	.100	.497
Policy liberalism	.647	.765
Urban=1	−.152	.296
Percent black≥50%	−.076	.325
Veteran=1	.619	.355*
Race organization=1	1.56	.658*
Racial identification	.485	.700
Church	1.09	.507*
Traditionalism	2.42	.662*
μ_1	−.485	1.11
μ_2	−.065	1.11
μ_3	.117	1.11
μ_4	1.07	1.12
Pseudo R^2	.122	
χ^2	59.46	
−2 Log likelihood	−213.11	
Cases	185	

Note: All cell entries are ordered logistic coefficients and standard errors. All tests are one-tailed, where (*) indicates significance at p<.05 or less. All variables are scaled 0–1.

Again, if the model is any indication, support for integration as policy received broad support. Regardless of age, educational attainment, party identification, and where one lived, among other factors, black Southerners supported attempts to integrate schools. Moreover, holding other variables at their respective means, the effect of military expe-

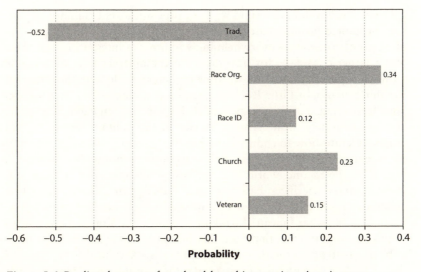

Figure 5.6. Predicted support for school-based integration. Age, income, education, and party identification are set to their respective means.

rience remains intact, as does membership in black civic institutions, religious and secular. However, given the interpretive limitations associated with the coefficients in table 5.8, I once again rely on the use of predicted probabilities to illustrate the substantive of various determinants on the concrete application of integration. Figure 5.6 displays the results.

As we move from someone who's a nonveteran to one with military experience, it increases the likelihood by 15 percent that black Southerners agreed that their children should be agents of change, integrating a white school. It seems that the challenges veterans endured in the military prepared them to confront the hostility of whites determined to forestall social progress. Group-based resources, once again, have great explanatory power, for those who belonged to black civic organizations or churches were the most likely by far to support the implementation of integration. Black Southerners who attended church regularly were 23 percent more likely to support the implementation of integration than those who attended less frequently. Likewise, membership in black secular organizations increased the probability that a respondent would support school integration by 34 percent. However, as one romanticized more about the South, preferring the status quo, it *decreased* the likelihood of supporting school-based integration by 52 percent!

Generally, my findings support the proposition that military experience promoted insurgent attitudes—or criticism, if you will. As a group, black Southerners were overwhelmingly in favor of integration, but there was a larger consensus for integration in the abstract than in concrete terms. I suspect that question wording had much to do with these results. Recalling images of Little Rock's Central High, many black Southerners must have cringed at the prospect of their own children being among the first to integrate a white school. Service in the military, however, had taught veterans how to endure hardship. If they were willing to fight and die overseas, they were no less willing to do so at home. Mr. Wilson, a veteran of the Second World War, expressed his opinion that black soldiers' military sacrifices had rewarded subsequent generations—their children, as well as others'—with improved life chances: "I think I paid for it. You see what I mean? I paid a price for it and I'm entitled to it, so I think my son, the fact that I see that he can look for a better job, hope to be in a better position than I was, and not work as hard for it, so all of that. I look at thousands of others like that, young men. The fact that you're here now in these surroundings, I think that's part of the price that . . . that's part of my pay."

His comment is pregnant with references to black republicanism. He felt entitled to the benefits of equality by virtue of his military service. He believes his son should benefit from his sacrifice. He even references me—someone with whom he had never come into contact before the interview, but someone who is also black—as a beneficiary of his sacrifice during the Second World War. After everything they were forced to endure, it seems, veterans felt that equality was owed them, their children, and their community. They were therefore committed to change, even if it meant accepting the risks associated with confronting whites over integration.

. . .

This chapter has illustrated the effect of military service on the adoption of insurgent attitudes, the desire for change, and criticism of the status quo. More important, it confirms some of the attitudes revealed in the interviews. Driven by black republicanism, evident by the republican rhetoric they used, veterans rejected traditional value orientations that promised to maintain the status quo.[13] They were also de-

---

[13] Furthermore, traditionalist orientations are injurious to democracy for two reasons. First, in a foundational sense, Southern traditionalism contaminated the conditions for full democracy. It abetted the practice of structural oppression from without and the experience of psychological oppression from within, neither of which are conducive to civic

termined to achieve integration, even if it meant enduring some of the unpleasant circumstances that accompanied school integration. They embraced policy liberalism and an interventionist central state, but they were relatively *less* likely than nonveterans to do so, perhaps because their experiences in the service had taught some of them to distrust the state.

These findings provide a window through which to view black republicanism's impact upon white domination—an internal threat to the republic. Veterans summarily rejected conditions that impeded liberty and equality, including the Southern status quo. For the same reason, subscription to black republicanism underwrote veterans' determination to achieve equality through integration. The results are similar to what one would expect from black liberals, particularly radical egalitarians, who are also critical of American social practices and push for equality (Dawson 2001). One can imagine that in the 1940s, '50s, and early '60s, radical egalitarians would have pushed for a change in the status quo and embraced integration. It is in the measure of support for liberal policy preference that differences between black republicanism and radical egalitarianism emerge, though this difference is rather small.

In addition to their distrust of the government and their subscription to the military ethic that promoted individual merit, it is possible that a source of these veterans' relative conservatism lay in their conception of masculinity. As the embodiment of black masculinity—a masculinity that takes pride in personal uplift (DuBois 1990)—some veterans may have disapproved of government involvement in the affairs of the community as an affront to their manhood. Recall, for instance, that in preceding chapters a number of veterans mentioned that the military made men of them or that fighting was a means of validating their manhood. This also reminds us of the gendered nature of black republicanism.

So far, we have seen that military service promoted insurgent attitudes and a desire for change among both the veterans I interviewed and the larger group sampled by the Negro Political Participation Study. But attitudes are one thing; acting on them is something quite different. Military service, I have argued, produced experiences so profound that they affected veterans' behavior. In the chapter that follows, I will test this proposition.

---

engagement. Second, even if we leave aside the Southern context, adherence to traditional beliefs militates against the practice of democracy at a more general level. As Inkeles (1969) indicates, men with traditionalist orientations are not well suited to the practice of democratic citizenship, because clinging to ways of the past is not conducive to an informed, civic-minded public.

CHAPTER 6

Dying to Participate

POLITICAL PARTICIPATION AS A FORM OF PROTEST

> You see, to come to back here to Mississippi and try to participate in politics meant your life. . . . Because to come back here to Mississippi . . . in order to try to participate, you'd be found floating down a river. You'd be found hung up in a tree. You'd be found burned, bombed, or killed.
> —State Stallworth, Mississippi Freedom Democratic Party, in a comment made to the media during the Democratic National Convention, 1964

> Since I lost a portion of my body to protect my own rights, I would die for my rights, and I would kill for my rights. And I was going to vote if I had to kill somebody to vote.
> —Doyle Combs, World War II veteran
> (quoted in Jennifer Brooks, *Defining the Peace: World War II Veterans, Race, and the Remaking of Southern Political Tradition*

In chapter 5, I illustrated the extent to which veterans held insurgent attitudes; how they were less inclined than other black Southern males to accept the conditions of domination. What remains to be seen, though, is how far they were willing to go in order to challenge white domination. Sociologist Aldon Morris suggests that black veterans contributed in no small way to black Southerners' resistance against white domination. "Black soldiers returning from the wars," he observes, "began urging their relatives and friends not to accept domination. In many instances black soldiers disobeyed the policy of bus segregation and refused to give up their seats long before Rosa Parks" (1984, 80). We have seen that this was the case even among the small group of black veterans I interviewed. Recent works on the social history of the civil rights movement suggest that veterans, as a group, were uncommonly active in the movement. Some occupied leadership positions in traditional civil rights organizations, heading up state and local chapters of the NAACP and serving in the leadership of the Student Nonviolent Coordinating Committee

(SNCC; see Carson 1981; Dittmer 1994; Henry 2000; Lipsitz 1988; Payne 1995; Tyson 1999; Tuck 2001). Others founded their own groups, such as the Mississippi Freedom Democratic Party; the Council of Confederated Organizations, the umbrella organization for civil rights groups in Mississippi; the Chatham Crusade for Voters; and the Georgia Voters League (Brooks 2004; Henry 2000; Hill 2004; Payne 1995).

While veterans appear to have embraced activism, there is reason to further interrogate the proposition insofar as many of these veterans were in some way associated with black civic organizations, institutions that promoted collective action. Indeed, a number of studies have shown that civic institutions such as black churches and civil rights organizations provided the emotional, motivational, and organizational resources that facilitated collective activism and mobilization (Gurin, Hatchett, and Jackson 1989; Harris 1999; McAdam 1999; Morris 1984). Group identification, moreover, constituted a sociopsychological component of these group-based resources in that the awareness of the illegitimacy of the group's position in society generated activism (Miller et al. 1981). More to the point, collective resources were critical to the success of the civil rights movement (Tate 1993). Since much black activism flowed through group resources, we cannot be confident that military service was an independent, additional source of resistance beyond black civic institutions and group solidarity. Moreover, the previous chapter clearly demonstrated the presence of attitudes consistent with black republicanism among veterans in the mass public, but it's a long way from holding critical attitudes to taking action.[1]

The present chapter examines the activism of black veterans. Those in chapter 4 who either agreed with, or participated in, activism during the civil rights movement did so using the rhetoric of black republicanism to justify their resistance. They all framed their claims on America and justified their postwar action by referring to their military service. While that chapter shows *why* they were active, the evidence is restricted to a handful of veterans. It is not clear, therefore, that activism is a tactic to which to which black veterans in the *mass public* turned in order to secure equality. Moreover, in my contention that military experience tended to promote activism among many black Southerners, I must also be sure to account for competing explanations for activism, including the influence of black civic institutions and solidarity.

Drawing upon the Negro Political Participation Study data used in the preceding chapter, I argue that black veterans' resistance was widespread in the South and largely independent of the group resources that mobilized

[1]For an extended discussion on the attitude-behavior link, see Fiske and Taylor (1991).

other black Southerners. To gain analytical leverage on the issue, I will again use male nonveterans as a baseline group against which to assess the activism of veterans. Since this requires the use of individual-level data, I turn to consideration of political participation in the South prior to the ratification of the Voting Rights Act of 1965. I do so for two reasons. First, studying participation in the political process permits us to gauge the extent of activism beyond protest, the principal means of political activism during the Jim Crow era (McAdam 1999; Morris 1984; Tate 1993). More to the point, adding conventional political participation to the roster of civil rights activities allows me to make more general claims about activism and resistance. It shows, for instance, that civil rights activism and resistance cannot be confined to *group-based* challenges to white supremacy, creating a space for agency at the *individual* level.[2] The second (and related) reason is that mainstream political participation can serve as an indicator of commitment to activism. As the first epigraph above states, participation in the political process was dangerous prior to the ratification of the Voting Rights Act in 1965, especially in areas where blacks were in the majority (Lawson 1976; Matthews and Prothro 1966; Woodward 1955). Accepting the physical and economic risks associated with political participation in the South in the late 1950s and early '60s was, I believe, indicative of one's commitment to activism.

This chapter begins with a short review of barriers to political participation with which black Southerners were forced to contend; this review helps to set the stage for defining virtually all political participation by black Southerners prior to 1965 as a form of activism. I then discuss competing explanations for the political participation of black veterans. The group-based resource model represents the conventional account in which the political participation of black veterans is explained in terms of the resources that stimulated mobilization among black Southerners. Alternatively, military experience and, by implication, black republicanism, predicts a unique effect of military service upon political participation. The second epigraph above says it all: black veterans' military experience committed them to exercising their rights, no matter the cost. I then make a theoretical distinction between voting and nonvoting participation. Among other factors, I argue that the former, because of its visibility, is a relatively risky form of activism. Like registering to vote, the voting act itself was at once "a momentous and potentially danger-

---

[2] Rochon (1998) also addresses the relationship between political participation and civil rights activism. He shows that those who were members of civil rights organizations also tended to be politically engaged, including participation in mainstream politics. However, the book fails to consider the residential context in which respondents lived. As I will show below, this is an important distinction.

ous act, a public challenge to the established order, and an invitation to violence or economic reprisals" (McAdam 1988, 80). Although the latter, nonvoting participation, such as attending political meetings in a segregated community, was less visible and arguably less risky than voting, it nevertheless remains consistent with activism (Harris et al. 2006). As such, it constitutes another important theoretical difference in these modes of activism. Finally, I test these propositions using the Negro Political Participation Study. The results permit me to conclude that, consistent with my interviews with veterans, military service predisposed black Southerners toward activism. In doing so, the findings allow me to move beyond what one might label anecdotal evidence as it pertains to my claims in chapter 4 regarding the activist component of black republicanism. Indeed, the findings place my proposition that black veterans were more likely than not to challenge Jim Crow on solid footing.

IMPEDIMENTS TO BLACK POLITICAL PARTICIPATION IN THE SOUTH

The modern political domination of black Southerners may be traced to the suffrage restrictions imposed upon black Mississippians in 1890. By 1910, all of the former Confederate states had adopted slick—if unconscionable—devices to dilute the black vote. In their efforts to get around the Fifteenth Amendment, white Southerners managed to create barriers to enfranchisement that were all but insurmountable. By making the franchise conditional on poll taxes, literacy, and residency requirements, property ownership, and grandfather and "good character" clauses, white legislatures avoided the explicit use of race as grounds for disqualification while managing to virtually eliminate black voting. Louisiana is a case in point. According to historian C. Vann Woodward (1955), 130,344 African Americans were registered to vote in 1896; by 1904, only 1,342 remained on the rolls.

In 1896, six years after the elected officials of the Mississippi statehouse circumvented the Constitution, South Carolina initiated a move that cemented white supremacy for almost two generations: it introduced the white primary, which the Democratic Party used to exclude African Americans from the political process in the South. The white primary was arguably more effective at excluding black voters than all other suffrage restrictions put together, all but rendering those restrictions moot (Key 1949; Matthews and Prothro 1966). Because African Americans were already registered with the party of Lincoln, local and state party committees of the Democratic Party—the party of white supremacy—simply barred any black Democrats from participating in the party primaries. Such a move was completely permissible because, according to statutory law, party committees could frame their own rules and regulations. Since the South was "solid" for the Democratic Party from the 1880s on, the exclusion of African Americans from the Democratic Party primary effectively excluded black voters from selecting the men who eventually, and inevitably, triumphed in the general election.[3] The institutionalization of the white primary summarily extinguished the political relevance of African Americans in the South (Frymer 1999; Kousser 1974).

The demise of the white primary in 1944 following the Supreme Court's decision in *Smith v. Allwright* momentarily boosted black political participation. By 1947, black voter registration had doubled from 250,000 before the *Smith* case to 500,000—though this figure still represented only 10 percent of the eligible African American electorate. To compensate for the elimination of the white primary, Southern whites reacquainted themselves with tried and true extralegal and illegal methods of diluting the black vote. First, they ratcheted up the enforcement of suffrage restrictions established during the early 1890s in state constitutions (Key 1949). Property and literacy requirements and the good character clause were dusted off and once again used to prevent blacks from voting.[4] Second, white Southerners revived the use of fear, threatening any blacks who possessed the temerity to exercise their rights with both physical and economic reprisals.

Retaliation against blacks who wished to exercise their civil rights was not limited to the acts of a few misguided white Southerners. In some cases, violence received public support from prominent politicians. In this regard, the sentiments of Georgia governor Eugene Talmadge and Mississippi senator Theodore Bilbo are illustrative. Talmadge is credited with "warning" African Americans to ignore the Supreme Court's decision to outlaw the white primary; if African Americans insisted upon voting, he suggested to whites, they were "fair game for whatever punishment white Georgians deemed necessary" (Anderson 2003). Bilbo similarly goaded Southern white Democratic partisans into violence, suggesting that " 'the best way to keep the nigger from voting . . . [was to] do it the night before the election.' " He advised, " 'If any nigger tries to organize to vote, use the tar and feathers and don't forget the matches' " (quoted in Anderson 2003, 63–64).

The new suffrage restrictions, when combined with violent coercion, effectively depressed the black vote. From 1940 to 1947, the registration

---

[3] With the exception of Florida, North Carolina, and Tennessee, the white primary was instituted at the state level.

[4] The grandfather clause was declared illegal in 1915 based upon a case originating in Oklahoma (Lawson 1976).

rate for black Southerners had more than doubled, from 5 percent to 12 percent. It reached 20 percent in 1952 before the rate of increase slowed; after 1952, the registration rate improved only 1 point per year, reaching its plateau at 28 percent in 1960 (Matthews and Prothro 1966). Leaving aside the complacency attributable to Southern tradition, which encouraged some black Southerners to cede the domain of politics to whites (Litwack 1998; Matthews and Prothro 1966), the principal reason for the decelerating rate of African American political participation was the coercion to which black Southerners were subjected in America after the Supreme Court's *Brown v. Board of Education of Topeka* decision.

If the volume of racist letters to Presidents Harry S. Truman and Dwight D. Eisenhower is in any way indicative of white Southern sentiment in the postwar South, something for which Taeku Lee (2002) makes a compelling case in his seminal work on the intersection of political activism and public opinion, it is no surprise that a reconstituted Ku Klux Klan intermittently patrolled the Deep South, purging the rolls of prospective black voters by lynching and shooting blacks who insisted on exercising their political rights. Once a few blacks had been made examples of, the threat of violence sufficed to prevent most others from voting. After the nullification of the white primary in 1944 and the *Brown* decision, the Citizens' Council emerged; economic reprisals (and the threat of them) gained favor in the mid- to late 1950s as the preferred means of impeding black political participation and organizational membership. For those who contemplated membership in the NAACP, registered to vote, or both (as was most often the case), economic retribution often awaited. While black entrepreneurs were threatened with high interest rates, being overcharged, or denied credit, wage earners faced termination (McMillen 1994; Payne 1995; Salamon and Van Evera 1973). In the late 1950s, the locus of terror moved from rural areas, where lynchings were commonplace, to Southern metropolises, as black Southerners in the city attempted to exorcise domination by exercising franchise (Matthews and Prothro 1963). By 1960, a full sixteen years after the burial of the white primary, only 28 percent of the Southern African American electorate was registered to vote (Matthews and Prothro 1966).

EXPLAINING BLACK POLITICAL PARTICIPATION IN THE SOUTH

Perhaps the best-known source of black resistance is also the oldest social institution in the black community: the church. In the context of Jim Crow, churches were places in which black Southerners were permitted to congregate without much interference (Harris 1999; Myrdal 1944). Hence, churches enjoyed enormous influence in the black community.

Because of their organizational infrastructure and ready-made membership base, churches were principal sites of insurgency and political mobilization in the South (McAdam 1999; Morris 1984). For these reasons, the Southern Christian Leadership Conference (SCLC) enjoyed great success in its early stages. Religion also furnished black Southerners with the strength to challenge Jim Crow. The belief that they were morally correct, that "God was on their side," gave many the courage to face and endure their fear of retaliation by white supremacists (Harris 1999).

Organizations committed to racial equality were another important source of black resistance in the South. Similar to churches and black colleges, local chapters of the NAACP supplied a ready-made pool from which the movement extracted members and leaders (McAdam 1999). Membership in black organizations also provided activists with an institutionalized base of social support through which sustained challenges to Jim Crow were made possible (Gurin et al. 1989). Based in the North, the NAACP worked from within the system, protesting the subordination of black Southerners in the courts instead of employing the direct-action tactics of students and churches. In the wake of the *Brown* decision, it was the only organization in the South with the wherewithal to oppose the hostility to which blacks were subjected (Morris 1984). Under the withering attack mounted by white supremacist groups such as the Klan and the Citizens' Council, Southern NAACP membership declined in the mid- to late 1950s, dropping from 128,000 in 1955 to 80,000 in 1957 (Morris 1984). Though weakened, the organization nonetheless remained committed to the fight for social justice and continued to mobilize blacks across the region. Along with fraternal organizations and women's groups, the NAACP encouraged African American movement participation and political mobilization (Dawson 1994, 2001; Heard 1952; McAdam 1999; Morris 1984; Rosenstone and Hansen 1993; Skocpol, Liazos, and Ganz 2006; Tate 1993).

According to the group-based resource model, perceived group membership also promotes activism. When group members become aware of the injustice of the group's position in society, a collective commitment to correct it ensues (Miller et al. 1981). Perhaps this is why blacks have proven to be more politically engaged than whites, all else equal (Shingles 1981; Verba and Nie 1972). If group identification is in fact related to perceptions of illegitimate treatment, we should expect to find that black veterans identified with other black Southerners. They certainly had grounds to question the legitimacy of Jim Crow; they did, after all, play by the rules of the game, serving in the military, proving their fitness for first-class citizenship. If black veterans recognized the illegitimacy of Jim Crow prior to serving, this recognition should have intensified upon their return to America (Brooks 2004; McMillen 1997; Nalty 1986).

There are several reasons, then, why black veterans' military service may not have had an independent effect upon their activism. For starters, black churches and civil rights organizations encouraged black Southerners to participate in the political process (Dawson 1994; Gurin et al. 1989; Harris 1999; Tate 1993). Black veterans, too, were often intimately involved in civil rights organizations, and, like many others in the black community in the South, most of them had been raised in the church. Additionally, black veterans should have strongly identified with other black Southerners as a group. These factors suggest that military experience may have had no effect on participation in the civil rights movement independent of more conventional explanations of insurgency.

The evidence I collected directly from veterans, on the other hand, suggests that military service increased the likelihood that black veterans would participate in civil rights activism independent of group resources. Indeed, as the interviews make clear, upon their return to the South, black veterans of both World War II and the Korean War believed their participation in the war effort would result in a better life for them and other black Southerners. Serving in the military had made them equal members of the political community, and they were determined to act in accordance with their standing as citizens. Convinced of the illegitimacy of white domination once they got a taste of race relations overseas, and more confident and courageous than other black Southerners as a result of their military experiences, black veterans were relatively insulated from the fear of confronting domination and of the coercion to which black Southerners were routinely subjected when they chose to participate in the political process. Thus, we have reason to expect that these veterans were driven to activism through a combination of the normative and experiential meanings associated with their military service. Nonetheless, it remains to be seen whether or not their military experience had an independent effect upon activism, once competing sources of activism are taken into account.

POLITICAL PARTICIPATION AND RISK: VOTING VERSUS POLITICAL ACTIVISM

Conventional participation in the political process is generally conceived as voting and nonvoting behavior.[5] Nonvoting political activity, such as donating money and time to a candidate, talking to others about voting,

---

[5] I emphasize conventional political participation to highlight the distinction between relatively conventional political activism and the more unconventional activism characterized by protest.

or attending a political meeting, is related to voting insofar as both are ultimately concerned with securing some mix of benefits and rewards, some of which are rooted in self-interest; others may be motivated by duty, friendship, or community recognition (Rosenstone and Hansen 1993). Having said that, one reason that the relationship between voting and nonvoting participatory behavior is at best moderate is in part because the latter requires, among other things, more initiative than voting (Milbrath 1965; Verba and Nie 1972; Verba, Schlozman, and Brady 1995). Indeed, some argue that nonvoting political participation is commensurate with grassroots activism (Harris, Sinclair-Chapman, and B. D. McKenzie 2006).

Another equally important difference emerges between these two types of political activity when we consider racial and regional factors during Jim Crow. Black participation in campaign activity, for instance, enjoyed a lower profile than voting and was therefore considered to be *less* risky (Matthews and Prothro 1966). Casting a ballot, on the other hand, entailed appearing at a specific location, on a specific date, a process that ultimately made it easier for white supremacists to intimidate those who sought to exercise their constitutional right. Indeed, as noted historian Leon Litwack comments, "voting and office holding simply became too risky, often fatal . . . [it] was a sign of assertiveness that few whites would tolerate" (1998, 365). As a result, dozens of black Southerners, many of whom were veterans, were killed attempting to register or attempting to cast a ballot, not to mention the economic reprisals visited upon black Southerners who were merely on voter rolls (Bunche 1973; Klinkner and Smith 1999; McMillen 1989, 1994; Payne 1995). Nonvoting political participation, on the other hand, was less visible, less public. Perhaps this is why it is so difficult to locate instances in which black Southerners endured much in the way of violence when, for instance, they attempted to sway someone's vote or opted to attend a political meeting.[6] In addition to serving as a form of grassroots activism, nonvoting participation, particularly when it was closely associated with a political party, served as a means of channeling black Southerners' frustration with being denied the right to vote (McMillen 1989).

A final distinction is possible between the two modes of political participation, one that's relevant for mobilizing the electorate. Making the decision to attend a political meeting, to help a campaign, to donate, to try to sway someone else's vote is for the most part encouraged by membership in social networks, in both private and associational life (Rosenstone and Hansen 1993). Much of the latter, at least for black Southerners, flowed principally through black religious and secular organizations

---

[6] E-mail exchanges with Steven Lawson and Jennifer Brooks confirmed this observation.

(McAdam 1999; Morris 1984; Skocpol et al. 2006). These organizational ties reinforced a sense of solidarity (Gurin et al. 1989), a unity underwritten by a feeling that "we're all in this together." Attending political meetings, perhaps the most public of the activities that constitute political activism, serves as an example. These were often convened in churches, the hub of black social life. As such, it was more or less a group-based activity, and helped overcome some of the fear associated with nonvoting political participation (Watters and Cleghorn 1967, chap. 6). This was not the case for voting, a more solitary undertaking in which *individuals*, not groups, were often targeted for harassment at the polls.[7]

For these reasons, to distinguish it from the act of voting, I refer to nonvoting political participation simply as political activism. Drawing once again on data collected for the Negro Political Participation Study, I turn first to voting behavior. Here I explore the proposition that veterans were more likely than nonveterans to pursue activism by visiting the polls. Respondents were asked how often they voted in presidential, gubernatorial, school board, and local elections. Using their answers, I created an index from the average score of the respondents on each item. If respondents reported voting at least once, they were coded as participants in the designated activity. Figure 6.1, however, reports the item-by-item results.

Consistent with Hanes Walton's (1985) conclusion, figure 6.1 indicates that black voter turnout was greater during high-profile contests. Not surprisingly, presidential and gubernatorial elections drew the largest proportion of voters, followed by local and school board elections. More important, however, black veterans appear to have voted more frequently than nonveterans in every type of election, and the distinction between veteran and nonveteran participation was greater in more visible elections. To illustrate, black veterans were far more likely to vote in presidential elections than nonveterans (a 30-point gap separates them), whereas they were only somewhat more likely than nonveterans (14 points) to vote in school board elections.

Turning now to political activism, we should expect differences between veterans and nonveterans to be smaller. To gauge the extent of less risky political participation, respondents were asked whether they had ever donated money to a candidate, attended a political meeting or campaign, worked for a candidate, or talked to others to influence votes. Each question required a yes or no response. Their responses are compared in figure 6.2.

---

[7] Factor analysis confirms the distinction between voting and political activism. The first factor yields an eigenvalue of 4; the second factor produced an eigenvalue of 1.4. The correlation between voting and political activism = .37.

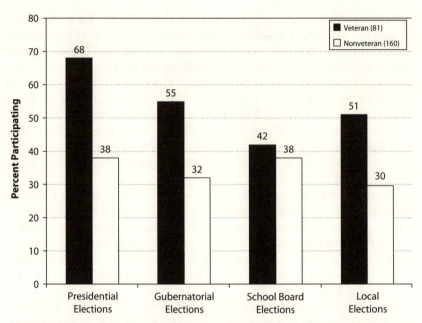

Figure 6.1. Voting behavior, by election type and veteran status. *Source:* Negro Political Participation Study 1961–62.

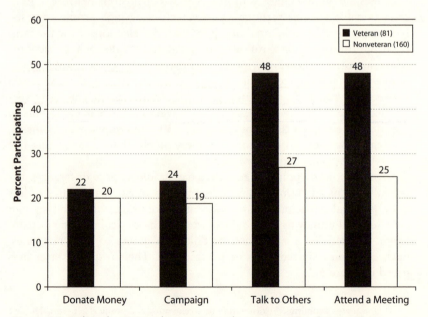

Figure 6.2. Political activism, by activity and veteran status. *Source:* Negro Political Participation Study 1961–62.

As the figure confirms, intergroup differences were indeed smaller for these less risky, grassroots modes of participation, though it is worth noting that more black Southerners preferred voting to political activism. Even here, however, we can see differences in veteran and nonveteran participation rates. The largest gaps between the two groups correspond with the most visible modes of participation: talking to others about voting and attending political meetings. Here, the difference between veterans and nonveterans is 21 and 23 percentage points, respectively. These differences shrink dramatically to 2 and 5 percentage points, however, for the less visible activities of donating money to candidates and working for candidates. The preliminary results for voting behavior and activism, then, are strikingly similar in that the largest gaps between veterans and nonveterans coincide with more visible, and therefore more risky, political acts. As a group, black veterans in the South seem to have been considerably more likely than nonveterans to engage in risky political activities, a sort of activism more likely to incur the wrath of white supremacists than less visible ones.

Although preliminary, these results are nonetheless fairly suggestive, and conform to expectations. They are limited, however, in that they are confined to single items. To increase theoretical traction, I constructed two indexes, one each for voting behavior and political activism. The indexes represent the summed and average responses for the items in figures 6.1 and 6.2.[8] I also consider the potentially confounding effect of education, perhaps the most important predictor of political participation of any kind (Nie, Junn, and Stehlik-Barry 1996). Figures 6.3 and 6.4 represent an assessment of mean group differences for voting behavior and political activism adjusted for years of formal schooling.

Figures 6.3 and 6.4 demonstrate similar patterns: regardless of the mode of activism, veterans participated in politics in all its forms more than did nonveterans—with the exception of college-educated nonveterans, whose participation slightly outstripped that of college-educated veterans. This suggests that even as I account for education, the gap in activism persists for many black Southerners because only 12 percent of this sample attended school beyond the twelfth grade. (See table A.1 in appendix A.)

So far, I have sought to assess whether or not veterans and nonveterans differ with respect to political activism and, in the context of white supremacy, resistance. I now attempt to account for factors beyond education that may have influenced this participation. Most important, in order to confirm that veteran/nonveteran differences are not spurious, I

---

[8] The coefficient for reliability, alpha, is .95 for voting behavior and .68 for political activism.

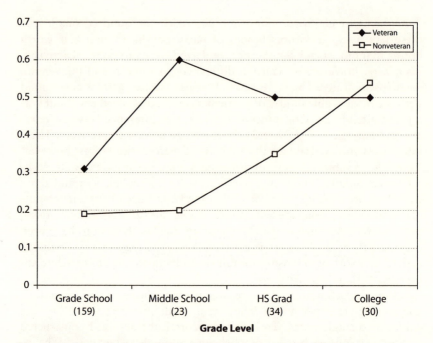

Figure 6.3. Mean level of voting behavior, by education and veteran status.

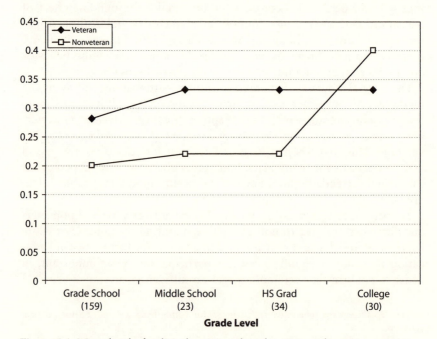

Figure 6.4. Mean level of political activism, by education and veteran status.

account for the possibility that veterans' organizational membership explains their activism, as well as the possibilities that threats of physical and economic coercion affected political participation and that identification with the race affected its likelihood. Accordingly, if veterans were truly more difficult to deter from exercising their constitutional rights than nonveterans, as the interviews indicate, we should expect the largest intergroup differences to have emerged at the polls, with black veterans being more likely to have engaged in this more visible act of resistance. By this logic, intergroup differences should be less apparent in relatively low-visibility, more grassroots political acts.[9]

Modeling Voting and Nonvoting Activism

The Negro Political Participation Study includes an array of items that permit me to model the effect of military service upon participation in the political process. For the dependent variables, voting behavior and political activism, I use the same composite indexes discussed above. To operationalize group resources, I draw upon four items. Answers to the question "How many race relations organizations do you belong to?" enable me to measure respondents' organizational membership. I use frequency of church attendance as a proxy for church membership and religiosity. To measure respondents' identification with the race, I use the questions "Would you say that you feel pretty close to other Negro Southerners in general, or that you don't feel much closer to them than you do to other people?" and "How much interest would you say you have in how Negro Southerners as a whole are getting along in this country?" (See appendix A for coding and question wording.)

Any discussion of political participation prior to the defeat of Jim Crow must also account for geographic context. The relative size of the black population in a given area often affected the ability of blacks to vote (Alt 1994; Matthews and Prothro 1963). In general, wherever blacks outnumbered whites in the South, the prospect of black political power and economic competition inspired fear among whites, often prompting them to resort to violence and intimidation as means of social control (Blalock 1967; Colby 1987). In counties in which black Southerners approached or exceeded the majority, therefore, blacks were less likely to participate in the political process (Alt 1994; Bunche 1973; Key 1949;

---

[9] Repression is not always an effective deterrent. When political participation is connected with the movement, white-on-black violence sometimes backfires, fueling more insurgency (Andrews 2004).

Lawson 1976; Matthews and Prothro 1966; Redding 2003).[10] Rural residency also dampened political participation among black Southerners, as rural blacks were more threatened by violence and more economically dependent on whites. At the same time, they had less access to activist churches and less extensive social networks, both of which were key to mobilization (Key 1949; Matthews and Prothro 1966; McAdam 1999; Morris 1984). Thus, in counties where the black population was either equal to or greater than the white population, we should expect black participation to have been depressed. We should also expect white domination in the rural South to have dampened black political participation in those areas.

Among demographic factors, we must consider the influence of age on political participation. In most cases, one's political appetite increases with age (Rosenstone and Hansen 1993; Verba and Nie 1972). This was true among white Southerners, but for black Southerners, participation actually *decreased* with age (Matthews and Prothro 1966). Once history is taken into account, this finding is easily explicable. As familiarity with the ways of Jim Crow increased, which it did with age, interest in political matters declined. Income and increments of formal schooling also predict the participatory levels of black Southerners (Matthews and Prothro 1966).

Table 6.1 displays the results of a test by which I estimated the effect of military upon voting behavior using four models. I did so in order to determine whether military service continues to *directly* predict political activism even as potential mediating factors are introduced. In the first model, I estimate the simple relationship between military service and voting behavior. In the second model, I add sociodemographic controls for age, education, and income. I account for possible confounds associated with contextual effects, such as areas in which African Americans made up at least half of the population, and whether one lived in a rural or urban area, in the third model. Finally, the fourth model considers the effects of group-based resources on voting behavior. This final specification is included to test the hypothesis that black veterans' activism is explained by their military experience—not group-based resources. If the effect of military service disappears on the introduction of group-based resources to the model, we can say that black veterans' military experience has no independent effect upon political activism. Otherwise, the

---

[10] Repression does not always succeed at reducing mobilization. In fact, sometimes white countermobilization backfired, actually increasing civil rights activism. This was most often the case during organized campaigns that generated great media interest (Andrews 2004).

TABLE 6.1
Determinants of Voting Behavior among Black Southerners

Variable	Model 1	Model 2	Model 3	Model 4
Service	.173*	.125*	.095*	.106*
	(.045)	(.047)	(.046)	(.045)
Sociodemographics				
Age		.062	.070	.027
		(.064)	(.062)	(.063)
Education		.188*	.216*	.117
		(.084)	(.081)	(.083)
Income		.246*	.166*	.149*
		(.091)	(.090)	(.088)
Context				
Black≥50%			−.193*	−.224*
			(.044)	(.043)
Rural=1			−.045	−.075
			(.045)	(.041)
Group resources				
Church				.150*
				(.065)
Black organizations				.320*
				(.081)
Group identification				.101
				(.083)
Intercept	.197*	.122*	.271*	.085
	(.026)	(.046)	(.055)	(.095)
Adj. R²	.057	.107	.174	.282
Root MSE	.332	.322	.311	.293
Cases	235	235	234	231

Note: All cell entries are unstandardized OLS coefficients and standard errors. All tests are one-tailed, where (*) indicates $p < .05$ or less. All variables are recoded 0–1.

case for military experience, and black republicanism, gathers more strength.[11]

[11] Another specification, one in which product terms are used to test the hypothesis of whether or not the effect of military service varies according to context, has been estimated elsewhere (Parker 2009). It's reasonable to consider the extent to which, say, rural residency and the black population relative to whites moderates the effect of military service on political activism. I did not do so here because theoretical priority resides with accounting for alternative hypotheses.

As Table 6.1 indicates, the results confirm black veterans' commitment to activism. The outcome for models 1 and 2 is consistent with expectations. Without controls, the positive relationship between military service and voting is easily discerned: having served in the military made black veterans more likely than nonveterans to engage in risky political participation. Introducing the sociodemographic controls failed to alter this result; moreover, as predicted—as education level and income increased—so too did the likelihood of voting. Model 3, in which contextual predictors were introduced, indicates that veterans' determination to vote did not disappear, even as "black belt" areas of the South loomed large in the model as deterrent to voting, as did whether or not one lived in the city or the country.

The fourth model introduced group-based resources. Even after accounting for all of the factors that inspired black activism, the effect of military service on relatively risky participation remains unmediated, continuing to exert a direct effect on black Southerners' voting behavior. Moreover, as we predicted, organizational membership encouraged voting. On the other hand, where black Southerners were in the majority, voting declined. While better-off black Southerners were more likely to cast ballots, the effect of education on risky participation ceases to be significant upon the introduction of group resources to the model. This indicates the likelihood that education works through group resources to affect voting behavior among black Southerners. It's likely that this result is a reflection of the presence of relatively educated black Southerners in black organizations.

Taken together, the four models tell us that black veterans engaged in risky political activity more frequently than did nonveterans and that this result cannot be explained away by their access to other, more conventional sources of activism or by veterans' sociodemographic profile. While it is the case that higher income, church membership, and membership in black organizations all influenced black Southerners to engage in relatively risky political activities, these are not the sole sources of such political activity.

I now turn to political activism. Recall that political activism differed from voting in that it did not require black Southerners to expose themselves to the wrath of white supremacists, as much as did attempting to vote, and that it reflected grassroots behavior. Relative to voting, we should therefore expect to find smaller differences between veterans and nonveterans. Table 6.2 provides confirmation.

While it is true that veteran/nonveteran differences are smaller for political activism, the groups remain distinct: veterans more so than nonveterans were moved to engage in nonvoting activity. In models 1 and 2, the connection between military service and political activism is as

TABLE 6.2
Determinants of Political Activism among Black Southerners

Variable	Model 1	Model 2	Model 3	Model 4
Service	.119*	.088*	.075*	.071*
	(.042)	(.044)	(.044)	(.043)
Sociodemographics				
Age		.061	.060	.017
		(.060)	(.060)	(.060)
Education		.127	.139*	.084
		(.078)	(.078)	(.079)
Income		.188*	.155*	.150*
		(.084)	(.085)	(.083)
Context				
Black ≥ 50%			−.111*	−.114*
			(.042)	(.041)
Rural = 1			−.010	−.005
			(.044)	(.041)
Group resources				
Church				.173*
				(.063)
Black organizations				.176*
				(.077)
Group identification				.031
				(.080)
Intercept	.229*	.165*	.243*	.106
	(.024)	(.043)	(.053)	(.091)
Adj. R^2	.028	.057	.099	.159
Root MSE	.308	.304	.301	.292
Cases	240	240	239	237

Note: All cell entries are unstandardized OLS coefficients and standard errors. All tests are one-tailed, where (*) indicates $p < .05$ or less. All variables are recoded 0–1.

predicted—military experience promoted engagement. Income is the sole sociodemographic predictor that registers anything meaningful: better-off black Southerners were more likely to engage in political activism than their poorer peers. In the third model, increasing education, income, and moving from nonveteran to veteran status all increase the likelihood of participating in civic activity. Context also matters in that black Southerners who lived in areas where they were the majority chose to participate less frequently, probably because they did not wish to risk retaliation from white supremacists. Urban/rural distinctions, however, had no bearing upon whether or not black Southerners participated in this dimension of the political process.

Model 4 tested the hypothesis that the veteran/nonveteran difference disappears once group resources are taken into consideration. The results indicate that while church membership and organizational membership were important, robust predictors of political activism, the relationship between military service and participation in this dimension of the political process remained unmediated, if somewhat diluted Geographical context is again shown to have affected levels of participation, as black Southerners living in areas where they constituted at least half of the local population avoided the political scene. Higher income is also shown in this model to have underwritten participation, while education drops out as a reliable predictor, again apparently working through (i.e., mediated by) group resources.

Overall, these results allow us to conclude that organizational involvement in churches and civil rights organizations were effective sources of political mobilization, and that the racial makeup of the population in a given area also figured prominently in convincing black Southerners to engage in political activism or deterred them from doing so. Even so, military service had a separate and independent effect as a catalyst for black political participation of all types, including less risky political behavior. In this case, on accounting for group-based resources, differences between veterans and nonveterans should have been more difficult to discern. Yet even here the effects of military service remain apparent.

Let me be clear; I do not mean to suggest that nonvoting political activism was without danger. Rather, the point is that black Southerners' attempts to both register to vote and to actually vote were relatively more visible and, therefore, more dangerous.[12]

These differences parallel Doug McAdam's distinction between low-risk activism and high-risk activism in which "risk refers to the anticipated dangers—whether legal, social, physical, financial, and so forth—of engaging in a particular type of activity" (1986, 67). Hence, these results suggest the strength of military experience as a means of stimulating activism and resistance beyond the conventional channels of insurgency such as black institutions—religious and secular—as well as racial solidarity. But why, exactly, were veterans so insistent upon political activism of this kind, especially when we recall the barriers to mainstream political participation—including violence and threats of economic reprisals—to

---

[12] At some point in the process, blacks encountered whites either formally (the registrar, the polling official), or informally (whites physically threatening black citizens during registration or at the polls).

which black Southerners were exposed? To the extent that conventional political participation is commensurate with resistance and activism in general, the interviews in chapters 3 and 4 provide answers. In chapter 3, in which I touch upon military experience, several veterans recounted the good and bad times associated with their service. It's likely that among other factors the self-efficacy and confidence generated from their military experience furnished the belief that they could be agents of change. After all, they had survived serving in a racist military in which they were often forced to wage two wars: one in the battlefield, the other on base. Moreover, if the sentiments and actions of these men are any indication, many of them, we learned, had no reservations about resisting racism in the ranks. These actions likely benefited them on returning to society, as many of the men had openly challenged whites and lived to tell about it.

Chapter 4 informs the results of the current chapter through the provision of a rationale by which veterans justified their criticism and activism. In light of their sacrifice, most of the men were critical of the social conditions to which they returned. Did they not earn, for themselves and for the black community, equal standing? Had they not performed their duty? Yes on both counts, they believed. And like good republicans, they undertook activism based, in large measure, on their critique of continuing white supremacy.

Returning to the survey data, the current chapter confirms the generalizability of the qualitative evidence. It shows that the mix of confidence and courage wasn't confined to my respondents, or even Medgar Evers and Hosea Williams, two of the civil rights icons and veterans mentioned in the introduction to this volume.[13] Likewise, the findings echo the activism of the veterans who spoke in chapter 4, suggesting that the attitudes and behavior of my respondents were nothing exceptional. The dialog between the qualitative and quantitative findings indicates a more general trend among black veterans of the era; that the social and political consequences of military service may be extended to veterans as a group, at the individual level.

• • •

Recently, scholars have begun to acknowledge the contributions of black veterans to social change in the South. At issue in this chapter was the question of whether veteran-activists were exceptional people who incidentally

---

[13] It's worth noting that veterans were also more likely than nonveterans to join civil rights organizations. For instance, almost twice as many veterans (at 21 percent) versus nonveterans (at 12 percent; p<.04) were members of at least one secular civil rights group.

happened to be veterans or whether willingness to fight Jim Crow was more common among veterans than it was among the black Southern population at large. We know, of course, that many nonveterans were moved to challenge Jim Crow when embedded within organizational structures. Thus, it was not at all that clear that veterans' motivation to challenge white supremacy differed in any way from that of nonveterans. This chapter's exploration of risky and less risky political behavior show that it did: military experience was salient. As the results indicate, it affected black veterans' activism independent of their involvement with civic or church organizations; independent of their age, economic status, or level of education; and independent of the relative size of the black population where they lived. The results point, in other words, to the influence of black republicanism on Southern veterans.

These results indicate that the political activism of these veterans went beyond that which was associated with group resources—that the activism of Medgar Evers, Hosea Williams, and others was not exceptional but something more like the rule. We must entertain the possibility that the military experience of black veterans provided them with the impetus to seek change, as the veterans I interviewed informed me that it did. Veterans' sense of what the nation owed them, we are told, fed into militant dispositions that made them determined to participate in the political process. In this way, the interviews validate Cynthia Enloe's (1980) work, which suggests that minorities who serve in the military become more likely than nonveteran minorities to challenge the status quo. The present volume takes her work a step further, however, by specifying a concrete mechanism by which minority veterans—at least in the American context—became militant.

One way to appreciate the effects of military service is to compare its explanatory power to that of what is perhaps the most consistent individual-level predictor of political participation and mobilization: education. For both voting behavior and political activism, the effects of military service remained intact through each model specification. The same cannot be said for education. When one controls for group resources, the substantive effect of education declines, suggesting that its role in motivating political activism is mediated by group-related activism. That military service maintains its independence even when group-based resources are accounted for indicates that there was something unique about black veterans' military experience that motivated their activism. That something, I argue, is that black veterans' military service produced something akin a republican worldview.

The results of this chapter also allow us to distinguish the effects of black republicanism from those of radical egalitarianism. To the extent that black radical egalitarians favored working through black organizations to realize their goals (Dawson 2001), the models enable us to measure, through the proxy of membership in black organizations, the extent to which radical egalitarians were activists, and to what degree this activism was explained by their ideology. To be sure, black republicanism and radical egalitarianism both predict activism. The fact that the effect of military service remains viable after controlling for the influence of black organizations, however, is another indication that black republicanism was the principal source of activism among black veterans.

Finally, in the absence of systematic evidence, there has been some disagreement about the role that veterans played in Southern social reform. Ronald Krebs (2006) doubts that black veterans were more politically active than nonveterans. His work is based largely upon an interpretation of anecdotal evidence, however, from which it is difficult to draw firm conclusions. Suzanne Mettler (2005a) has shown that black veterans were indeed politically active, but her work focuses upon the GI Bill. She argues that veterans who used the GI Bill were more politically engaged than veterans who elected not to take advantage of it. In fact, one of the shortcoming of the data on which I draw is that it does not allow me to control for GI Bill usage, which affected 56 percent of nonwhite veterans (Mettler 2005b). Still, while the use of the GI Bill boosted political activism, the absence of it from Matthews and Prothro's data set does not damage my argument. Indeed, the fact that 44 percent of the veterans did not use the GI Bill yet as a whole remained more committed to activism than did nonveterans strengthens my claim that military experience is an important predictor of political activism.

Taps for Jim Crow in the Postwar South

Black leaders Frederick Douglass and W.E.B. DuBois both recognized the value of military service in the pursuit of equal citizenship. Each hoped that the sacrifices made by African Americans would generate policy and legislation equal to their commitment to the nation. In Douglass's case, these hopes were realized. The service of African Americans was a key factor in the victory of the United States over the Confederacy, and it helped to spur postwar racial reform. Jim Crow settled in shortly thereafter, however, affecting the long-term consequences of reform in the South. DuBois, on the other hand, was bitterly disappointed with the results of the First World War, after which African Americans' situation grew worse. It would take another worldwide conflagration for DuBois's vision to be realized as black veterans, indeed, returned to fight. It is now clear that the black Southerners who were veterans of World War II and the Korean War did just that. Imagine the movement without Hosea Williams leading the "Bloody Sunday" march over the Edmund Pettus bridge between Selma and Montgomery, Alabama; without Aaron Henry's leadership of both the Mississippi Freedom Democratic Party and the NAACP of Mississippi consider the Student Nonviolent Coordinating Committee without the leadership of James Forman; and how can we forget the courage of James Meredith, Medgar Evers, and many other veterans?

This study has sought to explore two basic questions. First, did military service generate insurgency among black veterans at large, as opposed to among just a few prominent veterans, and if so, by what mechanism? Second, was the effect of military service independent of the conventional explanation of insurgency, which holds that veterans' activism was a product of their access to group-based resources? In response to these questions, I have argued that black veterans, driven by the rhetoric of black republicanism that developed at least in part as a result of their military experience, sought to challenge white supremacy upon separating from the military. This book illustrates that their activism had much to do with their military service and remained independent of the influence of black civic organizations or identification with the race.

These results confirm the recent accounts of several historians who have argued that veterans were important to African American resistance

(Brooks 2004; Dittmer 1994; Henry 2000; Hill 2004; Lawson 1991; O'Brien 1999; Payne 1995; Tyson 1999). *Fighting for Democracy* also extends historical accounts in at least two ways. First, this volume adds a theoretical dimension to the many fine narrative accounts on the subject, offering a more general framework within which these more specific historical narratives may fit. Second, through the use of survey data, this book adds an empirical dimension that heretofore has been missing. The ability to account for possible confounding influences upon the relationship between military service and militancy strengthens the historical accounts by using new evidence capable of ruling out alternative explanations for the activism of black veterans, especially for those who argued that these veterans were movement catalysts (Lawson 1991; Morris 1984). Indeed, even as we move beyond the aforementioned civil rights icons who were also veterans, we see that there were also "ordinary" veterans, much like Ivory Perry, a veteran movement activist and Korean War veteran who sought to contest white domination but never rose to national prominence (Lipsitz 1988).

One can even argue that black veterans' leadership during the early phases of the movement, depending upon how one chooses to date it, was crucial to sustaining the black freedom struggle. While the urban Southern black church wielded more power and resources than did its rural counterpart (McAdam 1999), it remained free of insurgent activity early on in the movement. Likewise, college students, black and otherwise, didn't become a force in the movement until the early 1960s (Carson 1981; Forman 1972; McAdam 1988). This leaves us with veterans. If we date the movement to the 1930s, as does Nikhil Singh (2005) in his account, we may cite the leadership of black veterans of the First World War. The efforts of Charles Hamilton Houston in the courts constructed the scaffolding for what would eventually follow. Of course, we cannot forget about other black officers who served during World War I. Several led the Committee for Participation of Negroes in the National Defense Program in 1938, which lobbied for more equal military service prior to the Second World War.

In the absence of an increasing presence of black Southerners in uniform, many of whom went on to provide leadership in the movement, it's possible that the fight for equality may have unfolded a bit differently, though still successfully. If the movement began to stir in the 1940s, as Taeku Lee (2002) argues, we must include black veterans of the Second World War. Medgar Evers, Amzie Moore, W. W. Law, and Robert F. Williams went on to head important NAACP chapters in Georgia, Mississippi, and North Carolina during the growth of the organization after the war. They were instrumental in transforming the venerable national organization into one with formidable local, grassroots power. Moreover, the leadership of veterans who stepped up to form the Georgia Veterans' League ultimately mobilized enough black voters in 1946 to threaten Governor Eugene Talmadge's bid to retake Georgia's statehouse (Brooks 2004) must certainly be considered an important forerunner to the Southern Christian Leadership Conference's campaigns in the late 1980s.

My results upset accounts in which the activism of black veterans is questioned. Ronald Krebs's (2006) approach is thoughtful, well executed, and long overdue. In striving for theoretical generality, however, he underestimates the importance of the historical relationship between African Americans and military service. The socialization mechanisms he outlines may have failed among American whites, and among the Druze in Israel, another group to which he applies his framework. The present study, however, casts doubt upon the conclusion that this failure applies to African Americans. Black veterans, at least in the South, were not forced to abandon the lessons of their military experience if they wished to conform to the norms of black civil society, as Krebs argues was the case for veterans generally. On the contrary, black veterans were esteemed by the black community *because of* their military experience. (See appendix B for the number of news articles in the *Chicago Defender* in which military service was emphasized.) They were a source of strength and pride for the black community, and they assisted in setting the tone for demands for citizenship long after the wars in which they served had ended (Fletcher 1968; Morris 1984; Reich 1996).

Principal Findings

Given everything black veterans endured while serving, it was an experience they did not soon forget. Often, veterans emerge more disciplined, confident, and mature from military experience than they were when they enlisted (Elder, Gimble, and Ivie 1986,1991). This is not an insignificant transformation, as traits learned in the military are frequently parlayed into life success (Moskos and Butler 1996). For black veterans, though—and especially for those who served prior to the Vietnam era— the military experience was even more significant, because it contained both positive experiences and traumatic struggles with discrimination and racism.

No one contests that black servicemen were subjected to racist treatment. We know less, though, about the positive aspects of their military service. The veterans I interviewed spoke of the myriad ways in which whites attempted to transport racism overseas, even attempting to co-opt locals. They also mentioned, however, how they actively attempted to buck racism, literally fighting back on several occasions, and they impressed upon me that the pride, confidence, and opportunities that they were supplied with in the military had positive effects on their lives. Add to this the sense of masculinity that accompanies arms bearing and we can account for why black veterans were willing to confront racism in the military. Overcoming the negative aspects of military service by drawing on its positive aspects symbolized, for black veterans, their achievement and courage.

Military service as a political symbol extended beyond the period of veterans' service to serve normative purposes. To black Southern veterans, their military service signified both their commitment to America and their entrance into the first rank of the political community. We know this because the veterans I interviewed almost always framed their claims on America, and those of the black community, in terms of their service. Upon returning to the South and finding that nothing had changed, these veterans referred to their sacrifices in the military as the basis for their criticism of Southern society and for their activism. To the extent that their experiences in uniform drove them to draw on the language of republicanism to frame their criticism and justify their resistance, I call the belief system to which black veterans appeared to adhere *black republicanism*.

Black republicanism represents an amended version of classical republicanism. Several of the veterans I interviewed were emphatic about their identification with the nation, a classical republican trait. Yet the frequency with which they invoked race in discussions of their identification, as well as their military experiences, is a telling sign that the experience of domination lurks in their memories as an integral part of what military service symbolizes for them. Though they rejected the label *African American*, these veterans were also committed to the black community, on behalf of which they were wiling to absorb insult while serving in a Jim Crow military. Both of these factors indicate veterans' ideological affiliation with black republicanism rather than classical republicanism. Likewise, black veterans expressed appreciation for the institution of citizenship, using republican rhetoric to define good citizenship by emphasizing its duties and obligations. Here, too, however, we see the specter of domination, for veterans also emphasize the importance of citizens' rights—anathema to classical republicanism—which they perceive to be a necessary counter to white domination, their domination by an internal enemy.

Black republicanism represents an addition to the roster of black political ideologies. It incorporates some of the tenets associated with black liberalism, particularly radical egalitarianism. Both are committed to making America realize its democratic promise. Each also subscribes to criticism and activism as modes of keeping the state honest. But the two ideologies part company in key areas—first among them their attitudes toward the state. Black republicans, as we have seen, are less willing to countenance state intervention than radical egalitarians. In addition, the two ideologies differ in the source of their criticism and activism. Black republicans' criticism and activism grows out of their critical and relatively organic attachment to the nation as a function of their military experience. The criticism and activism of radical egalitarianism, by contrast, is fueled more by strategic aims and liberal rhetoric. Perhaps more important, masculinity is a point of departure between the two ideologies. Black republicanism, like its mainstream counterpart, is gendered; radical egalitarianism, in theory if not in practice, is not.

Black republicanism is also associated with the adoption of insurgent attitudes and behavior. Upon returning home, many (but not all) black veterans declined to embrace the political culture of the South, in which traditionalism stifled change. They were also somewhat less politically liberal than nonveterans, though they were certainly more liberal than white Southerners. Given their poor treatment within a state institution, the military, they were less than enthusiastic about trusting the government—central or otherwise. And, as their subscription to black republicanism would predict, they were adamant about equality, even if achieving it required them to court the possibility of confronting hostile whites.

The adoption of insurgent attitudes, insofar as they ran counter to accepted Southern social practice, represented some progress in comparison to the relatively conservative attitudes toward change of many black Southerners (Marx 1967). Attitudes, however, may be concealed to avoid reprisals; activism cannot. To the extent that political participation of any kind was an attempt to dismantle white domination, whites forbade it. Attempts to participate in mainstream politics—voting, campaigning—were especially discouraged. By definition, then, black political participation constituted insurgent behavior in the South, for it sought to buck authority and convention. Black veterans were determined to exercise the rights for which they had served and fought, and they voted and engaged in nonvoting political participation at a higher rate than nonveterans, the baseline group against which comparisons were made.

It seems, then, that black republicanism is consistent with the type of oppositional ideology to which Cathy Cohen (1999) refers because it interrogates dominant belief systems, providing veterans a means of understanding their subordinate position in the American social order. In this way, black republicanism is similar to black liberal ideologies, including radical egalitarianism, insofar as it turns liberal political philosophy on itself using its own principles to challenge the dominant interpretation of liberalism and republicanism. Again, however, black republicanism differs because its appeals for redress were based upon sacrifice, particularly military service, whereas black liberalism's were based upon liberal universalism.

At this point it's fair to question whether or not the emancipatory effects of military service are confined to blacks. If Latinos are any indication, the answer is no: military experience has also helped to fuel insurgent behavior among some Latinos. As it turns out, World War II produced a cadre of Latino veterans who founded and led Latino organizations dedicated to fighting for their civil rights in the postwar West and Southwest (Muñoz 1989; Pycior 1997). Thus, the effects of military service for blacks and Latinos, at least during the postwar years, worked from the bottom up. In other words, reform was related to military service *through* veterans pressing for change. For women the story was a bit different. In the wake of their contributions to a winning effort during the Second World War, women emerged from it less better off than they were when the war began, their civic standing vis-à-vis men's injured by inaccessibility to combat (Ritter 2006).

As the women's movement gained momentum in the 1960s and '70s, however, women's military service had a shot at working from the top down. Indeed, one could argue that were it not for the issue of conscription in the early 1970s, women would have been closer to securing full equality with the Equal Rights Amendment (Kerber 1998; Mansbridge 1986), something that was ultimately rendered moot by statutes passed from the early 1970s through the early '80s that were geared to expand women's rights (Berry 1986). Even so, women continue to suffer discrimination and harassment, something that military experience may ultimately help them combat. One way it may do so is through a discovery of feminist consciousness from exposure to sexism in the military (Katzenstein 1998). Like black Southerners who became intolerant to mistreatment in the military, something that helped to push many of them into activism upon departing the military, it's possible that a similar experience may spark female veterans to contest sexism in their postservice lives. Moreover, as an institution that is known to foster political participation (Ellison 1992; Teigen 2006), the military, as a state institution, promises to close the gender gap in ways similar to its religious and economic counterparts (Burns, Schlozman, and Verba, 2002).

Military service also promises to make citizens out of immigrants, many of whom are of Latino descent. Here, however, the process is different. Unlike women and Latinos with citizenship, who at least formally enjoy full membership in the political community, immigrant soldiers, also known as "green card soldiers," are resident aliens. In return for serving in the military, president George W. Bush issued an executive order waiving the residency requirement for naturalization, something that normally requires living in the United States for at least five years. Thus, for immigrants, the process is top down versus bottom up.

Whether it works from the top down or the bottom up, there's evidence to support the proposition that the connection between military service and citizenship is neither bound to a particular group (African Americans) nor confined to the postwar South. Before moving on to discuss the broader implications of the present volume, I must first consider at least three possible objections to its findings. One charge to which some would say the book is vulnerable is that it ignores structural explanations of resistance. The argument here is that the conditions were ripe for activism across the board. In this account, veterans were no different than anyone else who participated in activism because these conditions increased the activism of everyone. But if the conditions were conducive to activism for most everyone, should not structural-level explanations by treated as a constant, not a variable? Moreover, this book shows that even with the ubiquity of activism, black veterans continued to stand out.

Another possible objection to this study is that the interviews may be subject to bias—specifically, the use of a snowball sample. It should be noted, however, that this was unavoidable given the increasing mortality rates of people who served during World War II and the Korean War. Even so, potential bias exists, which is a reason why I supplemented my interviews with survey data. Moreover, the interviews served two purposes. First, I sought to use them to illustrate how black veterans viewed military service and its consequences; second, they were a means by which to derive testable hypotheses for chapters 5 and 6. Having said that, the biases that may have affected the results culled from the interviews were corrected upon the introduction of controls into the survey. For instance, by virtue of their organizational membership, and the fact that voluntary organizations tend to encourage activism (Verba, Schlozman, and Brady 1995), I must consider that veterans in the snowball sample were inclined toward political engagement. Moreover, these black Southerners tended to be relatively well educated. (See appendix C for details.) Both are legitimate concerns. For these reasons, the data from The Negro Political Participation Study is important because it allows me to go beyond the individuals who were part of the snowball sample and generalize to the mass public. The data allows me to control for membership in black organizations. On the subject of educational disparities, almost to a man, veterans in the snowball sample increased their human capital either during or after serving in the armed forces. Nevertheless, the Negro Political Participation Study data allows me to correct for whatever educational disparities there were among black Southern men at the time by holding it constant. A final rationale for drawing on a snowball sample in the face of possible bias is the alternative, doing nothing at all. Clearly, this is no real alternative, especially if the objective is to gain leverage on why military service on the part of black Southerners was so effective at mobilizing segments of the black community.

The discerning critic may also raise a third objection. This one would contend that, while heroic, black veterans' relative insistence upon school-based integration, their rejection of traditionalism, and their willingness to participate in the political process fails to amount to systematic challenges to the ideology of white supremacy on which Jim Crow rested. No doubt, taken individually, adoption of these attitudes and undertaking this behavior—that is, political participation—may constitute heroism, but it doesn't rise to the level of a systematic challenge to Southern tradition. When taken together, however, these insurgent attitudes and behavior did, in fact, issue a resounding challenge to the ways of Jim Crow, thus threatening to undermine white supremacy in the postwar South. Rejecting traditionalism interrupted the maintenance of domination by causing folk to question "the way things were," while insisting upon school-based integration threatened to undermine the social, educational, and therefore economic foundations of white supremacy. Beyond signaling one's commitment to insurgent behavior, participation in the political process posed a threat to the political foundation of white supremacy. If black veterans were outstanding in only insurgent attitudes or behavior, but not both, it becomes easier for the critic to charge that black veterans were perhaps heroic, even brave, but no different than nonveterans in their push for systemic change. But since veterans were more determined than others to interrogate white domination, no matter its location, it suggests their commitment to wholesale change.

THE IMPLICATIONS OF FIGHTING FOR DEMOCRACY

Now that I've summarized the major findings, it's time to illustrate how they intersect with and inform cognate literatures. As we shall see, the book informs at least two fields in political science. The findings also promise to contribute to sociology and history as well.

Black Republicanism and Veterans' Civil Rights Activism

This study has confirmed the accuracy and generalizability of historical accounts of service-related insurgency. By drawing on individual-level data across the South, it shows that the effects of military service were relevant beyond, say, North Carolina or Mississippi. The book generalizes in another way: black republicanism encompasses a number of existing explanations for veterans' resistance across the South. Historians have explained the reasons why black veterans resisted in various ways, paying particular attention to veterans' race consciousness, their sense of masculinity, their personal efficaciousness, their shift in political identification while in the service, and their sense of entitlement (Brooks 2004; Dalfiume 1969; O'Brien 1999; Tyson 1999; Wynn 1993).

If we think about these explanations in terms of the components of black republicanism, we see that all of them are part of this study's model of veteran activism. The experiential component of military service provides an explanation for veterans' race consciousness, sense of masculinity, and efficaciousness. Race consciousness is, among other things, an *awareness* of the illegitimacy with which race structures life chances (Gurin, Hatchett, and Jackson 1989; Gurin, Miller, and Gurin 1980). Serving overseas made black veterans aware of the illegitimacy of Jim Crow, after which some blamed the limitations of their life chances on the persistence of white supremacy. Masculinity, as we have seen, is a product of military culture and arms bearing. Efficaciousness, finally, is produced by the confidence gained from a successful stint in the military, including the educational and vocational opportunities to which servicemen are exposed.

The normative meaning of military service, in turn, is responsible for veterans' sense of entitlement and the shifts in their political identity. American political culture prizes the contributions of veterans. Equity requires that individuals be rewarded in proportion to their contributions to the political community (Deutsch 1975; Hochschild 1981). By this criterion, veterans should be among the most rewarded citizens in American society. Black veterans expected equality as a reward for their service, to which they were entitled by virtue of their sacrifices. Black republicanism also explains veterans' shift toward a new, more American political identity insofar as the performance of military service resulted in identification—albeit a qualified, critical one—with the nation and its values. The veterans I interviewed insisted upon identifying as American and explained that they felt more American as a result of serving in the armed forces. This transformation in their political identification was caused by their military experiences and mediated by their encounters with racial discrimination.

The Military as a Source of Insurgency

Moving from the cultural to the institutional, the military was a source of active, public resistance. Scholars of African American insurgency in the South typically locate the agency for insurgency within black civic institutions (McAdam 1999; Morris 1984). The black church, black fraternal organizations, and civil rights organizations are rightfully recognized for their ability to mobilize protest. These institutions could recruit, organize, furnish leadership, and sow much-needed solidarity for the movement, all of which was part of a larger institutional script that all of them more or less followed. To be sure, each had its own organizational idiosyncrasies—different tactical approaches, for example—but they all had a common goal: the achievement of equality for African Americans.

In the early civil rights movement, black civic institutions were geared toward supporting insurgent activities. The same cannot be said of the military as an institution. Far from it: obedience and discipline are the hallmarks of the military's institutional culture. Yet, as the interviews in this book highlight, military experience continued to motivate black veterans' resistance for many years after their discharge from the military. Ironically, the institutional culture of the military helped to teach black veterans to balk at submitting to domination. The military's emphasis on masculinity, combined with its racist culture, all but guaranteed this result. Black servicemen were taught to not to cower in the face of fear. They were taught that wearing the same uniform as whites and bearing arms signified their equality. In this way, the military as an institution acted as the sponsor of veterans' insurgency.

War and Racial Reform

Another area of scholarly inquiry on which this book touches is the connection between war and racial reform. With the exception of Mark Sawyer's (2006) work, which examines the interplay of macro- and microlevels of analysis, scholarship that focuses upon war and reform typically analyzes data at the macrolevel. Some scholars, for instance, make the case that racial progress resulted when it was politically expedient to do so, a consequence of wartime domestic and international political concerns (Borstelmann 2001; Dudziak 2000; Kryder 2000; Plummer 1996; Skrentny 2002). For Gary Gerstle (2001), war was a means of incorporating non-American *ethnics*—not races—deemed worthy of assimilation. This excluded blacks, Latinos, and Asians from President Theodore Roosevelt's vision of a nation.[1] Macrohistorical explanations for racial progress in the period following World War II and the Korean War emphasize the importance of the rationales for war mobilization, the scope of mobilization, and the consequences attached to each (Klinkner

---

[1] Salyer's (2004) work on war and citizenship, however, shows how military service on the part of Asian Americans during the First World War allowed them to qualify for naturalization.

and Smith 1999; Kryder 2000). Manifestly structural factors that ultimately led to reform include economic aspects of making war that increased the political and economic power of African Americans (McAdam 1999; Wynn 1993).

This study does not claim to answer the question of how war effects social change. Rather, in tracing veterans' political activism, it offers an individual-level account of how war may tangibly produce reform. With its emphasis on microlevel processes, it highlights a path by which military service led to reform via black veterans' participation in the political process. Beyond serving as a proxy for insurgency, black participation in the mainstream political process in some cases helped to improve the circumstances of some black Southerners prior to the passage of the Voting Rights Act of 1965 (Button 1989; Keech 1968; Lawson 1985; Matthews and Prothro 1966). This study also indicates why black veterans sought change, and in doing so, it reveals how far they were willing to go in order to achieve it.

Black Republicanism and the Citizen-Soldier Ideal

One of the most enduring beliefs among republican theorists is that soldiering promotes courage, selflessness, fraternity, and patriotism—all virtues that are essential traits of good citizens in a democratic republic (Pocock 1975; Snyder 1999). Civic virtue is also very important, for in a democratic republic the welfare of the political community must take priority over individual interest lest the community court corruption and collapse. According to Niccolò Machiavelli, the citizen-soldier formed the backbone of the republic, for in time of war he fought for its preservation while in peacetime he exercised the discipline acquired in the military to produce the civic virtue required for the practice of republican citizenship (Pocock 1975).

In theory the citizen-soldier ideal is sound. Men are willing to bear arms to ensure liberty and avoid enslavement, particularly given that the decision to go to war in the first place is made collectively, arrived at through a deliberative process in which the citizen-soldier participates. But the republic about which Machiavelli theorized was more racially homogenous than the American republic. Though property was required for citizenship in Florence, only citizens went to war. This was fair, because propertied citizens had the most to lose from external conquest. Until the mid-1960s, on the other hand, when the federal assault on Jim Crow reached its zenith, black Americans, and especially black Southerners, had neither liberty nor property rights equal to those of white Americans. Yet African Americans served and fought, several times providing the deciding edge in battle—when they were allowed to do so.

If citizen-soldiers are moved to fight in order to avoid enslavement and retain their liberty, how does one understand the service of blacks who were the victims of domination? If citizen-soldiers participate in the decision to wage war, how do we account for the participation of blacks who were proscribed from voting? How, if at all, were they able to develop the patriotism necessary for the exercise of civic virtue in the absence of full citizenship? Black republicanism provides a way of amending the citizen-soldier ideal: black servicemen were not citizens before going to war, but, as we have seen, serving caused them to believe that they had earned equal citizenship. Believing that they were citizens, eventually, earned for them the equal citizenship to which they aspired.

Reconsidering Race and Nation

Finally, black republicanism represents a new conceptual lens through which to investigate the interface between race and nation. Perhaps the single most important insight DuBois provided in his pioneering work on the black experience, *The Souls of Black Folk* (1990), regards the collision between race and nation in the psyche of African Americans. Double consciousness is one of the consequences of this clash: African Americans are both black and American. But as Jim Sidanius and Felicia Pratto (1999) illustrate, these identities are often difficult to reconcile. Nonetheless, DuBois completed his volume in 1903, seven years after the Supreme Court's *Plessy v. Ferguson* decision and the institutionalization of segregation and seven years before the beginning of the Great Migration of African Americans from the South to the North (Gregory 2004). It must have appeared a dark time to him and the masses for whom he spoke.

Of course, other scholars have dealt with issues relating to race and nation both before and after 1903, some of whom argue that American universalism is capable of correcting the racist tendencies of the American nation-state. This argument posits that the liberal democratic principles upon which the American nation-state rests often win out over the more inegalitarian strains of American ideology, including racism (Fuchs 1990; Gleason 1980; Walzer 1992). Eventually, these scholars hold, everyone will gain admission to the political community, as long as they subscribe to the tenets of the creed. This view suggests that race and nation are one and the same, the "American race."

Following DuBois, other scholars have contested such idealizations of American nationality. American nationhood, they argue, was bought and paid for with the suffering of nonwhite people. Blacks and Native

Americans constituted the racialized other against which American (white) nationhood was constructed (Higginbotham 1996; Marx 1998).[2] Even in the twentieth century, race continued to be a metric by which national belonging was measured (Gerstle 2001; Smith 1997).

Nikhil Singh (2005) argues that for African Americans to become "just Americans," as membership in the national community implies, the role of race must be banished from discussions about national unity in the public sphere. The reason for this is that race "remains a code for histories of color: legacies of conquest, enslavement . . . whose narratives must be silenced within public culture or hived off from the national story into a separate world of their own" (42). In the absence of the imposition of national amnesia, Singh argues, we cannot have national unity. Thus, race and nation remain incompatible, as they were in DuBois's day.

The military, as an institution, provided veterans with a means of at least mediating the relationship between race and nation. As Douglass and DuBois's insistence upon the importance of black military service suggests, by proving black Americans' loyalty to the national community, military service promised to allow them to become "just Americans," shorn of the civic and social inferiority they had been assigned. And service had just this effect on at least two occasions, in the aftermath of both the Revolutionary War and the Civil War. It failed to work following World War II and the Korean War, however. Thus, well into the twentieth century, black Southerners remained beyond the bounds of American nationhood, especially if the unfettered ability to vote and equal treatment constituted first-class membership in the national community (Karst 1989; Shklar 1991).

That the state failed to recognize African American military service, however, does not mean that service failed to affect the relationship between race and nation. In fact, the evidence of this study suggests that race and nation are not necessarily incompatible. Several of the veterans I interviewed rejected hyphenated identification, preferring—indeed, insisting—that they were simply American. But they also identified with other black Southerners, lamenting the absence of social progress for all on their return to the South. And there is evidence that wearing the uniform, on some occasions, elevated the status of blacks in the eyes of white Southerners.

If one considers patriotism, especially the type consistent with a critical understanding of American values, and how military service stimulates this critical view, race and nation appear to be quite compatible. Indeed, black Southerners who fought for the country epitomized Ameri-

[2] See Gilroy (1991) for a similar perspective as it pertains to Great Britain.

can ideals. They sacrificed much in the fight for freedom at home and abroad. Examining their struggles furnishes a new perspective that is central to understanding race and politics in the twentieth century.

FUTURE DIRECTIONS

Black Southerners were not the only ones who were affected by their military experiences. White Southerners, too, were moved by their service in the armed forces. For some of them, fighting for freedom and equality overseas during the Second World War changed their views on civil rights upon returning to the United States: they wished to see blacks enjoy freedom and equality at home (Brooks 2004). For other white veterans, it took fighting alongside black servicemen to moderate their racial views (Bogart 1969; Stouffer et al. 1949). Military service failed to work its magic on all white Southerners, however. These veterans were too wedded to regional values to care about the national values for which they fought. They wished to preserve the "Southern way of life," which included keeping blacks in their "place" (Brooks 2004; McMillen 1994). Such thinking produced the founder of the Citizens Council, and Medgar Evers' assassin, both of whom were veterans. Which version comes closest to reality? Were white Southerners, who fought for democracy, more likely to return from service more racially tolerant? Or, did their experiences during war merely ossify prior attitudes toward racial equality? We don't know—yet.

The template from *Fighting for Democracy* can also be fruitfully extended beyond the South, to the North and elsewhere. After all, the ratification of the Voting Rights Act is commonly viewed as the culmination of the Southern phase of the civil rights struggle. But where did black veterans stand as the movement's theme shifted from "We shall overcome" to "Black power?" The former connotes righteous struggle through relatively peaceful means, with the political system remaining intact. The latter didn't rule out violence and called for the system to be restructured (Carmichael and Hamilton 1967). Where did veterans come down on this? Many, though certainly not all, had served and fought in the hopes of achieving unfettered access to the ballot and better jobs. Would they support a radically restructured America? Would they support efforts to achieve it? Would they subscribe to the "By any means necessary" mantra made famous by Malcolm X, and perhaps participate in achieving a radically restructured America? Again, we don't know—yet!

Study Description, Coding, Question Wording, and Other Estimates from Chapters 5 and 6

The data used in chapters 5 and 6 are drawn from the Negro Political Participation Study (ICPSR Study 7255; Matthews and Prothro 1966). Two samples were drawn: one from black Southerners, and one from white Southerners. The sampling is drawn from the adult, noninstitutionalized population of the eleven former Confederate states. From the population of black Southerners, 618 adults were interviewed. Approximately 87 percent of the interviews were completed, all of which were conducted by black interviewers. However, for the current analyses, only the responses from the male interviewees are included. Accordingly, for black Southerners I had 246 observations at my disposal. The study also consists of a sample of white Southerners as well as a sample of black college students. There were 694 completed interviews of whites, and 264 were completed by college students, most of whom were attending school at historically black colleges and universities. Finally, the study also includes in-depth interviews of respondents in four counties. This appendix contains the distribution of selected demographic variables and the data and models for chapters 5 and 6 of the present volume, including question wording and coding. At the very end of this appendix, the reader will find the estimates for the measurement models in chapter 5.

Donald Matthews and James Prothro's book (1966), based on a massive study—perhaps the most comprehensive data collected on Southerners and the political process—was principally exploratory, one that sought to investigate the contours of the political participation of black (and white) Southerners instead of testing a series of claims based on an overarching theory. Among other things, Matthews and Prothro sought to explore the parameters of Southern politics. On a general level, they sought to gauge what constituted political normalcy in the South at the time. Another, more specific goal was an assessment of how much Southern blacks participated in Southern politics, and in "what ways" (1966, 9). Matthews and Prothro thought it possible to account for the political attitudes and behavior of black Southerners by exploring four criteria: (1) the socioeconomic structure of which they were a part; (2) the local political system in which they lived; (3) their socioeconomic status; and (4) their attitudes and beliefs. Together, these criteria account for almost

TABLE A.1
Selected Demographic Characteristics

	Veteran	Nonveteran
Education		
Grade (0–6 years)	46.9%	74.5%
Middle (7–9)	8.6%	4.8%
High school (10–12)	27.0%	10.5%
Beyond high school	17.0%	3.0%
Income		
Under $1000	70.4%	81.4%
$1000–$1999	16.0%	10.5%
$2000–$5999	6.8%	6.2%
Above $6000	7.4%	1.2%

Source: Negro Political Participation Study 1961–1962

fifty variables, ultimately allowing this depiction of politics among black Southerners to explain 63 percent of the variation in their political participation. In the end, attitudes and beliefs represent the only explanation that *directly* informed black Southerners' political participation.[1]

DEPENDENT VARIABLES

Traditionalism

1. If you start trying to change things very much, you usually make them worse.
2. If something grows up over a long period of time, there will always be much wisdom in it.
3. It's better to stick by what you have than to be trying new things you don't really know about.
4. We must respect the work of our forefathers and not think that we know better than they did.
5. A man doesn't really get to have much wisdom until he's well along in his years.

---

[1] Examples of variables from the various groups include: percentage of the labor force engaged in agriculture (socioeconomic structure), degree of party competition (community political system), education (socioeconomic status), and strength of party identification (attitudes and cognitions).

All items were recoded on a 4-point 0–1 interval from "disagree quite a bit" to "agree quite a bit." For each item, pro–status quo=1.

Policy Liberalism

1. The government in Washington ought to see to it that everyone who wants to work can find a job.
2. If cities and towns around the country need help to build more schools, the government in Washington ought to give them the money they need.
3. The government ought to help people get doctors and hospital care at low cost.

All items were recoded on a 4-point 0–1 interval from "disagree quite a bit" to "agree quite a bit." For each item, proliberal=1.

Integration in Principle

This question was used to measure respondent's views regarding integration:

Are you in favor of integration, strict segregation, or something in between?

Pro-integration response=1.

Integration in Practice

Suppose that you are married and have small children. Then you decided that the white school closest to where you live is much better than the Negro school. Would you want your children to go there, even if they were among the first few Negroes to attend the school?

Response options: children already attends integrated school; definitely would want children to go; probably would want children to go; it makes no difference; probably would not want children to go; definitely would not want children to go.

Pro-integration response=1.

Voting Behavior

The voting behavior index is the average score of respondents who were asked the following:

Number of times voting in presidential election.

Number of times voting in gubernatorial elections.
Number of times voting in school board elections.
Number of times voting in local elections.

Response options: none of them=0; some of them=.33; most of them=.67; all of them=1.

Political Activism

Have you ever donated money to a candidate?
Have you ever attended a political meeting or campaign?
Have you ever worked for a candidate?
Did you talk to people to influence votes?

Response options: yes=1; no=0

PREDICTORS

Church

Church attendance is measured by the following:
   Would you say you go to church services—regularly, often, seldom, or never?

All items recoded on a 4-point 0–1 interval from "never attend" to "regularly attend." Regularly attend=1.

Urban

This question was used to measure where respondents grew up:
   Were you brought up mostly on a farm, in a town, in a small city, or in a large city?

Recoded such that 1=large city; elsewhere=0.

Racial Identification

Racial identification is indexed by the following items:

1. Would you say that you feel pretty close to other Negro Southerners in general, or that you don't feel much closer to them than you do to other people?

Recoded to a 4-point 0–1 interval from "feel pretty close" to "not closer than to others."

2. How much interest would you say you have in how Negro Southerners as a whole are getting along in this country? Do you have a good deal of interest in it, some interest, or not much at all?"

Recoded to a three-point 0–1 interval from "not much at all" to "a good deal."
Reliability: α=.40
Pro-identification=1.

Party Identification

Strong Republican–Strong Democrat

Strong Democrat=1.

Education

These questions determined the respondent's highest level of education:

1. How many grades of school did you finish?
2. Do you have a college degree?

Recoded 0–1 scale, with four categories in which some college/college degree=1.

Age

Actual age in years, compressed into four cohorts, where oldest cohort=1.

Income

This question measured the income of the respondent:
How much income have you and your family made altogether during the last year, 1960–1961, before taxes?

All items recoded on a nine-point scale from $0 to $7,500+; $7,500+=1.

Service

Service=1; otherwise=0.

Percent Black ≥50

This is measured with county-level data in which black Southerners account for at least 50 percent of the population. Of the twenty counties in which samples were drawn, there were eight in which blacks constituted at least 50 percent of the population.

Coded such that 1=counties where blacks were at least 50 percent of the population; else=0.

Organizational Membership

This question measured organizational membership:
How many race-relations organizations do you belong to
Actual number, rescaled to 0–1.

TABLE A.2
Measurement Model: Support for Traditionalism

Latent variable	Item	Unstandardized λ (se)	Standardized λ
Traditionalism			
A man really doesn't get to have much wisdom until he's well along in years.	X_1	.87 (.08)	.76
We must respect the work of our forefathers and not think that we know better.	X_2	.92 (.10)	.88
It's better to stick by what you have than to be trying new things you don't know about.	X_3	.67 (.08)	.59
If something grows up for over a long time, there will always be much wisdom to it.	X_4	.92 (.07)	.81
If you start trying to change things very much, you usually make them worse.	X_5	—	—

n=246; χ^2=1.34, df=5, p=.93, AGFI=.99; α=.80

Source: Negro Political Participation Study.
Notes: PRELIS 2.x and LISREL 8.5x were used for the estimation of confirmatory factor models. The covariance structures are computed with the assistance of matrices designed for use with ordinal variables. The weighted least squares estimator is used to compute the covariance structures (Bollan 1989). The dashed line for X_5 identifies it as the scaling variable. The errors for X_1 and X_5 are correlated; as are X_2 and X_4.

TABLE A.3
Measurement Model: Support for Policy Liberalism

Latent variable	Item	Unstandardized λ (se)	Standardized λ
Policy Liberalism			
The government in Washington ought to see to it that everyone who wants to work can find a job.	X_1	1.72 (.10)	.91
If cities and towns around the country need help to build more schools, the government in Washington ought to give them the money they need.	X_2	1.83 (.13)	.85
The government ought to help people get doctors and hospital care at low cost.	X_3	1.64 (.12)	.78

n=246; χ^2=.26, df=3, p=.90, AGFI=.99; α=.68

Source: Matthews and Prothro 1966.

Notes: PRELIS 2.x and LISREL 8.5x were used for the estimation of confirmatory factor models. The covariance structures are computed with the assistance of matrices designed for use with ordinal variables. The weighted least squares estimator is used to compute the covariance structures. Since there are only three parameters in the lambda matrix, I declined to use one of these as a scaling variable. Instead, I set the variance = 1.

Content Analysis of the *Chicago Defender*

We now know why African Americans often relied upon military service as a means of advancing claims against the state: they held a belief, deeply rooted in American political culture and borne out in past practices, that military service would be rewarded by more equal treatment. What remains to be seen, however, is how the African American public at large made this connection. The answer, simply put, is that many blacks were willing to make the ultimate sacrifice at least in part because influential members of the black elite made a strong case for doing so.

As we saw in chapter 1, both Frederick Douglass and W.E.B. DuBois—perhaps the two most visible black leaders during their respective eras—recognized the efficacy of republican rhetoric. On the eve of the Civil War, Douglass drew on black gains in the aftermath of the American Revolution and the War of 1812 to justify black participation in the coming war. Implicitly referring to the citizen-soldier ideal, DuBois later used republican rhetoric to mobilize African American support for World War I, observing that "the man who fights the battles of America may claim America as his country—and have that claim respected." Nothing in the way of tangible benefits resulted from black mobilization during that war, but the bitter experience of returning to race riots in the North and lynchings in the South raised the ire of black veterans, several of whom later pushed for the racial reform that resulted in the Selective Service Act of 1940.

Extracting concessions at the elite level was only part of the campaign for African American progress during and after World War II. Another facet involved informing the masses of their stake in the war. For this, the black elite turned to the black press. Since its institutionalization in 1827, the black press has supported protest movements by increasing race consciousness and keeping African Americans abreast of current issues (O'Kelly 1982). To be sure, black churches were spaces in which racial solidarity was nurtured and issues of the day were discussed (Dawson 1994; Harris 1999). Nonetheless, it was the black press—and the black press alone—that enjoyed the ability to forge an "imagined community" on a national level, bridging both sectional and class-based divides in the black community.[1]

---

[1] Here I refer to Benedict Anderson's (1983) proposition that the print media, due to its wide dissemination and readership, contributed to the formation of national consciousness.

During World War II, 169 black newspapers circulated in weekly, semimonthly, or daily editions. The *Pittsburgh Courier*, the Baltimore *Afro-American*, the *Chicago Defender*, and the New York *Amsterdam News* serviced the vast majority of the black newspaper audience, with a total of 812,700 faithful subscribers. Two of the most enduring works on race to emerge during the war were quick to recognize the scope of the influence enjoyed by the black press. In *Black Metropolis*, a monumental study of race in Chicago, St. Claire Drake and Horace Cayton (1945) indicated that the black press was the most effective means of molding and reflecting opinion in the black community. Gunnar Myrdal agreed, commenting that "the press more than any other institution, has created the Negro group as a special and psychological reality to the individual Negro. By expressing the protest, the press also magnifies it, acting like a huge sounding board" (1944, 911). For these reasons, the black press was important to the formation of a "black counterpublic."

The term *counterpublic* derives from the Jürgen Habermas's (1989) idea of the bourgeois public sphere. The Habermasian version necessarily excluded marginalized social groups as participants in the critical public discourse that took place in the coffeehouses and parlors of Europe. But women and African Americans formed their own indigenous *counter*public spheres, within which they participated in public discourse and developed oppositional ideologies and strategies (Dawson 2001; Fraser 1992). Historically, the black counterpublic served as an oppositional space in which the dominant narratives of mainstream American society were challenged. One example is the liberal consensus: through the black counterpublic, black commentators launched critiques of liberal institutions and liberal practices, revealing the flaws of liberalism to all who chose to listen to them (Dawson 1995; Mills 1998). In addition to its ability to facilitate criticism, the counterpublic functioned as the principal site for the formation of countervailing political discussion, strategizing, and the "activation" of mass opinion (Lee 2002). Criticism and countervailing political discussion took place within a number of venues constitutive of the black counterpublic, including fraternal organizations, civil rights groups, and churches.

It was the press, though, that had the ability, more so than the other organs of the counterpublic, to set the terms of debate within these other spaces. This was the case because the media's ability to both set the agenda for public debate and frame issues is difficult to match (Iyengar and Kinder 1987; McCombs and Shaw 1972; Nelson et al. 1997). The media not only informs us about *what* to think about an issue (agenda setting) but also suggests *how* we should think about it (framing). Interpretive frames, moreover, are tangible representations of cognitive schema, which, in turn, are based upon cultural referents (Archer 1988;

Lee 2002; Sewell 1992). More practically, frames function as a bridge between elite discourse and the formation of mass opinion, highlighting existing beliefs and ways to think about the world (Gamson 1992; Nelson et al. 1997).

To assess the extent to which the black press emphasized the citizenship-service frame during World War II and the Korean War, I draw upon content published in the *Chicago Defender* from 1941 through 1953. I do so because of the *Defender*'s political views and because of its circulation. While the South produced 45 percent of the black papers in America (Walton 1985), white resistance and economic instability affected the political content of the indigenous Southern black press. If black publishers, editors, and reporters wished to avoid reprisals of any sort, they were forced to steer clear of interrogating the racial status quo (Thompson 1993). For this reason, black papers were not produced in the rural South, where blacks were most heavily concentrated (Walton 1985).

White supremacy failed to prevent black Southerners from reading papers produced elsewhere, however. Among these papers, the *Defender* enjoyed the heaviest circulation of any single paper in the South—including those indigenous to the region—where, two years after World War II, its Southern readership was approximately 85,000 (Oak 1970).[2] Since the *Defender* was a weekly paper, subscribers tended to retain it and pass it along to interested parties (Finkle 1975). We must assume, moreover, that the contents of the *Defender* became known through "everyday talk" (Harris-Lacewell 2004), beyond those who actually read it. While the *Pittsburgh Courier* issued the most strident criticism of white domination (Finkle 1973), the *Defender* was also known for its strong antisegregationist views (Brooks 1959).

Taeku Lee's (2002) work provides a model for the content analysis of the *Defender* that follows. Black Southerners who wrote to the president, he found, often framed their grievances in terms of cherished values. Considered broadly, one set of values emphasized democratic rights; the other, political principles. Democratic rights index support for civil rights based upon appeals to equality and justice. Political principles index frames in which references to freedom and liberty are dominant. I use both sets of values to gauge the extent to which the black counterpublic drew on American cultural beliefs in order to challenge white domination. To these I add two frames for understanding: discrimination (particularly in the defense industry) and patriotism. Discrimination is useful as a distinct frame because it spoke specifically to economic rights. It is useful to look at patriotism, moreover, for the obvious reason: the nation

---

[2] Since Northern newspapers enjoyed far more latitude than their Southern counterparts and were better financed, there was a healthy demand for them in the South.

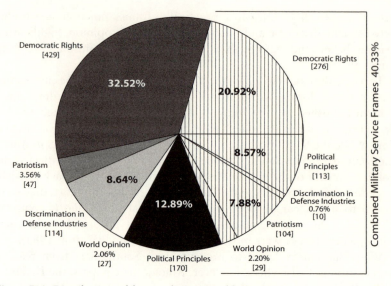

Figure B.1. Distribution of frames during World War II. *Source: Defender.* The numbers in brackets represent the total number of articles collected; the relevant articles sum to 1,319.

was at war. I also include world opinion as a frame. These five frames are what I call *baseline frames*. When the subject of military service accompanied any of the four basic themes in an article or editorial, I classified the piece as having a *republican* frame. Since democratic rights are an essential concept to the military service–citizenship tradeoff, we should expect to find that this is the most prevalent republican frame. We turn to figure B.1 to observe the results for World War II.

As the figure makes clear, the *Defender* often referenced racial justice independent of military service during the Second World War. Approximately one-third of the content in the *Defender* dedicated to raising black consciousness, through its interrogation of racial injustice, did so by referring to black Americans' democratic rights. Nevertheless, over 40 percent of the frames were linked in some way to military service, and half of those were linked to democratic rights. Discrimination in the defense industries—to which discrimination in the military was often tied at the outset of the war—was rarely mentioned alongside military service, however. In hindsight, this makes sense. Without doubt, discrimination is at its core a violation of egalitarianism. But compared with the more familiar rights and political ideals discourse, discrimination in defense failed to fit within a republican framework, because military service has most often been paired with rights in the abstract.

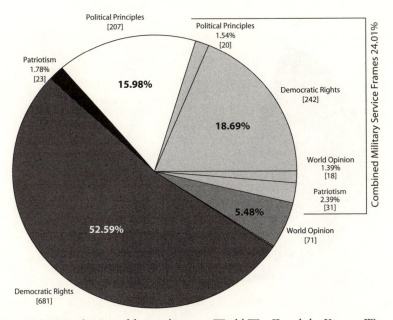

Figure B.2. Distribution of frames between World War II and the Korean War. *Source: Defender*. The numbers in brackets represent the total number of articles collected; the relevant articles sum to 1,295.

To provide contrast, I also examined how the *Defender* framed racial injustice during the three-year interim between World War II and the Korean War. As figure B.2 indicates, the frequency with which the press employed republican frames declined by 40 percent, to a point at which military service was associated with only 24 percent of the coverage identifying racial injustice.

One explanation for the reduction in frequency of republican frames is fairly simple: it was peacetime. Leveraging military service is understandably a more effective tactic when the nation is at war. It is also possible that the shift away from republican frames was part of a larger strategy aimed at capitalizing upon Cold War liberalism with an emphasis on rights (Krebs 2006). Patriotism, too, faded from the discourse; again, the absence of a hot war may explain this result. Apart from these observations, the chart is interesting for other reasons. Democratic rights, for instance, dominated the conversation about racial reform after World War II. While the spotlight on democratic rights grew brighter than it had been during the war, the focus on discrimination in defense industries disappeared, at least in the *Defender*, after the war ended.

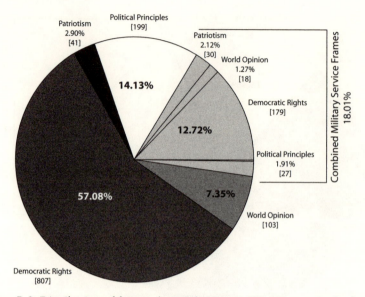

Figure B.3. Distribution of frames during the Korean War. Source: *Defender*. The numbers in brackets represent the total number of articles collected; the relevant articles sum to 1,416.

Shifting, finally, to the Korean War years, several trends continued, as figure B.3 shows. While military service continued to be linked, in the main, with rights, attention to it declined again as a proportion of overall frames. During the Korean War, the *Defender* mentioned military service approximately once for every five articles or editorials that framed racial injustice, approximately half the number dedicated to it during the Second World War.

Among the nonrepublican frames, rights-based frames were by far the most common. While these articles were only slightly more frequent than those about political principles during the Second World War and the interwar years, in the Korean War era the gap widened fourfold. Perhaps this shift may be explained in terms of the national need during the Second World War to draw near and close ranks. Once the threat of Adolf Hitler was extinguished, the black press refocused its critical gaze upon long-festering issues such as equal justice and equal rights.

Overall, the black press impressed upon the mass public the import of conditional support for war and the necessity of pushing for democratic rights. Insofar as democratic rights are a safeguard against lynching and discrimination, it is no mystery that the *Defender* directed most of its attention toward this issue. Blacks in the military, however, constitute the second largest issue by means of which the black press interrogated domination. Linking military service to more general criticism accomplished at least three things. First, it alerted the black community to the mistreatment of black soldiers and marines (the latter during the Korean War). Second, it made it possible for the black community to appreciate the sacrifices undertaken for them. And finally, it facilitated the construction of a republican frame. This frame, I argue, was critical, because it informed the meaning of military service, helping to transform veterans into a viable social group.

Methodology

Sampling

Between 1941 and 1953 the *Chicago Defender* was strictly a weekly newspaper, and thus the number of issues per month varied between four and five. During periods where more than one edition of the *Defender* was published (for example a Gary, Indiana, edition or a "Golden West" edition) the national edition was always selected. Two issues out of every month were sampled; thus, twenty-four out of fifty-two papers were sampled per year. For the period of 1941 through 1946, the first and third weeks were sampled; the second and fourth issues of a particular month were sampled for the remaining papers, from 1947 through 1953. This selection was done in order to achieve a sample that is uniformly representative of the entire year.

Units of Analysis

The units of analysis were entire articles. These included editorials, opinion columns, news articles, and less frequently entertainment or sports articles. They were coded according to the interpretive frame into which they fit. While some articles appeared to show elements of more than a single frame, they were categorized according to the single most dominant frame. The inter-coder reliability, based on three coders, is .85.

The Typology of Interpretive Frames

DEMOCRATIC RIGHTS

This describes support for civil rights and racial equality based on appeals to justice and equality. Articles generally cite the idea of equality explicitly; they frequently referred to equality of opportunity (often in the case of employment, service at public establishments, or in education), or called for equal protection under the law (protesting "Southern justice," unduly harsh sentences for black defendants, lack of legal protection from white-on-black violence). Also included in this frame are articles describing and protesting segregation, discrimination, and Jim Crow.

POLITICAL PRINCIPLES

This describes articles in support of civil rights and racial equality based on an appeal to the core tenants of democracy. Articles included frequently cited political principles such as those of freedom and liberty as well as egalitarianism. Also, articles included often referred to foundational texts in American history (the Declaration of Independence, the Bill of Rights, the Constitution, and in later years the Universal Declaration of Human Rights). Generally the articles would highlight the contradictions and discrepancies between American ideals and democracy as practiced in the United States.

PATRIOTISM AND LOYALTY

This frame describes articles in favor of civil rights and racial equality based on the patriotism and loyalty of African Americans, or the national interest of the United States. Articles of this type often cited the historical patriotism of blacks (history of military service in every American war, lack of African American traitors, and the role of African Americans in the American Revolution), or contemporary accounts of patriotism (heroism in World War II or the Korean War). Also included in this frame were articles that urge racial integration and reconciliation for the purpose of furthering national interests, most often as the need for national unity and strength in times of international uncertainty.

DISCRIMINATION IN WAR INDUSTRIES

This frame describes articles that called for racial integration of war industries and the end of discrimination by federal war contractors. Included were articles that called for strengthened fair employment practices legislation, the right of all citizens to work, and the need for increased production for the war efforts. These appeals varied, yet the main calling for more employment opportunities for black Americans in helping the national war effort was the dominant theme.

WORLD OPINION

This describes support for a civil rights and racial equality based on the need to maintain American credibility and prestige internationally for foreign policy considerations. Articles frequently referred to the damage done to American international leadership (moral leadership, democratic leadership) by domestic race policy. Other articles cited the effectiveness of fascist or communist propaganda in hurting U.S. prestige by referring to racism in America. Also included were articles that emphasized the racial composition of the world and the need for sound racial policy in order to court the favorable opinion of the world's populations of color.

MILITARY SERVICE

This describes articles that fit one of the issue frames above, in addition to references to military service by African Americans. Included were articles that dealt with African Americans fighting for the protection of the American way of life and democracy. Also included were articles about the mistreatment of black servicemen in the United States or abroad (incidents on Southern army bases, unjustified court-martials, discrimination), as well as articles about discrimination faced by colored veterans in civilian life and the segregation of the soldiers slain in the line of duty. Articles tended to emphasize the sacrifices made by the servicemen for rights they were not able to enjoy.

Interview Methodology and Material

This appendix contains information relevant to the interviews on which I draw in chapters 3 and 4. I begin with a brief discussion of the methodology, after which I include the interview schedule. The final portion of this appendix contains selected information on each subject.

The respondents were produced through a snowball sample drawn from randomly selected members of the Ninth and Tenth (Horse) Cavalry Association, one in Houston, Texas, the other in New Orleans, Louisiana. It's based upon two of the four permanent African American regiments resulting from the Military Reorganization Act of 1866. Members are generally African American veterans of the army.

From the membership lists of both locations, I selected three members at random from Houston and another three at random from New Orleans. I then asked these members to provide me names of other veterans who had served between 1941 and 1953, the period encompassing the Second World War and the Korean War. From this arrangement, I conducted a total of twenty-five complete interviews. However, space limitations permitted me to use only seventeen of the completed interviews. All respondents *were not* members of the organization; half had no formal affiliation with it. Nonetheless, I am aware of some of the biases that may affect this data, something that I have addressed in this volume's conclusion.

Interview Questionnaire

I am researching the life experiences of Black Southern veterans who served in World War II and the Korean War. More specifically, I'm interested in the role your generation played in social change in the Civil Rights South. In addition to conducting interviews like this one, I also use a large-scale survey of black Southerners. I will write a book based on my findings.

This interview contains several questions. Please feel free to skip any questions that you are not comfortable answering. If you wish to return to any question or wish to elaborate upon questions not answered to your satisfaction, please don't hesitate. All answers are anonymous and confidential. This means that your full name will not appear anywhere and no one will know about your specific answers except me.

I. FAMILY AND BACKGROUND

A) Where were you born? Where did you grow up?
B) Can you tell me about your family? How much education did your parents have? What were their occupations?
C) How would you describe your family's financial situation when you were growing up? What were your home and neighborhood like?

II. CITIZENSHIP

A) What does it mean to you to be an American citizen?
B) What does the term "citizenship" mean to you? What is a "good citizen"?
C) Has citizenship been important in your life? How?
D) What, if anything, does America owe its citizens? Why?
E) What, if anything, does American owe veterans? Why?
F) Looking back, as a veteran, did feel you deserved more, the same, or less than those who chose not to serve?
G) Does military service affect the way you view yourself as a citizen? As an American?

III. LIFE EXPERIENCES AND TURNING POINTS

A) As you look back over the course of your life, certain events or opportunities may stand out as highly significant or as turning points. What might these be?

IV. MILITARY SERVICE

A) How did you come to be in the military? Were you drafted?
B) [If volunteered] Why?
C) What was your attitude, at the time, about serving in the armed forces?

D) Which branch? Where were you stationed?

E) Did you serve with white troops?

F) If overseas, how, if at all, did it affect your views on American society? The South?

G) What were your primary duties? Were you in combat?

H) How long did you serve?

I) What was your rank upon discharge?

J) Did you sustain any service-connected disabilities?

K) What was your overall attitude about your years if service? Was it a privilege to serve? Did you see it as your duty to society, a necessary obligation? Or, was it a burden?

L) Looking back, how did the time you spent in the armed services affect your life?

M) How, if at all, did the service affect the way that you view yourself? Are you proud, angry, frustrated with your service? Why?

N) How, if at all, did the service affect the way you view American society and the South—particularly whites?

V. RETURNING TO THE SOUTH

A) Looking back, what, if anything, did you expect to come from the war for blacks in the South?

B) What were the conditions of the South upon your return? Had anything changed for blacks? How did this make you feel? Why?

C) How about you? How were you treated? Were you satisfied with your treatment as a returning veteran? If so, why? If not, why not?

D) Did military service affect your desire for equal rights? Why?

VI. MILITANCY/SOCIAL IDENTIFICATION

A) Were you an active participant in the civil rights movement? Why? Why not?

B) Looking back, did you agree with the protests as they got underway?

C) Were they, in your estimation, necessary? Or do you believe that black Southerners should have relied more upon prayer than protest?

D) Did you prefer peaceful demonstrations or something more drastic?

E) Looking back, at the time, were you satisfied with the speed of change?

F) Do you feel that African Americans share a common fate?

G) Do you see yourself as first black, then American? American, then black? One or the other? Why? Do you feel simply American? Why?

H) Do you see yourself as a black veteran? Or, simply as an American veteran? Why?

I) Does your military service affect the extent to which you identify with either race or country?

J) How often do you reflect on your wartime experiences?

VII. EDUCATION AND TRAINING

A) What is your highest level of education? How does this compare with those in your immediate family?

B) How much education or vocational training did you have prior to your service?

C) What kind of employment/training were you involved in prior to service?

D) Did you receive any of your college education while in the armed services?

E) Did you go to school, return to work, or take time off upon your return? Why?

F) If advanced studies, why? What was your degree/vocational training in?

G) Was any of your training after the service funded by the GI Bill?

H) How did you consider the GI Bill? Was it a right, a reward for military service, or a privilege? Why? After receiving these benefits, did you feel as though you owed anything to society? Why or why not?

VIII. DEMOGRAPHICS

A) In what year were you born?

B) Were you raised in a particular religion?

IX. IS THERE ANYTHING ELSE YOU'D LIKE TO TELL ME?

TABLE C.1
Selected Military and Demographic Characteristics of Interviewees

Name	Branch	Service Period	Drafted?	Combat?	Officer?	Year of birth	Education	Interview location
Baines	Army	Korea	Yes	Yes	No	1928	18	TX
Bashful	Army	WWII	Yes	Yes	Yes	1917	20	LA
Baskin	Army	WWII	No	No	No	1919	13	TX
Carey	Army	Korea	Yes	Yes	No	1933	20	LA
Carter	Army	WWII–Korea	No	Yes	Yes	1918	18	LA
Fuller	Army	Korea	Yes	No	No	1933	18	TX
Grant	Army	WWII	Yes	Yes	No	1918	12	TX
McWilliams	Army	WWII–Korea	No	Yes	Yes	1927	16	LA
Moret	Army (AC)	WWII	No	No	Yes	1925	12	LA
Pete	Army	Korea	No	Yes	No	1927	18	TX
Shaw	Army	WWII–Korea	No	Yes	Yes	1926	20	TX
Stewart	Army	WWII	Yes	No	No	1927	11	TX
Thomas	Army (AC)	WWII	Yes	No	No	1917	18	LA
Thornton	Army	Korea	Yes	Yes	No	1933	15	TX
Williams	Army	Korea	No	Yes	No	1935	13	TX
Wilson	Army	WWII–Korea	Yes	Yes	Yes	1914	16	LA
Womack	Army	Korea	No	Yes	No	1934	16	TX

Notes: Data collected by the author 2003–4. AC = Army Air Corps.

Profiles of Selected Black Veteran Activists

In the text of the book, I have alluded to black veterans' leadership in the movement. Chapter 4 even leads off with a snapshot of Aaron Henry, the World War II veteran who was integral to the movement's success in Mississippi (Dittmer 1994; Payne 1995). In this appendix, I have selected a few other veterans, some of whom were mentioned in the introduction or chapter 1, who were also important. The purpose for doing so is to reveal the scope of their activism, as well as introducing a few who were not mentioned. In the interest of saving space, several black veterans who were also activists are not listed, including Harry Belafonte, Ossie Davis, James Meredith, Ivory Perry, and Bobby Seale, a founding member of the Black Panthers, among many others.

Medgar and Charles Evers were both born in Decatur, Mississippi, Charles in 1922 and Medgar in 1925. Both served in the army during the Second World War, with Medgar rising to the rank of sergeant and serving as part of the Red Ball Express, a post–D-Day logistical operation during the Battle of Normandy that helped win the war in Europe. On his return from war, Medgar attended Alcorn State where he received a degree in business. Sometime after being rejected from the University of Mississippi's Law School in an effort to integrate it, he was named the first field secretary for the NAACP. Among other things, he investigated the murder of Emmett Till and helped set up chapters of the NAACP throughout the state. On his brother's death in 1963, Charles returned to the South and assumed Medgar's post as field secretary. He later won election as the first black mayor in the post-Reconstruction South when he was elected in the late 1960s in Fayette, Mississippi.

James Forman was born in Chicago in 1928, but moved to Mississippi as a child to live with his grandmother. After serving in the air force during the Korean War, he became involved in the movement upon visiting Robert Williams in North Carolina in 1960, who was under fire for his continuing advocacy of armed self defense. After narrowly escaping death at the hands of irate whites during a demonstration, and being jailed, he decided to join the Student Nonviolent Coordinating Committee's efforts in the South. He assumed the role of SNCC's executive secretary from 1961 to 1965. In that capacity he provided much of the leadership that contributed to their success (Carson 1981). Without Forman's leadership and concomitant discipline, SNCC's efforts to revive the movement, and energize the activists, would have been far more difficult. Consider the impact of Freedom Vote, easing the fear associated with voting for black Mississippians, and voter registration drives. SNCC's examples, challenging white supremacy, inspired many black Southerners to do the same (Carson 1981). Forman was a big part of this.

W. W. Law was born in Georgia in 1923. A veteran of World War II, he was a longtime postal employee who was once fired for his activism. He presided over the statewide Georgia NAACP from 1953 to 1966. Law ran the Savannah branch for twenty-six years. He led voter registration drives, the integration of schools, housing, and public facilities in the city.

Floyd B. McKissick, whose father was a World War I veteran, was born in Asheville, North Carolina, in 1922. After serving in the Army in Europe during World War II, he was the first African American to attend law school at the University of North Carolina–Chapel Hill, graduating in 1951. McKissick would later successfully defend those who participated in sit-ins, and integrated local tobacco unions. He later became a leader in the Congress of Racial Equality, rising to national chairman in 1966. On his watch, CORE scrapped its interracial, integrationist, and nonviolent orientation toward a more militant approach, adopting black power as an organizational philosophy.

Amzie Moore was born in Mississippi in 1911. An army veteran of the Second World War, in 1951 Moore helped to organize the Regional Council of Negro Leadership. The group preached self-help, entrepreneurship, and fighting for civil rights. He later presided over the Cleveland, Mississippi branch of the NAACP. In the 1960s he teamed with SNCC's Bob Moses to organize voter registration drives. In fact, Freedom Summer grew from Moore's desire to defeat segregation through enfranchisement, in part by having students staffing the operation (Carson 1981). He was also an entrepreneur whose house also served as the headquarters for strategy sessions among the Mississippi movement's leadership. Without Moore's work, among others, the Mississippi movement would not have happened (Dittmer 1994).

Earnest "Chilly Willy" Thomas was born in Jonesboro, Louisiana, in 1935. After serving almost four years in an Army Airborne unit, he returned to Jonesboro, and with Charlie Sims, another veteran of World War II, founded Deacons for Defense and Justice in 1964 with chapters throughout the South. Their working-class composition and willingness to use force were significant departures from the more well-known civil rights organizations. They were formed in response to a reconstituted Ku Klux Klan, which resurfaced after the demise of the Citizens' Council and the failure of the state to enforce the Civil Rights Act (Hill 2004). Beyond protecting the black community and civil rights workers from the Klan, the Deacons compelled the state of Louisiana to enforce the Civil Rights Act in Jonesboro, and forced city leaders in Bougalosa to abolish segregation laws and provide equal protection for protestors (Hill 2004).

Robert F. Williams was born in 1925 and raised in Monroe, North Carolina. After serving in the army during the latter stages of World War II, and serving a stint in the marines from 1954 to 1957, he returned to the South and founded the Black Armed Guard in response to Klan violence. In the process, he received a charter from the National Rifle Association. He led perhaps the most militant branch of the NAACP, from which he was suspended in the late 1950s. He led a campaign to desegregate a public swimming pool after black children had drowned in a swimming hole. However, he received international attention for publicizing a case in which two little black boys were charged with assault for kissing a white girl. In the midst of the Cold War, the state was forced to drop the charges because Williams, without the help of the NAACP, launched a publicity campaign that embarrassed the United States. Eventually, Williams was forced into exile, first to Cuba, where he criticized U.S. race relations. He then moved to China. He later returned to the United States, where he lived for many years before his death. His program of armed self-defense and open defiance of white supremacy inspired many, including Huey P. Newton, co-founder of the Black Panther Party, as well as members of SNCC's inner circle (Tyson 1999).

Hosea Williams was born in Attapulgus, Georgia in 1926. He served in the army during World War II, part of an all-black unit attached to General George Patton's Third Army. Highly decorated, he returned to the South after the war, earning his high school diploma at age twenty-three. Williams later earned bachelor's and master's degrees in chemistry, after which he was hired as a chemist for the U.S. Department of Agriculture. He joined the movement after realizing that his children could not have a sandwich at a local drug store. He led the political arm of the Savannah, Georgia, branch of the NAACP, helped desegregate schools and pools in the city, and led the "Bloody Sunday March" over the Edmund Pettus Bridge between Selma and Montgomery, Alabama, that resulted in the Voting Rights Act. Moore was jailed no less than 125 times for challenging white supremacy.

References

Abdul-Jabbar, K. 2004. *Brothers in Arms: The Epic Story of the 761st Tank Battalion, WWII's Forgotten Heroes*. New York: Broadway Books.

Abrahamsson, B. 1970, August. "Some Elements of Military Conservatism." Paper presented at the Seventh World Congress of Sociology, Varna, Bulgaria.

Adorno, T., E. Frenkel-Brunswick, D. Levinson, and N. Sanford. 1950. *The Authoritarian Personality*. New York: Harper and Row.

Allen, R. L., M. C. Dawson, and R. E. Brown. 1989. "A Schema-Based Approach to Modeling an African-American Belief System." *American Political Science Review* 83(2): 421–41.

Almond, G., and S. Verba. 1963. *The Civic Culture: Attitudes and Democracy in Five Nations*. Princeton: Princeton University Press.

Alt, J. E. 1994. "The Impact of the Voting Rights Act on Black and White Voter Registration in the South." In *Quiet Revolution in the South: The Impact of the Voting Rights Act, 1965–1990*, ed C. Davidson and. B. Grofman, 341–77. Princeton: Princeton University Press.

Anderson, B. 1983. *Imagined Communities: Reflections on the Origin and Spread of Nationalism*. London: Verso.

Anderson, C. 2003. *Eyes off the Prize: The United Nations and the African American Struggle for Human Rights, 1944–1955*. New York: Cambridge University Press.

Andrews, K. T. 2004. *Freedom Is a Constant Struggle: The Mississippi Civil Rights Movement and Its Legacy*. Chicago: University of Chicago Press.

Archer, M. S. 1986. *Culture and Agency: The Place of Culture in Social Theory*. New York: Cambridge University Press.

Baas, L. R. 1979. "The Constitution as Symbol: The Interpersonal Meaning of a Secondary Symbol." *American Journal of Political Science* 23(10): 101–20.

Bachman, J. G., and M. K. Jennings. 1975. "The Impact of Vietnam on Trust in Government." *Journal of Social Issues* 31(4): 141–56.

Bailyn, B. 1967. *The Ideological Origins of the American Revolution*. Cambridge, Mass.: Harvard University Press.

Bandura, A. 1982. "Self-Efficacy Mechanism in Human Agency." *American Psychologist* 37: 122–47.

———. 1986. *Social Foundations of Thought and Action*. Englewood Cliffs, N.J.: Prentice Hall.

Barbeau, A. E., and F. Henri. 1974. *The Unknown Soldiers: African-American Troops in World War I*. Philadelphia: Temple University Press.

Bartley, N. V. 1969. *The Rise of Massive Resistance: Race and Politics in the South during the 1950s*. Baton Rouge: Louisiana State University Press.

Bass, J., and W. DeVries. 1976. *The Transformation of Southern Politics: Social Change and Political Consequence since 1945*. Athens: University of Georgia Press.

Berlin, I. 1969. *Two Concepts of Liberty*. Oxford: Clarendon Press.

Berns, W. 2002. *Making Patriots*. Chicago: University of Chicago Press.

Berry, M. F. 1977. *Military Necessity and Civil Rights Policy: Black Citizenship and the Constitution, 1861–1868*. Port Washington, N.Y.: Kennikat Press .

———. 1986. *Why the ERA Failed: Politics, Women's Rights, and the Amending Process of the Constitution*. Bloomington: University of Indiana Press.

Binkin, M. 1993. *Who Will Fight the Next War? The Changing Face of the American Military*. Washington, D.C.: Brookings Institution.

Black, E., and M. Black. 1987. *Politics and Society in the South*. Cambridge, Mass.: Harvard University Press.

Blalock, H. M. 1967. *Toward a Theory of Minority-Group Relations*. New York: John Wiley and Sons.

Blight, D. W. 1989. "For Something beyond the Battlefield: Fredrick Douglass and the Struggle for the Memory of the Civil War." *Journal of American History* 75: 1157–77.

Bock, G., Q. Skinner, and M. Viroli. 1990. *Machiavelli and Republicanism*. New York: Cambridge University Press.

Bogart, L. 1969. *Social Research and the Desegregation of the U.S. Army*. Chicago: Markham.

Bollen, K. A. 1989. *Structural Equations with Latent Variables*. New York: John Wiley and Sons.

Borstelmann, T. 2001. *The Cold War and the Color Line: American Race Relations in the Global Arena*. Cambridge, Mass.: Harvard University Press.

Bound, S., and J. Turner. 2002. "Closing the Gap or Widening the Divide: The Effects of the G.I. Bill and World War II on the Educational Outcomes of Black Americans." NBER Working Paper 9044. Washington, D.C.: National Bureau of Economic Research.

Brewer, M. 2001. "Ingroup Identification and Intergroup Conflict: When Does Ingroup Love Become Outgroup Hate?" In *Social Identity, Intergroup Conflict, and Conflict Reduction*, ed. L. J. Richard, D. Ashmore, and D. Wilder, 17–41. New York: Oxford University Press.

Broman, C. L., H. W. Neighbors, and J. S. Jackson. 1988. "Racial Group Identification among Black Adults." *Social Forces* 67(1): 146–58.

Brooks, J. E. 2004. *Defining the Peace: World War II Veterans, Race, and the Remaking of Southern Political Tradition*. Chapel Hill: University of North Carolina Press.

Brooks, M. 1959. *The Negro Press Re-examined*. Boston: Christopher.

Brophy, A. L. 2002. *Reconstructing the Dreamland: The Tulsa Race Riots of 1921*. New York: Oxford University Press.

Brown, R. A., and T. C. Shaw. 2002. "Separate Nations: Two Attitudinal Dimensions of Black Nationalism." *Journal of Politics* 64: 22–44.

Brown, S. 1997. "African American Soldiers and Filipinos: Racial Imperialism, Jim Crow, and Social Relations." *Journal of Negro History* 82: 42–53.

Browning, H., S. C. Lopreato, and D. L. Poston Jr. 1973. "Income and Veteran Status." *American Sociological Review* 38: 74–85.

Bunche, R. J. 1973. *The Political Status of the Negro in the Age of FDR*. Chicago: University of Chicago Press.

Burk, J. 1995. "Citizenship Status and Military Service: The Quest for Inclusion by Minorities and Conscientious Objectors." *Armed Forces and Society* 21: 503–29.

———. 2002. "Theories of Democratic Civil-Military Relations." *Armed Forces and Society* 29: 7–29.

Burns, N., K. L. Schlozman, and S. Verba. 2002. *The Private Roots of Public Action: Gender, Equality, and Political Participation.* Cambridge, Mass.: Harvard University Press.

Butler, J. S., and K. L. Wilson 1978. "The American Soldier Revisited: Race Relations and the Military." *Social Science Quarterly* 59: 451–67.

Button, J. W. 1989. *Blacks and Social Change: Impact of the Civil Rights Movement in Southern Communities.* Princeton: Princeton University Press.

Carby, H. V. 1998. *Race Men.* Cambridge, Mass.: Harvard University Press.

———. 1999. *Cultures in Babylon: Black Britain and African America.* London: Verso.

Carmichael, S., and C. Hamilton. 1967. *Black Power: The Politics of Liberation in America.* New York: Vintage Books.

Carmines, E., and J. Stimson 1989. *Issue Evolution: Race and the Transformation of American Politics.* Princeton: Princeton University Press.

Carson, C. 1981. *In the Struggle: SNCC and the Black Awakening of the 1960s.* Cambridge, Mass.: Harvard University Press.

Cash, W. F. 1941. *The Mind of the South.* New York: Alfred A. Knopf.

Cassel, C. A. 1979. "Change in Electoral Participation in the South." *Journal of Politics* 41: 907–17.

Chambers, J. W. 1987. *To Raise an Army: The Draft Comes to Modern America.* New York: Free Press.

Chen, A. S. 2007. "The Party of Lincoln and the Politics of State Fair Employment Practices and Legislation in the North, 1945–1964." *American Journal of Sociology* 112: 1713–74.

———. 2009. *The Fifth Freedom: Jobs, Politics, and Civil Rights in the United States, 1941–1972.* Princeton: Princeton University Press.

Christian, G. L. 1995. *Black Soldiers in Jim Crow Texas, 1899–1917.* College Station: Texas A&M University Press.

Christie, R. 1952. "Changes in Authoritarianism as Related to Situational Forces." *American Psychologist* 7(2): 307–8.

Citrin, J., C. Wong, and B. Duff. 2001. "The Meaning of American National Identity." In *Social Identity, Intergroup Conflict, and Conflict Reduction,* ed. L. J. Richard, D. Ashmore, and D. Wilder, 71–100. New York: Oxford University Press, .

Cobb, R. W., and C. D. Elder. 1972. "Individual Orientations in the Study of Political Symbolism." *Social Science Quarterly* 53(1): 79–90.

Cohen, C. J. 1999. *The Boundaries of Blackness: AIDS and the Breakdown of Black Politics.* Chicago: University of Chicago Press.

Cohen, E. A. 1984. *Citizens and Soldiers: The Dilemmas of Military Service.* Ithaca, N.Y.: Cornell University Press.

Cohen, J., R. L. Warner, and D. R. Segal. 1995. "Military Service and Educational Attainment in the All-Volunteer Force." *Social Science Quarterly* 76: 88–103.

Colby, D. 1987. "White Violence in the Civil Rights Movement." In *Blacks in Southern Politics*, ed. L. W. Moreland, R. P. Steed., and T. A. Baker, 31–48. New York: Praeger.

Conover, P. 1991. "Political Socialization: Where's the Politics?" In *Political Behavior*, vol. 3, ed. W. J. Crotty, 125–52. Evanston, Ill.: Northwestern University Press.

———. 1995. "Citizen Identities and Conceptions of the Self." *Journal of Political Philosophy* 3: 133–65.

Conover, P., I. V. Crewe, and D. D. Searing. 1991. "The Nature of Citizenship in the United States and Great Britain: Empirical Comments on Theoretical Themes." *Journal of Politics* 53: 800–832.

Conover, P., D. D. Searing, and I. V. Crewe. 2004. "The Elusive Ideal of Equal Citizenship: Political Theory and Political Psychology in the United States." *Journal of Politics* 66(4): 1036–68.

Converse, P. 1964. "The Nature of Mass Belief Systems in Mass Publics." In *Ideology and Discontent*, ed. D. Apter, 206–61. New York: Free Press.

Cornish, D. 1987. *The Sable Arm: Black Troops in the Union Army, 1861–1865*. Lawrence: University Press of Kansas.

Costa, D. L., and M. E. Kahn. 2005. "Forging a New Identity: The Costs and Benefits of Diversity in Civil War Combat Units for Black Slaves and Freedmen." *Journal of Economic History* 66(4): 936–62.

Dalfiume, R. 1969. *Desegregation of the U.S. Armed Forces: Fighting on Two Fronts, 1939–1953*. Columbia: University of Missouri Press.

———. 1971. "The 'Forgotten' Years of the Negro Revolution." *Journal of American History* 55: 90–106.

Davis, D. W., and R. E. Brown. 2002. "The Antipathy of Black Nationalism: Behavioral and Attitudinal Implications of an African American Ideology." *American Journal of Political Science* 46: 239–52.

Dawson, M. C. 1994. *Behind the Mule: Race and Class in African-American Politics*. Princeton: Princeton University Press.

———. 1995. "A Black Counterpublic? Economic Earthquakes, Racial Agenda(s) and Black Politics." In *The Black Public Sphere*, ed. Black Public Sphere Collective, 199–228. Chicago: University of Chicago Press.

———. 2001. *Black Visions: The Roots of Contemporary African-American Political Ideologies*. Chicago: University of Chicago Press.

Demo, M., and D. Hughes. 1989. "Self-Perceptions and Black Americans." *American Journal of Sociology* 95: 132–59.

Deutsch, M. 1985. *Distributive Justice*. New Haven, Conn.: Yale University Press.

Devos, T., and M. R. Banaji. 2005. "American=White?" *Journal of Personality and Social Psychology* 88(3): 447–466.

Dietz, M. 2002. "Patriotism: A Brief History of the Term." In *Patriotism*, ed. I. Primoratz, 201–16. New York: Humanity Books.

DiMaggio, P., and W. W. Powell. 1991. "Introduction." In *The New Institutionalism in Organizational Analysis*, ed. W. W. Powell and P. DiMaggio, 1–39. Chicago: University of Chicago Press.

Dittmer, J. 1994. *Local People: The Struggle for Civil Rights in Mississippi*. Urbana: University of Illinois Press.

Dittmer, L. 1977. "Political Culture and Political Symbolism: Toward a Theoretical Synthesis." *World Politics* 29(4): 552–83.

Dorman, J. E. 1976. "ROTC Attitudes: A Product of Socialization or Self-Selection?" *Journal of Political and Military Sociology* 4(2): 203–16.

Douglass, F. 1852, July 5. "Fourth of July Oration, 1852." Speech delivered at Corinthian Hall, Rochester, New York.

———. 1865. "What the Black Man Wants." Speech delivered at the Annual Meeting of the Antislavery Society, Boston.

Drake, S., and H. R. Cayton. 1945. *Black Metropolis: A Study of Negro Life in a Northern City*. Chicago: University of Chicago Press.

Dred Scott v. Sandford, 60 U.S. 393 (1857).

Dubois, W.E.B. 1918. "The Reward." *Crisis* 16: 217.

———. 1919. "Returning Soldiers." *Crisis* 18: 13.

———. 1935. *Black Reconstruction in America*. New York: Atheneum.

———. 1990 [1903]. *The Souls of Black Folk*. New York: Vintage Books.

Ducksworth, S. M. 1994. "What Hour of the Night: Black Enlisted Men's Experience and the Desegregation of the Army during the Korean War, 1950–1951." PhD diss., Ohio State University.

Dudziak, M. 2000. *Cold War Civil Rights*. Princeton: Princeton University Press.

Edelman, M. 1985. *The Symbolic Uses of Politics*. Urbana: University of Illinois Press.

Edgerton, R. B. 2002. *Hidden Heroism: Black Soldiers and America's Wars*. Boulder, Colo.: Westview Press.

Elder, G., and E. Clipp. 1989. "Combat Experience and Emotional Health." *Journal of Personality* 57(2): 311–41.

Elder, C. D, and R. W. Cobb. 1983. *The Political Uses of Symbols*. New York: Longman.

Elder, G., C. Gimble, and R. Ivie. 1986. "Military Times and Turning Points in Men's Lives." Developmental *Psychology* 22: 233–45.

———. 1991. "Turning Points in Life: the Case of Military Service and War." *Military Psychology* 3(4): 215.

Ellis, M. 1992. "Closing Ranks and Seeking Honors: W.E.B. DuBois in World War I." *Journal of American History* 79(1): 96–124.

———. 1995. " 'W.E.B. DuBois and the Formation of Black Opinion in World War I: A Commentary on the 'Damnable Dilemma.' " *Journal of American History* 81(4): 1583–90.

Ellison, C. G. 1992. "Military Background, Racial Orientations, and Political Participation among Adult Black Males." *Social Science Quarterly* 73: 360–77.

Elshtain, J. B. 1987. *Women and War*. Chicago: University of Chicago Press.

Enloe, C. E. 1980. *Ethnic Soldiers: State Security in Divided Societies*. New York: Penguin Books.

———. 1993. *The Morning After: Sexual Politics at the End of the Cold War*. Berkeley and Los Angeles: University of California Press.

Erbing, L., and A. Miller. 1979. "Type-Set Politics: Impact of Newspapers on Public Confidence." *American Political Science Review* 73: 67–84.

———. 1980. "Front-Page News and Real-World Cues: A New Look at Agenda Setting by the Media." *American Political Science Review* 24: 16–49.

Ernest, E. G., and R. R. French 1955. "The Relationship between Authoritarian-ism and Acceptance of Military Ideology." *Journal of Personality* 24(1): 181–91.

Fairclough, A. 1995. *Race and Democracy: The Civil Rights Struggle in Louisiana, 1915–1972.* Athens: University of Georgia Press.

Finkle, L. 1973. "The Conservative Aims of Militant Rhetoric: Black Protest during World War II." *Journal of American History* 60(3): 692-713.

———. 1975. *Forum for Protest: The Black Press during World War II.* Cranbury, N.J.: Associated Universities Press.

Firth, R. 1973. *Symbols: Public and Private.* Ithaca, N.Y.: Cornell University Press.

Fiske, S., and V. Taylor. 1991. *Social Cognition.* New York: McGraw-Hill.

Fletcher, M. E. 1968. "The Negro Volunteer in Reconstruction, 1865–66." *Military Affairs* 32: 124–31.

———. 1974. *The Black Soldier and Officer in the United States Army: 1891–1917.* Columbia: University of Missouri Press.

Foner, E. 1988. *Reconstruction: The Unfinished Revolution.* New York: Harper and Row.

Foner, J. D. 1974. *Blacks and the Military in American History: A New Perspective.* New York: Praeger.

Forman, J. 1972. *The Making of a Black Revolutionary.* Seattle: University of Washington Press.

Franklin, J. H. 1961. *Reconstruction after the Civil War.* Chicago: University of Chicago Press.

———. 2002 [1956]. *The Militant South: 1861–1880.* Urbana: University of Illinois Press.

Fraser, N. 1992. "Rethinking the Public Sphere: A Contribution to a Critique of Actually Existing Democracy." In *Habermas and the Public Sphere*, ed. C. Calhoun, 109–42. Cambridge, Mass.: MIT Press

Frazier, F. E. 1942. "Ethnic and Minority Groups in Wartime, with Special Reference to the Negro." *American Journal of Sociology* 48: 369–77.

Frederickson, K. 2001. *The Dixiecrat Revolt and the End of the Solid South, 1932–1968.* Chapel Hill: University of North Carolina Press.

Fredrickson, G. M. 1981. *White Supremacy: A Comparative Study in American and South African History.* New York: Oxford University Press.

Frymer, P. 1999. *Uneasy Alliances: Race and Party Competition in America.* Princeton: Princeton University Press.

Fuchs, L. 1990. *The American Kaleidoscope: Race, Ethnicity, and the Civic Culture.* Hanover, N.H.: Wesleyan University Press.

Gage, R. W. 1964. "Patriotism and Military Discipline as a Function of Military Training." *Journal of Social Psychology* 64(1): 101–11.

Galston, W. A. 1991. *Liberal Purposes: Goods, Virtues, and Diversity in the Liberal State.* New York: Cambridge University Press.

Gamson, W. 1992. *Talking Politics.* New York: Cambridge University Press.

Gatewood, W. B. 1987a. *"Smoked Yankees" and the Struggle for Empire: Letters from Negro Soldiers.* Fayetteville: University of Arkansas Press.

———. 1987b. "Black Americans and the Quest for Empire." *Journal of Southern History* 545–66.

Gecas, V. 1982. "The Self-Concept." *American Review of Sociology* 8: 1–33.

Gecas, V., and M. Schwalbe. 1983. "Beyond the Looking Glass." *Social Psychology Quarterly* 46: 77–88.

Geertz, C. 1973. *The Interpretations of Cultures: Selected Essays.* New York: Basic Books.

Gerstle, G. 2001. *American Crucible: Race and Nation in the Twentieth Century.* Princeton: Princeton University Press.

Gill, L. 1997. "Creating Citizens, Making Men: The Military and Maculinity in Bolivia." *Cultural Anthropology* 12(4): 527–50.

Gillin, J. 1955. "National and Regional Cultural Values in the United States." *Social Forces* 34(2): 107–13.

Gilroy, P. 1991. *"Ain't no Black in the Union Jack": The Cultural Politics of Race and Nation.* Chicago: University of Chicago Press.

Glatthaar, J. T. 1990. *Forged in Battle: The Civil War Alliance of Black Soldiers and White Officers.* Baton Rouge: Louisiana State University Press.

Gleason, P. 1980. "American Identity and Americanization." In the *Harvard Encyclopedia of American Ethnic Groups*, ed. A. Thernstrom, A. Orlof, and O. Handlin, 31–58. Cambridge, Mass.: Harvard University Press.

Goffman, E. 1974. *Frame Analysis: An Essay on the Organization of Experience.* Cambridge, Mass.: Harvard University Press.

Goldstein, J. S. 2001. *War and Gender: How Gender Shapes the War System and Vice Versa.* New York: Cambridge University Press.

Grant, C. 2008. *Negro with a Hat: The Rise and Fall of Marcus Garvey.* New York: Oxford University Press.

Grasmick, H. G. 1973. "Social Change and Modernism in the American South." *American Behavioral Scientist* 16(1): 137–58.

Gregory, J. N. 2004. *The Southern Diaspora: How the Great Migrations of Black and White Southerners Transformed America.* Chapel Hill: University of North Carolina Press.

Gurin, P., S. Hatchett, and J. S. Jackson. 1989. *Hope and Independence: Blacks' Response to Electoral and Party Politics.* New York: Russell Sage Foundation.

Gurin, P., A. H. Miller, and G. Gurin. 1980. "Stratum Identification and Consciousness." *Social Psychology Quarterly* 43: 30–57.

Habermas, J. 1989 [1962]. *The Structural Transformation of the Public Sphere.* Translated by T. Burger. Cambridge, Mass.: MIT Press.

Hahn, S. 2003. *A Nation under Our Feet: Black Political Struggles from Slavery to the Great Migration.* Cambridge, Mass.: Harvard University Press.

Halliburton, R. 1972. "The Tulsa Race War of 1921." *Journal of Black Studies* 2(3): 333–57.

Hamby, A. 1995. *Man of the People: A Life of Harry S. Truman.* New York: Oxford University Press.

Hamilton, A. 2005. "Concerning the Militia" [Federalist Paper 29]. In Alexander Hamilton, James Madison, and John Jay, *The Federalist*, ed. J. R. Pole, 152–58. Indianapolis: Hackett.

Handley, L., and B. Grofman. 1994. "The Impact of the Voting Rights Act on Minority Representation: Black Officeholding in Southern State Legislatures." In *Quiet Revolution in the South: The Impact of the Voting Rights Act, 1965–1990*, ed. C. Davidson and B. Grofman, 335–30. Princeton: Princeton Univesity Press.

Hansen, J. 2001. *The Lost Promise of Patriotism*. Chicago: University of Chicago Press.

Hardy, M. A. 1993. *Regression with Dummy Variables*. Newbury Park, Calif.: Sage.

Harris, F. C. 1999. *Something Within: Religion in African-American Political Activism*. New York: Oxford University Press.

Harris, F. C., V. Sinclair-Chapman, and B. D. McKenzie. 2006. *Countervailing Forces in African-American Political activism, 1973–1994*. New York: Cambridge University Press.

Harris-Lacewell, M. V. 2004. *Barbershops, Bibles, and BET: Everyday Talk and Black Political Thought*. Princeton: Princeton University Press.

Heard, A. 1952. *A Two-Party South?* Chapel Hill: University of North Carolina Press.

Henry, A. 2000. *The Fire Ever Burning*. Jackson: University Press of Mississippi.

Herzog, D. 1986. "Some Questions for Republicans." *Political Theory* 14: 473–93.

Higginbotham, A. L. 1996. *Shades of Freedom: Racial Politics and Presumptions of the American Legal Process*. New York: Oxford University Press.

Higham, J. 1997. Coda: "Three Reconstructions." In *Civil Rights and Social Wrongs: Black-White Relations since World War II*, ed. J. Higham, 179–90. University Park: Pennsylvania State University Press.

Hill, L. 2004. *The Deacons for Defense: Armed Resistance and the Civil Rights Movement*. Chapel Hill: University of North Carolina Press.

Hochschild, J. L. 1981. *What's Fair? American Beliefs about Distributive Justice*. Cambridge, Mass.: Harvard University Press.

———. 1995. *Facing Up to the American Dream: Race, Class, and the Soul of the Nation*. Princeton: Princeton University Press.

Hockey, J. 2003. "No More Heroes: Masculinity in the Infantry." In *Military Masculinities: Identity and the State*, ed. P. R. Higate, 15–26. New York: Praeger.

Holt, T. C. 1977. *Black over White: Negro Political Leadership in South Carolina during Reconstruction*. Urbana: University of Illinois Press.

Horton, C. A. 2005. *Race and the Making of American Liberalism*. New York: Oxford University Press.

Howard-Pitney, D. 2005. *The African American Jeremiad: Appeals for Justice in America*. Philadelphia: Temple University Press.

Hughes, D., and M. Demo. 1990. "Socialization and Racial Identity among Black Americans." *Social Psychology Quarterly* 53: 364–74.

Hughes, E. 1942. "The Impact of War on American Institutions." *American Journal of Sociology* 48: 398–403.

Huntington, S. P. 1957. *The Soldier and the State: The Theory and Politics of Civil-Military Relations*. Cambridge, Mass.: Harvard University Press.

Hurlbert, J. S. 1989. "The Southern Region: A Test of the Hypothesis of Cultural Distinctiveness." *Sociologocial Quarterly* 30: 245–66.

Inkeles, A. 1969. "Making Men Modern: On the Causes and Consequences of Individual Change in Six Developing Countries." *American Journal of Sociology* 75: 208–25.

Isaacs, A. R. 1997. *Vietnam Shadows: The War, Its Ghosts, and Its Legacy*. Baltimore: Johns Hopkins University Press.

Iyengar, S., and D. R. Kinder. 1987. *News that Matters: Television and American Opinion*. Chicago: University of Chicago Press.

James, D. R. 1988. "The Transformation of the Southern Racial State: Class and Race Determinants of Local State Structures." *American Sociological Review* 53: 199–208.

Janowitz, M. 1960. *The Professional Soldier: A Social and Political Portrait*. Glencoe, Ill.: The Free Press.

———. 1976. "Military Institutions and Citizenship in Western Societies." *Armed Forces and Society* 2: 185–203.

———. 1977. *Military Institutions and Coercion in the Developing Nations*. Chicago: University of Chicago Press.

———. 1978. *The Last Half-Century*. Chicago: University of Chicago Press.

———. 1980. "Observations on the Sociology of Citizenship: Obligations and Rights." *Social Forces* 59: 1–24.

———. 1983. *The Reconstruction of Patriotism: Education for Civic Consciousness*. Chicago: University of Chicago Press.

Jaynes, G., and R. Williams Jr. 1989. *A Common Destiny: Blacks and American Society*. Washington, D.C.: National Academy Press.

Jenkins, J. C., and J. Argonne. 2003. "Political Opportunities and African-American Protest." *American Journal of Sociology* 109(2): 277–303.

Jennings, M. K., and G. B. Markus. 1976. "Political Participation and the Vietnam War Veterans: A Longitudinal Study." In *The Social Psychology of Military Service*, ed. N. L. Goldman and D. R. Segal, 175–200. Beverly Hills, Calif.: Sage.

———. 1977. "The Effect of Military Sevice on Political Attitudes: A Panel Study." *American Political Science Review* 71(1): 131–47.

———. 1981. *Generations and Politics: A Panel Study of Young Adults and Their Parents*. Princeton: Princeton University Press.

Jennings, M. K., and R. Niemi. 1974. *The Political Character of Adolescence*. Princeton: Princeton University Press.

Jordan, W. 1995. "The Damnable Dilemma: African-American Accommodation and Protest during World War I." *Journal of American History* 81(4): 1562–83.

Joseph, J., and N. Alex. 1972. "The Uniform: A Sociological Perspective." *American Journal of Sociology* 77: 719–30.

Karst, K. 1989. *Belonging to America: Equal Citizenship and the Constitution*. New Haven, Conn.: Yale University Press.

Karsten, P. 1966. "The American Democratic Citizen Soldier: Triumph or Disaster?" *Military Affairs* 30: 34–40.

Kasarda, W. 1976. "Veteran Status and Socioeconomic Attainment." *Armed Forces and Society* 2: 407–19.

Katznelson, I. 2005. *When Affirmative Action Was White: An Untold History of Racial Inequality in Twentieth-Century America*. New York: W. W. Norton.

Katznelson, I., K. Geiger, and D. Kryder. 1993. "Limiting Liberalism: The Southern Veto in Congress, 1933–1950." *Political Science Quarterly* 108: 283–306.

Katzenstein, M. F. 1998. *Faithful and Fearless: Moving Feminist Protest inside the Church and Military*. Princeton: Princeton University Press.

Keech, W. R. 1968. *The Impact of Negro Voting: The Role of the Vote in the Quest for Equality*. Chicago: Rand McNally.

Kelley, R.D.G. 1990. *Hammer and Hoe: Alabama Communists during the Great Depression*. Chapel Hill: University of North Carolina Press.

———. 1993. "We Are Not What We Seem: Rethinking Working-Class Opposition in the Jim Crow South." *Journal of American History* 80: 75–112.

———. 1994. *Race Rebels: Culture, Politics, and the Black Working Class*. New York: Free Press.

Kerber, L. K. 1997. "The Meanings of Citizenship." *Journal of American History* 84: 833–54.

———. 1998. *No Constitutional Right to Be Ladies: Women and the Obligations of Citizenship*. New York: Hill and Wang.

Key, V. O., Jr. 1949. *Southern Politics in State and Nation*. New York: Alfred A. Knopf.

Keyssar, A. 2000. *The Right to Vote: The Contested History of Democracy in the United States*. New York: Basic Books.

Kinder, D. R., and L. M. Sanders. 1996. *Divided by Color: Racial Politics and Democratic Ideals*. Chicago: University of Chicago Press.

King, D. 1995. *Separate and Unequal: Black Americans and the U.S. Federal Government*. Oxford: Clarendon Press.

Klarman, M. J. 2006. *From Jim Crow to Civil Rights: The Supreme Court and the Struggle for Equality*. New York: Oxford University Press.

Klinkner, P., and R. M. Smith. 1999. *The Unsteady March: The Rise and Decline of Racial Equality in America*. Chicago: University of Chicago Press.

Kohn, R. H. 1981. "The Social History of the American Soldier: A Review and Prospects for Research." *American Historical Review* 86(2): 553–67.

Kousser, J. M. 1974. *The Shaping of Southern Politics*. New Haven, Conn.: Yale University Press.

———. 2000. "What Light Does the Civil Rights Act of 1875 Shed on the Civil Rights Act of 1964?" In *Legacies of the 1964 Civil Rights Act*, ed. B. Grofman, 33–42. Charlottesville: University of Virginia Press.

Krebs, R. R. 2004. "A School for the Nation? How Military Service Does Not Build Nations, and How it Might." *International Security* 28: 85–124.

———. 2006. *Fighting for Rights: Military Service and the Politics of Citizenship*. Ithaca, N.Y.: Cornell University Press.

Krosnick, J. A., and D. F. Alwin. 1989. "Aging and Susceptibility to Attitude Change." *Journal of Personality and Social Psychology* 57(3): 416–25.

Krosnick, J. A., and R. E. Petty. 1995. "Attitude Strength: An Overview." In *Attitude Strength: Antecendents and Consequences*, ed. R. E. Petty and J. A. Krosnick, 1–24. Mahwah, N.J.: Lawrence Erlbaum Associates.

Kruse, K. 2005. *White Flight: Atlanta and the Making of Modern Conservatism.* Princeton: Princeton University Press.

Kryder, D. 2000. *Divided Arsenal: Race and the American State during World War II.* New York: Cambridge University Press.

Laitin, D. 1988. "Political Culture and Political Preferences." *American Political Science Review* 82(3): 589–93.

Lane, R. 1962. *Political Ideology: Why the American Common Man Believes What He Does.* New York: Free Press.

Lanning, M. L. 1997. *The African-American Soldier: From Crispus Attucks to Colin Powell.* Secaucus, N.J.: Birch Lange.

Laufer, R. 1989. "The Aftermath of War: Adult Socialization and Political Development." In *Political Learning in Adulthood*, ed. R. S. Sigel, 1–10. Chicago: University of Chicago Press.

Lawson, S. F. 1976. *Black Ballots: Voting Rights in the South, 1944–1969.* New York: Columbia University Press.

———. 1985. *In Pursuit of Power: Southern Blacks and Electoral Politics, 1965–1982.* New York: Columbia University Press.

———. 1991. *Running for Freedom: Civil Rights and Black Politics in America since 1941.* Philadelphia: Temple University Press.

———. 2004. *To Secure These Rights: The Report of Harry S. Truman's Committee on Civil Rights.* Boston: Bedford/St. Martin's Press.

Leal, D. 1999. "It's Not Just a Job: Military Service and Latino Political Participation." *Political Behavior* 21(2): 153–74.

Lee, T. 2002. *Mobilizing Public Opinion: Black Insurgency and Racial Attitudes in the Civil Rights Era.* Chicago: University of Chicago Press.

Lee, U. 1966. *The Employment of Negro Troops.* Washington, D.C.: Center of Military History.

Lentz-Smith, A. D. 2005. "The Great War for Civil Rights: African American Politics and World War I, 1916–1920." PhD diss., Yale University.

Levi, M. 1997. *Consent, Dissent, and Patriotism.* New York: Cambridge University Press.

Lewis, D. L. 2000. *W.E.B. Du Bois: The Fight for Equality and the American Century, 1919–1963.* New York: Henry Holt.

Lieberman, R. C. 1998. *Shifting the Color Line: Race and the American Welfare State.* Cambridge, Mass.: Harvard University Press.

———. 2005. *Shaping Race Policy: The United States in Comparative Perspective.* Princeton: Princeton University Press.

Linder, D. O. 2000. *Before Brown: Charles H. Houston and the Gaines Case.*

Lippert, E., P. Schneider, and R. Zoll. 1978. "The Influence of Military Service on Political and Social Attitudes." *Armed Forces and Society* 4(2): 265–81.

Lipsitz, G. 1988. *A Life in the Struggle: Ivory Perry and the Culture of Opposition.* Philadelphia: Temple University Press.

Little, R. D., and J. E. Fredland. 1979. "Veteran Status Earnings, and Race." *Armed Forces and Society* 5: 244–60.

Litwack, L.. 1979. *Been in the Storm So Long: The Aftermath of Slavery*. New York: Vintage Books.

———. 1998. *Trouble in Mind: Black Southerners in the Age of Jim Crow*. New York: Vintage Books.

Lopreato, S., and D. L. Poston Jr. 1977. "Difference in Earnings and Earnings Ability between Black Veterans and Non-Veterans in the United States." *Social Science Quarterly* 57: 750–66.

Lovell, J. P., and J. H. Stiehm. 1989. "Military Service and Political Socialization." In *Political Learning in Adulthood*, ed. R. S. Sigel, 415–57. Chicago: University of Chicago Press.

Machiavelli, N. 1970. *The Discourses*. Translated by L. Walker. New York: Penguin Books.

MacGregor, M. 1981. *Integration of the Armed Forces: 1940–1965*. Washington, D.C.: Center of Military History.

MacIntyre, A. 2002. "Is Patriotism a Virtue?" In *Patriotism*, ed. I. Primoratz, 43–58. New York: Humanity Books.

MacLean, N. 2006. *Freedom Is Not Enough: The Opening of the American Workplace*. New York: Russell Sage Foundation.

Major, B. 1994. "From Social Inequality to Personal Entitlement." In *Advances in Experimental Psychology*, ed. M. P. Zanna, 293–355. New York: Academic Press, .

Mansbridge, J. 1986. *Why We Lost the ERA*. Chicago: University of Chicago Press.

Mansfield, H. C. 2006. *Manliness*. New Haven, Conn.: Yale University Press.

Markell, P. 2008. "The Insufficiency of Domination." *Political Theory* 36: 9–36.

Marwick, A. 1974. *War and Social Change in the Twentieth Century: A Comparative Study of Britain, Germany, France, Russia, and the United States*. New York: St. Martin's Press.

Marx, A. W. 1998. *Making Race and Nation: A Comparison of the United States, South Africa, and Brazil*. New York: Cambridge University Press.

Marx, G. T. 1967. *Protest and Prejudice: A Study of Belief in the Black Community*. New York: Harper and Row.

Matthews, D. R., and J. Prothro. 1963. "Political Factors and Negro Voter Registration in the South." *American Political Science Review* 57: 355–67.

———. 1966. *Negroes and the New Southern Politics*. New York: Harcourt Brace.

McAdam, D. 1986. "Recruitment to High Risk Activism." *American Journal of Sociology* 92: 64–90.

———. 1988. *Freedom Summer*. New York: Oxford University Press.

———. 1999. *Political Process and the Development of Black Insurgency, 1930–1970*. Chicago: University of Chicago Press.

McClosky, H. 1958. "Conservatism and Personality." *American Political Science Review* 52(1): 27–45.

McCombs, M. E, and D. L. Shaw. 1972. "The Agenda-Setting Function of Mass Media." *Public Opinion Quarterly* 36: 176–87.

McCracken, G. 1988. *The Long Interview*. Newbury Park, Calif.: Sage.

McGuire, P. 1983. *Taps for a Jim Crow Army: Letters from Black Soldiers in World War II*. Lexington: University Press of Kentucky.

McMillen, N. R. 1989. *Dark Journey: Black Mississippians in the Age of Jim Crow*. Urbana: University of Illinois Press.

———. 1994. *The Citizens' Council: Organized Resistance to the Second Reconstruction, 1954–64*. Urbana: University of Illinois Press.

———. 1997. "Fighting for What We Didn't Have: How Mississippi's Black Veterans Remember World War II." In *Remaking Dixie: The Impact of World War II on the American South*, ed. N. R. McMillen, 91–110. Jackson: University Press of Mississippi.

McNeil, G. R. 1983. *Groundwork: Charles Hamilton Houston and the Struggle for Civil Rights*. Philadelphia: University of Pennsylvania Press.

Mershon, S., and S. Schlossman. 1998. *Foxholes and Color Lines: Desegregating the U.S. Armed Forces*. Baltimore: Johns Hopkins University Press.

Mettler, S. 2002. "Bringing the State Back into Civic Engagement." *American Political Science Review* 96: 351–66.

———. 2005a. " 'The Only Good Thing Was the G.I. Bill': Effects of the Education and Training Provisions on African-American Veterans' Political Participation." *Studies in American Political Development* 19: 31–52.

———. 2005b. *Soldiers to Citizens: The G.I. Bill and the Making of the Greatest Generation*. New York: Oxford University Press.

Meyer, J. W., and B. Rowan. 1991. "Institutionalized Organizations: Formal Structure as Myth and Ceremony." In *The New Instutionalism in Organizational Analysis*, ed. W. W. Powell and P. DiMaggio, 41–62. Chicago: University of Chicago Press.

Mickey, R. W. Forthcoming. *Paths out of Dixie: The Democratization of Authoritarian Enclaves in America's Deep South, 1944–1972*. Princeton: Princeton University Press.

Milbrath, L. 1965. *Political Participation: How and Why Do People Get Involved in Politics?* Chicago: Rand McNally.

Miller, A. H., P. Gurin, G. Gurin, and O. Malanchuk. 1981. "Group Consciousness and Political Participation." *American Journal of Political Science* 25: 494–511.

Mills, C. W. 1998. *Blackness Visible: Essays on Philosophy and Race*. Ithaca, N.Y.: Cornell University Press.

Mississippi Humanities Council et al. N.d. "Mississippi Freedom Democratic Party." Retrieved January 12, 2009 from http://www.usm.edu/crdp/html/cd/mfdp.htm.

Modell, J., M. Goulden, and S. Magnusson. 1989. "World War II in the Lives of Black Americans: Some Findings and Interpretations." *Journal of American History* 76: 839–848.

Moore, B. L. 1987. "Effects of the All-Volunteer Force on the Civilian Status Attainment of Black Men and Women." PhD diss., University of Chicago.

———. 1996. *To Serve My Country, to Serve My Race: The Story of the Only African-American WACS Stationed Overseas during World War II*. New York: New York University Press.

Morris, A. 1984. *The Origins of the Civil Rights Movement: Black Communities Organizing for Change.* New York: Free Press.

———. 2000. "Reflections on Social Movement Theory: Criticisms and Proposals." *Contemporary Sociology* 29: 445–54.

Moskos, C. 1970. *The American Enlisted Man: Rank and File in Today's Military.* New York: Russell Sage.

———. 1976. "The Military." *Annual Review of Sociology* 2: 55–77.

Moskos, C., and J. S. Butler. 1996. *All That We Can Be: Black Leadership and Racial Integration the Army Way.* New York: Basic Books.

Muñoz, C. 1989. *Youth, Identity, Power: The Chicano Movement.* London: Verso.

Myrdal, G. 1944. *An American Dilemma: The Negro Problem and Modern Democracy.* New York: Harper and Brothers.

Nalty, B. C. 1986. *Strength for the Fight: A History of Black Americans in the Military.* New York: Free Press.

Nelson, T. E., R. A. Clawson, and Z. M. Oxley. 1997. "Media Framing of a Civil Liberties Conflict and Its Effect on Tolerance." *American Political Science Review* 91(3): 567–83.

Nie, N. H., J. Junn, and K. Stehlik-Barry. 1996. *Education and Democratic Citizenship and America.* Chicago: University of Chicago Press.

Oak, V. 1970. *The Negro Newspaper.* Westport, Conn.: Negro Universities Press.

O'Brien, G. W. 1999. *The Color of the Law: Race, Violence, and Justice in the Post–World War II South.* Chapel Hill: University of North Carolina Press.

Odum, H. 1948. "Social Change in the South." *Journal of Politics* 10: 242–58.

O'Kelly, C. G. 1982. "Black Newspapers and the Black Protest Movement: Their Historical Relationship, 1827–1945." *Phylon* 43(1): 1–14.

O'Leary, C. E. 1999. *To Die For: The Paradox of American Patriotism.* Princeton: Princeton University Press.

Oliver, M., and T. Shapiro. 1995. *Black Wealth–White Wealth: A New Perspective on Racial Inequality.* New York: Routlege.

Omi, M., and H. Winant. 1994. *Racial Formation in the United States.* New York: Routledge.

Onkst, D. H. 1998. "First a Negro . . . Incidentally a Veteran: Black World War II Veterans and the G.I. Bill of Rights in the Deep South, 1944–1948." *Journal of Social History* 31: 517–27.

Orfield, G. 2000. "The 1964 Civil Rights Act and American Education." In *Legacies of the 1964 Civil Rights Act,* ed. B. Grofman, 89–128. Charlottesville: University of Virginia Press.

Page, B. I., and R. Y. Shapiro. 1992. *The Rational Public: Fifty Years of Trends in American Policy Preferences.* Chicago: University of Chicago Press.

Parker, C. 2001. "War, What Is It Good For? Race, Military Service, and Social Change, 1945–1995." PhD diss., University of Chicago.

———. 2009, in press. "When Politics Becomes Protest: Black Veterans and Political Activism in the Postwar South." *Journal of Politics* 71: 113–31.

Patten, A. 1996. "The Republican Critique of Liberalism." *British Journal of Political Science* 26: 24–44.

Payne, C. M. 1995. *I've Got the Light of Freedom: The Organizing Tradition and the Mississippi Freedom Struggle*. Berkeley and Los Angeles: University of California Press.

Pettit, P. 1997. *Republicanism: A Theory of Freedom and Government*. New York: Oxford University Press.

Phillips, R. L., and C. Gilroy. 1992. "The Economic Returns to Military Service: Race-Ethnic Differences." *Social Science Quarterly* 73: 340–57.

Plummer, B. G. 1996. *Rising Wind: Black Americans and U.S. Foreign Affairs, 1935–1960*. Chapel Hill: University of North Carolina Press.

Pocock, J.G.A. 1975. *The Machiavellian Moment: Florentine Political Thought and the Atlantic Republican Tradition*. Princeton: Princeton University Press.

Pratt, M., and A. Rafaeli. 1997. "Organizational Dress as a Symbol of Multilayered Social Identities." *Academy of Management Journal* 40: 862–98.

Price, H. D. 1955. "The Negro and Florida Politics, 1944–1954." *Journal of Politics* 17: 198–220.

Purcell, S. 2002. *Sealed with Blood: War, Sacrifice, and Memory in Revolutionary America*. Philadelphia: University of Pennsylvania Press.

Putnam, R. 1993. *Making Democracy Work: Civic Traditions in Modern Italy*. Princeton: Princeton University Press.

Pycior, J. L. 1997. *LBJ and Mexican Americans*. Austin: University of Texas Press.

Quarles, B. 1948. *Frederick Douglass*. New York: Da Capo Press.

———. 1961. *The Negro in the American Revolution*. Chapel Hill: University of North Carolina Press.

Ransby, B. 2003. *Ella Baker and the Black Freedom Movement: A Radical Democratic Vision*. Chapel Hill: University of North Carolina Press.

Ransom, R. L., and R. Sutch. 2001. *One Kind of Freedom: The Economic Consequences of Emancipation*. New York: Cambridge University Press.

Redding, K. 2003. *Making Race, Making Power: North Carolina's Road to Disfranchisement*. Urbana: University of Illinois Press.

Reich, S. A. 1996. "Soldiers of Democracy: Black Texans and the Fight for Citizenship, 1917–1921." *Journal of American History* 83: 1478–1590.

Reisberg, D., and F. Heuer. 1992. "Remembering the Details of Emotional Events." In *Affect and Accuracy in Recall: Studies of "Flashbulb" Memories*, ed. E. Winograd and U. Neisser, 162–92. New York: Cambridge University Press.

Ritter, G. 2006. *The Constitution as Social Design: Gender and Civic Membership in the American Constitutional Order*. Stanford, Calif.: Stanford University Press.

Robinson, C. J. 1997. *Black Movements in America*. New York: Routledge.

Rochon, T. R. 1998. *Culture Moves: Ideas, Activism, and Changing Values*. Princeton: Princeton University Press.

Rogers, M. L. 2008. "Republican Confusion and Liberal Clarification." *Philosophy and Social Criticism* 34: 799–824.

Roghmann, K., and W. Sodeur. 1972. "The Impact of Military Service on Authoritarian Attitudes: Evidence from West Germany." *American Journal of Sociology* 78(2): 418–33.

Rokeach, M. 1968. *Beliefs, Attitudes, and Values: A Theory of Organizational Change*. San Francisco: Jossey-Bass.

Rosenberg, G. N. 1991. *The Hollow Hope: Can Courts Bring About Social Change?* Chicago: University of Chicago Press.

Rosenstone, S., and J. M. Hansen. 1993. *Mobilization, Participation, and Democracy in America*. New York: Macmillan.

Ryan, J. G. 1977. "The Memphis Riots of 1866: Terror in a Black Community during Reconstruction." *Journal of Negro History* 62: 243–57.

Salamon, L., and S. Van Evera. 1973. "Fear, Apathy, and Discrimination." *American Political Science Review* 67: 1288–1306.

Salyer, L. E. 2004. "Baptism by Fire: Race, Military Service, and Citizenship Policy." *Journal of American History* 91: 847–76.

Sampson, E. E. 1975. "Justice as Equality." *Journal of Social Issues* 31: 45–61.

Sampson, R. J., and J. H. Laub. 1996. "Socioeconomic Achievement in the Life Course of Disadvantaged Men: Military Service as a Turning Point, circa 1940–1965." *American Sociological Review* 61: 347–67.

Sawyer, M. Q. 2006. *Racial Politics in Post-Revolutionary Cuba*. New York: Cambridge University Press.

Schama, S. 2006. *Rough Crossings: Britain, the Slaves, and the American Revolution*. New York: HarperCollins.

Schreiber, E. M. 1979. "Enduring Effects of Military Service? Opinion Differences between U.S. Veterans and Nonveterans." *Social Forces* 57: 825–39.

Schuman, H. 2008. *Method and Meaning in Polls and Surveys*. Cambridge, Mass.: Harvard University Press.

Schuman, H., and J. Scott. 1989. "Generations and Collective Memory." *American Sociological Review* 54: 359–81.

Schuman, H., C. Steeh, and L. Bobo. 1985. *Racial Attitudes in America: Trends and Interpretations*. Cambridge, Mass.: Harvard University Press.

Schuman, H., C. Steeh, L. Bobo, and M. Krysan. 1997. *Racial Attitudes in America: Trends and Interpretations*. Cambridge, Mass.: Harvard University Press.

Sears, D. O. 1993. "Symbolic Politics: A Social-Psychological Theory." In *Explorations in Political Psychology*, ed. S. Iyengar and W. J. MacGuire, 113–49. Durham, N.C.: Duke University Press.

Sears, D. O., C. A. Henslee, and L. K. Speer. 1979. "Whites' Opposition to Busing: Self-Interest or Symbolic Politics?" *American Political Science Review* 73(2): 369–74.

Segal, D. R., P. Freedman-Doan, J. G. Bachman, and P. O'Malley. 2001. "Atttitudes of Enlisted-Level Personnel: Pro-Military and Mainstreamed." In *Soldiers and Civilians:The Civil-Military Gap and American National Security*, ed. P. Fever and R. Kohn, 163–212. Cambridge, Mass: MIT Press.

Segal, D. R., and M. W. Segal. 1976. "The Impact of Military Service on Trust in Government, International Attitudes, and Social Status." In *The Social Psychology of Military Service*, ed. N. L. Goldman and D. R. Segel, 201–11. Beverly Hills, Calif.: Sage.

Sewell, W. H. 1992. "A Theory of Structure: Duality, Agency, and Transformation." *American Journal of Sociology* 98(1): 1–29.

Shaver, P., J. Schwartz, D. Kirson, and C. O'Connor. 1987. "Emotion Knowledge: Further Exploration of a Prototype Approach." *Journal of Personality and Social Psychology* 52: 1061–86.

Shelby. T. 2005. *We Who Are Dark: The Philosophical Foundations of Black Solidarity*. Cambridge, Mass.: Havard University Press.

Shils, E. 1971. "Tradition." *Comparative Studies in Society and History* 13: 122–59.

Shingles, R. D. 1981. "Black Consciousness and Political Participation: The Missing Link." *American Political Science Review* 75: 76–91.

Shklar, J. N. 1991. *American Citizenship: The Quest for Inclusion*. Cambridge, Mass.: Harvard University Press.

Sidanius, J., S. Feshbach, S. Levin, and F. Pratto. 1997. "The Interface between Ethnic and National Attachment: Ethnic Pluralism or Ethnic Dominance?" *Public Opinion Quarterly* 61(1): 102–133.

Sigel, R. S., ed. 1989. *Political Learning in Adulthood*. Chicago: University of Chicago Press.

Singh, N. P. 2005. *Black Is a Country: Race and the Unfinished Struggle for Democracy*. Cambridge, Mass.: Harvard University Press.

Sitkoff, H. 1971a. "Racial Militancy and Interracial Violence in the Second World War." *Journal of American History* 58: 661–81.

———. 1971b. "Harry Truman and the Election of 1948: The Coming Age of Civil Rights in American Politics." *Journal of Southern History* 37: 595–616.

———. 1978. *A New Deal for Blacks: The Emergence of Civil Rights as a National Issue*, vol. 1, *The Depression Decade*. New York: Oxford University Press.

———. 1997. "African American Militancy in the World War II South: Another Perspective." In *Remaking Dixie: The Impact of World War II on the American South*, ed. N. R. McMillen, 70–92. Jackson: University Press of Mississippi.

Skinner, Q. 1998. *Liberty before Liberalism*. New York: Cambridge University Press.

———. 2002. "A Third Concept of Liberty." *Proceedings of the British Academy* 117: 237–68.

Skocpol, T., A. Liazos, and M. Ganz. 2006. *What a Mighty Power We Can Be: African American Fraternal Groups and the Struggle for Racial Equality*. Princeton: Princeton University Press.

Skocpol, T., Z. Munson, A. Karch, and B. Camp. 2002. "Patriotic Partnership: Why Great Wars Nourished American Civic Volunteerism." In *Shaped by War and Trade: International Influences on American Political Development*, ed. I. Katznelson and M. Shefter, 134–80. Princeton: Princeton University Press.

Skrentny, J. D. 1996. *The Ironies of Affirmative Action: Politics, Culture, and Justice in America*. Chicago: University of Chicago Press.

———. 1998. "The Effect of the Cold War on African-American Civil Rights." *Theory and Society* 27(2): 237–85.

———. 2002. *The Minority Rights Revolution*. Cambridge, Mass.: Harvard University Press.

Small. S. 1994. *Racialized Barriers: The Black Experience in the United States and England*. New York: Routlege.

Smith, R. M. 1988. "The 'American Creed' and American Identity: The Limits of Liberal Citizenship in the United States." *Western Political Quarterly* 41: 225–51.

———. 1992. "If Politics Matters: Implications for a 'New Institutionalism.'" *Studies in American Political Development* 6: 1–36.

———. 1993. "The Multiple Traditions in America." *American Political Science Review* 87: 549–67.

———. 1997. *Civic Ideals: Conflicting Visions of Citizenship in U.S. History.* New Haven, Conn.: Yale University Press.

Snow, D. A., and R. D. Benford. 1988. "Ideology, Frame Resonance, and Participant Mobilization." In *From Structure to Action: Comparing Social Movements Research across Cultures*, ed. B. Klanderman, H. Kriesi, and S. Tarrow, 197–218. International Social Movement Research 1. Greenwich, Conn.: JAI Press, .

———. 1992. "Master Frames and Cycles of Protest." In A. D. Morris and C. M. Mueller, eds., *Frontiers in Social Movement Theory.* New Haven, Conn.: Yale University Press.

Snow, D. A., E. Rochford Jr., S. Worden, and R. Benford. 1986. "Frame Alignment Processes, Micromobilization, and Movement Participation." *American Sociological Review* 51: 464–81.

Snyder, R. C. 1999. *Citizen-Soldiers and Manly Warriors: Military Service and Gender in the Civic Republican Tradition.* Oxford: Rowman and Littlefield.

———. 2003. "The Citizen–Soldier Tradition and Gender Integration of the U.S. Military." *Armed Forces and Society* 29: 185–204.

Stouffer, S., L. C. DeVinney, S. A. Star, and R. Williams Jr. 1949. *The American Soldier.* vol. 2. Princeton: Princeton University Press.

Stouffer, S. A. 1992. *Communism, Conformity, and Civil Liberties.* New Brunswick, N.J.: Transaction.

Sullivan, P. 1996. *Days of Hope: Race and Democracy in the New Deal Era.* Chapel Hill: University of North Carolina Press.

Sunstein, C. R. 1988. "Beyond the Republican Revival." *Yale Law Journal* 97: 539–90.

Swidler, A. 1986. "Culture in Action: Symbols and Strategies." American Sociological Review 51(2): 273–86.

Tajfel, H. 1981. *Social Identity and Intergroup Relations.* New York: Cambridge University Press.

Tarrow, S. 1992. "Mentalities, Political Structures, and Collective Action Frames." In *Frontiers in Social Movement Theory*, ed. A. D. Morris and C. M. Mueller, 174–202. New Haven, Conn.: Yale University Press.

Tate, K. 1993. *From Protest to Politics: The New Black Voters in American Elections.* New York: Russell Sage Foundation.

———. 2004. "Will America Ever Pay? Racial Justice and Reparations." *Forum* 2(3): 1040.

Teigen, J. 2006. "Enduring Effects of the Uniform: Previous Military Experience and Voter Turnout." *Political Research Quarterly* 59(4): 601–7.

Thomas, J. 1993. "The Double V Was for Victory: Black Soldiers, the Black Protest, and World War II." PhD diss., Ohio State University.

Thompson, J. E. 1993. *The Black Press in Mississippi, 1865–1985*. Gainesville: University of Florida Press.

Tolnay, S. E., and E. M. Beck. 1995. *A Festival of Violence: An Analysis of Southern Lynching, 1882–1930*. Urbana: University of Illinois Press.

Tourangeau, R., L. J. Rips, and K. Rasinski. 2000. *The Psychology of the Survey Response*. New York: Cambridge University Press.

Tuck, S.G.N. 2001. *Beyond Atlanta: The Struggle for Racial Equality in Georgia*. Athens: University of Georgia Press.

Tyson, T. 1999. *Radio Free Dixie: Robert F. Williams and the Roots of Black Power*. Chapel Hill: University of North Carolina Press.

U.S. Bureau of the Census. 1943. *Sixteenth Census of the United States: 1940*. Washington, D.C.: GPO.

Valelly, R. M. 2004. *The Two Reconstructions: The Struggle for Black Enfranchisement*. Chicago: University of Chicago Press.

Verba, S., and N. H. Nie. 1972. *Participation in America: Political Democracy and Social Equality*. Chicago: University of Chicago Press.

Verba, S., K. Schlozman, and H. Brady. 1995. *Voice and Equality: Civic Voluntarism in American Politics*. Cambridge, Mass.: Harvard University Press.

Viroli, M. 1995. *For Love of Country: An Essay on Patriotism and Nationalism*. New York: Oxford University Press.

———. 2002. *Republicanism*. New York: Hill and Wang.

Von Eschen, P. M. 1997. *Race against Empire: Black Americans and Anti-Colonialism*. Ithaca, N.Y.: Cornell University Press.

Waldron, J. 1991. *Liberal Rights*. New York: Cambridge University Press.

Walton, H. 1985. *Invisible Politics: Black Political Behavior*. Albany: State University of New York Press.

Walzer, M. 1970. *Obligations: Essays on Disobedience, War, and Citizenship*. New York: Simon and Schuster.

———. 1992. *What It Means to Be An American: Essays on the American Experience*. New York: Marsilio.

Washington, J. M. 1986. *The Essential Writings and Speeches of Martin Luther King, Jr*. New York: HarperCollins.

Watter, P., and R. Cleghorn. 1967. *Climbing Jacob's Ladder: The Arrival of Negroes in Southern Politics*. New York: Harcourt, Brace and World.

Wedeen, L. 2002. "Conceptualizing Culture: Possibilities for Political Science." *American Political Science Review* 96: 713–28.

Weiss, N. 1983. *Farewell to the Party of Lincoln: Black Politics in the Age of FDR*. Princeton: Princeton University Press.

Williams, C. L. 2007. "Vanguards of the New Negro: African American Veterans and Post–World War I Racial Militancy." *Journal of African American History* 92: 347–70.

Williams, D. 1991. "Civic Republicanism and the Citizen Militia." *The Yale Law Journal* 101: 551–615.

Williams, R. 1998. *Negroes with Guns*. Detroit: Wayne State University Press.

Winant, H. 2001. *The World Is a Ghetto: Race and Democracy since World War II*. New York: Cambridge University Press.

Wolseley, R. E. 1971. *The Black Press U.S.A.* Ames: Iowa State University Press.

Wood, G. 1969. *The Creation of the American Republic, 1776–1787.* Chapel Hill: University of North Carolina Press.

Woodward, C. V. 1951. *Origins of the New South: 1877–1913.* Baton Rouge: Louisiana State University Press.

———. 1955. *The Strange Career of Jim Crow.* New York: Oxford University Press.

Wynn, N. A. 1993. *The Afro-American and the Second World War.* New York: Holmes and Meier.

Xie, Y. 1992. "The Socioeconomic Status of Young Male Veterans, 1964–1984." *Social Science Quarterly* 73: 379–95.

Young, I. M. 1990. *Justice and the Politics of Difference.* Princeton: Princeton University Press.

———. 2000. *Inclusion and Democracy.* New York: Oxford University Press.

Zald, M. N. 1996. "Culture, Ideology, and Strategic Framing." In *Comparative Perspectives on Social Movements*, ed. D. McAdam, J. D. McCarthy, and M. N. Zald, 261–74. New York: Cambridge University Press.

Zaller, J, 1992. *The Nature and Origin of Mass Opinion.* New York: Cambridge University Press.

Index

Note: Page numbers in **bold** refer to illustrations and tables.

PRINCETON STUDIES IN AMERICAN POLITICS
HISTORICAL, INTERNATIONAL, AND COMPARATIVE PERSPECTIVES

Managing the President's Program: Presidential Leadership and Legislative Policy Formulation by Andrew Rudalevige

Shaped by War and Trade: International Influences on American Political Development edited by Ira Katznelson and Martin Shefter

Dry Bones Rattling: Community Building to Revitalize American Democracy by Mark R. Warren

Disjointed Pluralism: Institutional Innovation and the Development of the U.S. Congress by Eric Schickler

The Forging of Bureaucratic Autonomy: Reputations, Networks, and Policy Innovations in Executive Agencies, 1862–1928 by Daniel P. Carpenter

The Rise of the Agricultural Welfare State: Institutions and Interest Group Power in the United States, France, and Japan by Adam D. Sheingate

In the Shadow of the Garrison State: America's Anti-Statism and Its Cold War Grand Strategy by Aaron L. Friedberg

Stuck in Neutral: Business and the Politics of Human Capital Investment Policy by Cathie Jo Martin

Uneasy Alliances: Race and Party Competition in America by Paul Frymer

Faithful and Fearless: Moving Feminist Protest inside the Church and Military by Mary Fainsod Katzenstein

Forged Consensus: Science, Technology, and Economic Policy in the United States, 1921–1953 by David M. Hart

Parting at the Crossroads: The Emergence of Health Insurance in the United States and Canada by Antonia Maioni

Bold Relief: Institutional Politics and the Origins of Modern American Social Policy by Edwin Amenta

The Hidden Welfare State: Tax Expenditures and Social Policy in the United States by Christopher Howard

Morning Glories: Municipal Reform in the Southwest by Amy Bridges

Imperiled Innocents: Anthony Comstock and Family Reproduction in Victorian America by Nicola Beisel

The Road to Nowhere: The Genesis of President Clinton's Plan for Health Security by Jacob Hacker

The Origins of the Urban Crisis: Race and Inequality in Postwar Detroit by Thomas J. Sugrue

Party Decline in America: Policy, Politics, and the Fiscal State by John J. Coleman